The Upper Limit

The Upper Limit

How Low-Wage Work Defines Punishment and Welfare

François Bonnet

UNIVERSITY OF CALIFORNIA PRESS

University of California Press, one of the most distinguished university presses in the United States, enriches lives around the world by advancing scholarship in the humanities, social sciences, and natural sciences. Its activities are supported by the UC Press Foundation and by philanthropic contributions from individuals and institutions. For more information, visit www.ucpress.edu.

University of California Press
Oakland, California

Library of Congress Cataloging-in-Publication Data

Names: Bonnet, François, author.
Title: The upper limit : how low-wage work defines punishment and welfare / François Bonnet.
Description: Oakland, California : University of California Press, [2019] | Includes bibliographical references and index. | Identifiers: LCCN 2018060707 (print) | LCCN 2019001514 (ebook) | ISBN 9780520973305 (ebook) | ISBN 9780520305212 (cloth : alk. paper) | ISBN 9780520305229 (pbk. : alk. paper)
Subjects: LCSH: Public welfare—New York (State)—History. | Criminal justice, Administration of—New York (State)—History. | Minimum wage—Social aspects—New York (State) | East New York (New York, N.Y.)
Classification: LCC HV98.N7 (ebook) | LCC HV98.N7 B66 2019 (print) | DDC 362.5/56109747—dc23
LC record available at https://lccn.loc.gov/2018060707

Manufactured in the United States of America

26 25 24 23 22 21 20 19
10 9 8 7 6 5 4 3 2 1

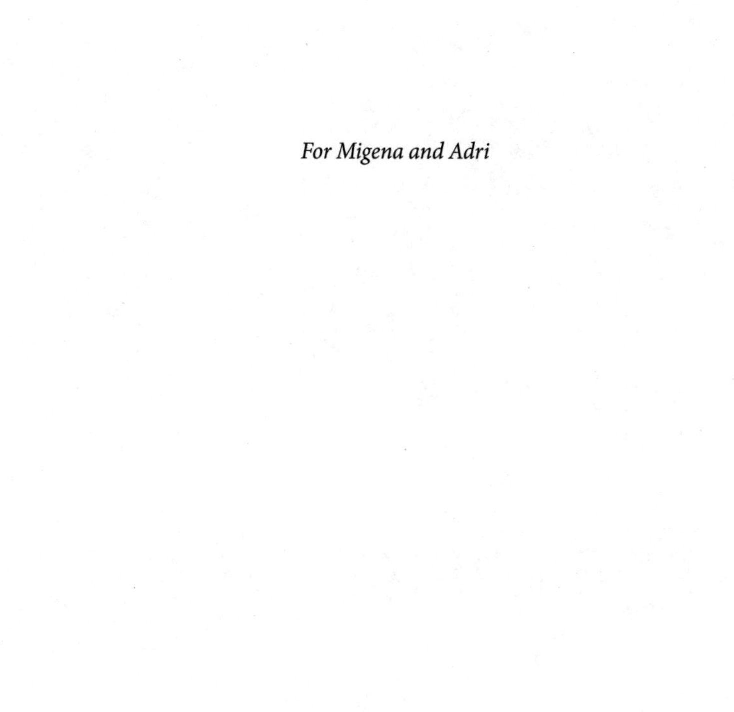

For Migena and Adri

Once upon a time there were two beggars. They were in rags, starving, freezing to death in the winter. Suddenly a good fairy appeared. She told them: "I can grant you one wish." The beggars were entranced.

The good fairy added: "There is a condition. The first one who shall ask, the second one shall get twice as much." The two beggars looked at each other, hesitated, and finally one spoke: "Good fairy, poke one of my eyes out."

—TWELFTH-CENTURY FRENCH FOLKTALE

CONTENTS

ILLUSTRATIONS

Introduction

Since 1993, crime in the United States has fallen to historic lows. This has provided extraordinary legitimacy to the peculiar mix of welfare and punishment that the country enforces, with ever stingier social programs for the poor and the highest rates of incarceration in the world. This book sets out to explain this peculiar mix.

There is amazing variation in how different countries arrange welfare and punishment. The Western European safety net is vastly more generous than the American one, which is still far superior to Brazil's. Punishment is equally diverse. In the United States, police officers kill about 900 civilians in the streets per year; police in Japan, France, Germany, and the United Kingdom put together barely kill thirty.[1] Prison conditions offer a range of experiences: in Brazil, "at one prison in Manaus, severed heads and limbs were stacked on the floor" after a riot.[2] In Finland, prisoners can go to the sauna.

The Upper Limit proposes a new theory of welfare and punishment that explains why such variations exist. This theory is an original reformulation of the Victorian principle of "less eligibility": every society has to make welfare less attractive than minimum-wage work and arrange punishment so that crime is less attractive than welfare.[3] The living standards of the lowest class of workers in a society determine the upper limit for the generosity of welfare and for the humanity of punishment in that society. This new theory provides an elegant and compelling framework to make sense of why societies manage their poor the way they do. In Scandinavian countries, the minimum wage is so high that the upper limit for welfare and punishment allows for generous subsidies toward the poor and lenient punishment; in the United States, generalized low-wage work at the bottom of the labor market only allows for stingy welfare and harsh punishment. In Brazil the poor survive through the informal economy and under the threat of death squads.[4]

The Upper Limit puts this theory to work to explain the rise of mass incarceration and the transformations of the welfare state in the United States. Doing so, it contributes to the rich literature on the transformations of American punishment. Many of the recent studies have promoted two competing accounts, the exceptionalism and the convergence theses. Exceptionalists have documented sequences of historical events, typically policy decisions, that have led to the present situation and the political actors that have been influential in adopting three-strikes-and-you're-out or mandatory minimums.[5] These accounts tend to present the American case as an outlier among other developed countries. By nature, histories of policy decisions tend to draw on historical contingencies and national specificities. In this respect the legacy of slavery for American punishment is enormous. Many of these political histories have emphasized the racist nature of the criminal justice system, in particular Michelle Alexander's *The New Jim Crow*.[6] Another body of work, represented by David Garland's *The Culture of Control* and Loïc Wacquant's *Punishing the Poor*, presents the United States as the vanguard of a global movement of penal convergence, where the rest of the world is supposed to follow American penal footsteps.[7]

This book's starting point is a triple observation: penal convergence didn't happen, sequential histories of policy decisions are not explanations, and racism doesn't explain why the United States incarcerates its whites at a rate probably ten times greater than Western Europeans incarcerate their own whites. A quick glance at history makes it unclear that Western European countries (or Japan) are any less racist than the United States. Against both the exceptionalism and the convergence theses, *The Upper Limit* provides a structural explanation for patterns of punishment and welfare in time and space. All societies have to deal with their poor, and where the poor are comparatively better off, welfare is more generous and punishment more lenient. Because the United States is a more unequal society, where low-wage workers struggle to a degree unknown in most Western European countries, social policy is less generous and penal policy less humane.

The Upper Limit proposes a new interpretation of postwar American history based on a close tracking of low-wage living standards. In short, rising living standards during postwar affluence made for the policy breakthroughs of the 1960s (the Great Society), and declining living standards since the 1970s have lowered the upper limit, forcing all-too-happy policy makers to enforce a punitive adjustment. This adjustment started in the 1970s, in the context of rising crime rates and widening fears among conservatives about the collapse of social order. Between the 1960s and the early 1990s, homicide rates doubled in the United States. During the 1970s and 1980s, crime became a central concern in American life. Punishment became more severe. The rate of incarceration increased sharply in the 1980s, to become the highest in the world. Meanwhile, states and federal government reforms radically downgraded social policy in an effort that culminated with the 1996 welfare reform, which was explicitly designed to get the poor out of welfare and into labor markets.

At the same time, in the 1990s, crime fell in the United States in historic proportions. Homicides dropped by almost half between 1990 and 2010. Violent and property crime, as registered by victimization surveys, dropped in similar proportions.[8] This decrease in crime is one of the great social facts of the turn of the millennium, but ascertaining its causes is extraordinarily difficult. The consequences of the crime drop for the population have been immense: "the poorest Americans are now victimized at about the same rate as the richest Americans were back at the start of the 1990s."[9] The effects of the crime drop were particularly visible in large cities like New York, where there was an 82 percent decline in homicides between 1990 and 2009.[10] The crime drop steered criticism away from mass incarceration and normalized the welfare reform, by implying that a weakened safety net was compatible with restored public order.

In short, over the past thirty years, American policy makers have made welfare less generous and punishment harsher. Such a trend seems like a recipe for disaster, or so twentieth-century social scientists might think. Yet American society has not collapsed, to the chagrin of progressives around the world. In fact, while many see the American mix of welfare and punishment as aberrant, irrational, and unsustainable, it is hailed by American conservatives as a historic policy success.[11] In their view, crime, riots, and general mess were born out of the optimistic policies of the 1960s (the Great Society, the War on Poverty). Mass incarceration and welfare reform have (seemingly) restored order. Crime is now at historical lows; urban nuisances such as panhandlers and homeless people are pushed out of the way of the well-to-do; cities have become transformed for consumerist enjoyment. No expensive social redistribution was needed, just a strong police force and courts willing to enforce the full extent of the law. In American and international policy circles, the crime drop in the United States has strengthened the idea that punitive law enforcement and restrictive access to poor relief is a perfectly adequate way to handle the nuisances of poverty.

A key assumption of this book is the importance of crime's role in shaping societies. When bodies start piling up in the streets, the daily lives of people across social groups are completely transformed. People suddenly need to take costly precautions that dramatically diminish their quality of life.[12] Conversely, declining crime rates are highly consequential in everyday life.[13] This assumption sets me apart from scholars who harbor a systematic suspicion of crime statistics. Their perspective, often labeled "constructivism" in social scientific circles, sees statements of fact about crime and welfare as using the authority of seemingly neutral knowledge for possibly nefarious political ends. Constructivists typically analyze fear of crime as an illusion manipulated by the media and politicians.[14] They are quick to dismiss empirical data on sensitive topics as normative or conceptual non sequiturs.[15] It is true that in public discourse, crime and welfare are used as coded innuendoes to stigmatize people and communities of color. But this cannot prevent social scientists from addressing the world as it is. This point was made thirty years ago by William Julius Wilson. In *The Truly Disadvantaged* he sought to explain why "joblessness, out-of-wedlock births, single families, welfare dependency, and serious crime" had increased in black neighborhoods.[16] He regretted that "liberal scholars shied away from researching behavior construed as unflattering or stigmatizing."[17] I believe social scientists need to take seriously variations in crime rates and other social problems as clues to assess the workings of a given mix of welfare and punishment.

To this end I propose a theory of unusual range. The only way to falsify the theory is the "Piketty option": to collect data in dozens of countries over six centuries and to systematically prove its universal validity. This strategy poses overwhelming empirical challenges, and I will not pursue the Piketty option in *The Upper Limit*. Instead, I will use the theory to make sense of the history of punishment and welfare in the postwar United States and, in particular, of the punitive adjustment that happened from the 1970s on. I will then explore the local consequences of this punitive adjustment in a poor urban neighborhood called East New York in Brooklyn (New York City), where I conducted field research from 2006 to 2011. This book is thus about the mix of social and penal policies that are implemented to enforce a measure of civil peace that allows for the continuation of normal economic activity, where "normal economic activity" is insufficient to integrate large swaths of the population. East New York was a high-crime neighborhood between the 1960s and the 1990s, before becoming one of the places where crime has fallen most since the early 1990s. East New York is a neighborhood where unemployment is high; that is, the labor market on its own has been unable to provide for social order. Instead, order comes about through the iron fist of social and penal policy. The case of this neighborhood forces us to take seriously the benefits of falling crime rates, along with the costs of implementing a harsher mix of welfare and punishment.

A WORD ON METHOD

I did most of my fieldwork in East New York with a nonprofit organization called Family Justice, which is part of a huge industry of nonprofits delivering direct services in poor neighborhoods. Family Justice was initially based in Manhattan's Lower East Side, where it ran a program to reduce drug abuse. As the Lower East Side achieved near-complete gentrification in the 2000s, Family Justice's customer base shrank. In 2006 Family Justice's founder and CEO, Carol Shapiro, planned an outreach phase in East New York and tasked a young project manager, Jenn, to establish ties with community stakeholders. The plan was to open an office to help the families of prisoners, in response to growing concerns over prisoner reentry. Because of mass incarceration, one-fourth of all black children born in 1990 have had a parent incarcerated.[18] Family Justice thus worked at the intersection of welfare and punishment.

This outreach phase involved working with other organizations in East New York, such as law enforcement agencies, other nonprofits, housing authorities, churches, and so forth. Carol Shapiro and Jenn both agreed to let me follow Jenn on a daily basis in East New York, and I am thankful to them for this. During 2006 I spent six months with Jenn, meeting people and attending community events in East New York on a daily basis. We met with people involved with various aspects of social and penal policy: policing, reentry, social services delivery, homelessness. We attended police-community meetings, talked to officers, and did ride-alongs in police patrol cars. We met with homeless shelter operators, politicians, public housing administrators, and pastors. While I was embedded with Family Justice I also observed the inner workings of a nonprofit. Family Justice did not pay me or refund anything that I can recall; I maintained full financial independence throughout my fieldwork. I came back on my own once a year between 2007 and 2011 for periods of two weeks to three months and revisited former respondents. In total I have about eighty interviews and notes from thirty meetings in East New York.

The Upper Limit draws on this fieldwork to illuminate what the principle of less eligibility means for ordinary individuals after a punitive adjustment. My East New York fieldwork will not prove the validity of the principle of less eligibility. But it will show why American policing is so brutal and why policing cannot be courteous and debonair in a violent, unequal society. It explains why the experience of returning prisoners is made so vexing: it is impossible to give to former criminals what is routinely denied to law-abiding citizens, even if this means more recidivism. It demonstrates how New York City's homelessness policy wastes a great deal of money to make shelters unpleasant and to force people back to paying rent in the private market. It explains how the rise of nonprofits delivering social services is the symptom of an inferior welfare state, belonging to a society without a meaningful minimum wage.

Unlike other scholars who have shadowed nonprofit organizations,[19] I do not intend to document the substance of Family Justice's work or the effect it is supposed to have on clients. Nor am I trying to describe the "ghetto." I am after the big picture of the mix of punishment and welfare and its overarching logic. My neighborhood focus has enabled me to observe the common patterns organizing different sectors of policy. I followed an organization dealing with other organizations, and my interest is in the objective logic of organized systems, not in individual experiences.[20] This is why I avoid long quotes or careful descriptions of what people did and what they said. East New York is a setting where I observe the consequences of an adjustment of less eligibility.

The empirical chapters of this book are based primarily on notes taken during my fieldwork in East New York. Ethnography has recently come under fire for loose accuracy standards. According to some, ethnographers are less rigorous in the presentation of evidence than reporters, are held to weaker standards of evidence, and don't have editors or fact-checkers who will look into their stories.[21] Although there is no newsworthy revelation in this book, there is a concern for accuracy. This is why I have used a wealth of contemporary news reports, policy documents, and blog posts related to crime and welfare to back up my claims and analysis. I have benefited in this procedure from New York's special situation. On any given day there are thousands of journalists writing stories about the city, with informative press articles available on any given topic appearing in publications ranging from upscale magazines to local blogs. The reliance on journalism in my work, which sometimes relegates my original data to the background, is a deliberate attempt to consolidate the veracity of my own field research.

In addition to my own notes, I have used Jenn's field notes. Jenn worked for Family Justice as a project manager, but she also was curious about social science. I did not see her as a research subject and don't have a single interview with her in my files. Instead, we spent countless hours discussing our interviews and observations. I even lent her a copy of Emerson's *Writing Ethnographic Field Notes*. So she wrote field notes for a number of interviews and meetings. We wrote our notes on the same file, which we sent back and forth over email a few hundred times. For some of the events we both attended, I have both our accounts; for most, only mine; and for the events when she went alone, her account. Each of these accounts was read by the other at the time, commented on, amended, corrected, and discussed over lunch or during commutes. This gives me hope that "my" notes are not unchecked solipsism and that trivial misunderstandings and English language mistakes are under control. The interpretations of the notes I make today, almost 10 years later, are mine. I am deeply thankful to Jenn for her contribution to this book.

CHAPTER OVERVIEW

The first chapter of *The Upper Limit* is about the big picture, and it rests on conceptual work and comparative-historical studies of welfare and punishment. The concept of less eligibility has been around for about two hundred years but had yet to be properly formulated. This chapter explains the logic of the evolution of social and penal policy across societies. For a society to function, welfare must be less attractive than low-wage work, and punishment must make crime less attractive than welfare. Punishment and welfare are capped by the situation of the lowest class of workers on the labor market—the upper limit of social and penal policy. The principle of less eligibility explains, for instance, why relief for the English poor in 1834 was meager and why today's Finnish prisons have saunas. The logic of less eligibility, I argue, has been at work for centuries and can help us understand recent patterns of welfare and punishment.

Chapter 2 narrows the focus to the evolution of social and penal policy in the United States and offers a reinterpretation of recent American history. Before the 1960s there were two separate societies in the United States, with two distinct structures of welfare and punishment. One was for whites and followed the European trajectory; the other was for southern blacks and, with slavery followed by Jim Crow laws, was horrifically cruel. The unification of these two societies through the Great Migration of southern blacks to the largely white North and West caused a breakdown in less eligibility, with both crime and welfare rolls increasing sharply. The range of options available to solve this breakdown in less eligibility was restricted by economic transformations: since the 1970s, structural change had caused living standards to decline for low-income Americans across the board. The upper limit for welfare and punishment was being brought down at a moment of crisis and only allowed for a thorough reengineering of less eligibility, which subsequently followed an ever less generous, ever more punitive route.

In chapter 3 I propose an empirical investigation of the outcome of this punitive adjustment of less eligibility in East New York, Brooklyn. Its residents, mostly poor and low-income, have suffered the most from welfare retrenchment and punitive penal policies, but they have also benefited from the ensuing crime drop, improving conditions, and rising property values that have transformed their daily lives. East New York exemplifies the implementation of a mix of social and penal policy that "works," in the sense that crime is contained.

But at what price? The four remaining chapters document the social and human cost of implementing tough punishment and meager welfare, with a particular focus on East New York. Punishment consists not only of incarceration rates but also of everyday police work. An extraordinary number of police killings have begun to shed light on the reality of policing in the United States. Chapter 4 explains how the crime drop has brought tremendous legitimacy to the New York Police Department (NYPD) and documents how police abuse and misconduct have led to discontent among many in East New York. Yet as the crime drop increases the value of their homes, many others in the neighborhood, especially homeowners, demand more policing. The chapter shows that police behavior is to be understood in its structural context.

One consequence of aggressive policing and mass incarceration that is observable in a neighborhood is prisoner reentry. Many prisoners means many people returning from prison. They need housing, but it is forbidden for people with a criminal record to live in public housing, and leaseholders may be evicted for granting hospitality to a husband or a son who comes back from prison. I explain in chapter 5 why this ban is counterproductive for law enforcement agencies, and I document how parole and the New York City Housing Authority (NYCHA) have worked with a nonprofit—Family Justice—to circumvent the law and reach out to parolees and their families in public housing. I then turn to explaining the logic of how vexing the reentry experience is made to be.

In chapter 6 I discuss the rise and significance of nonprofits such as Family Justice in delivering welfare services. Nonprofits are products of the privatization and devolution of the welfare state. The way contracts are distributed and the legal constraints on government spending have created a situation where two types of nonprofits survive: highly professional, managerial ones (such as Family Justice), on one hand, and gritty, politically connected local ones, on the other. The vast majority of both types of nonprofits do their best to meaningfully help the poor. But because resources are scarce, nonprofits tend to send their clients into endless loops of referrals while administrators try frantically to meet performance indicators. This organization of relief is the symptom of a society where living conditions at the bottom of the labor market are so bad that welfare generosity has to be reduced accordingly.

Chapter 7 argues that New York City's right-to-shelter policy creates a rift in less eligibility: given New York City's astronomical housing costs, right-to-shelter makes relief dangerously attractive. I therefore document how the city both upholds the law (to provide shelter) and reengineers less eligibility on the housing market by spending a lot of money to make shelter deliberately unpleasant. Shelter policy is designed to make the shelter experience less appealing than renting a private apartment at market rate. For those sleeping rough, there is always jail and prison—which underlines the continuity in social and penal policy on which the theory of the upper limit rests.

I reflect on policy implications in the conclusion. The principle of less eligibility is in itself conceptually agnostic about which mix of welfare and punishment should be implemented. The theory of the upper limit suggests that only when the living conditions of the lowest paid workers improve will the upper limit of welfare and punishment rise. This means that change is dependent on higher wages for low-income workers. I submit that the theory of the upper limit is one small step in the direction of acknowledging the world as it is.

1

The Upper Limit

But in no part of Europe except England has it been thought fit that the provision, whether compulsory or voluntary, should be applied to more than the relief of indigence, *the state of a person unable to labour, or unable to obtain, in return for his labour, the means of subsistence. It has never been deemed expedient that the provision should extend to the relief of* poverty; *that is, the state of one, who, in order to obtain a mere subsistence, is forced to have recourse to labour.*

—POOR LAW COMMISSIONERS' REPORT OF 1834

The major function of criminal law in a capitalist society is to prevent people from bypassing the system of voluntary, compensated exchange—the "market." . . . When transaction costs are low, the market is, virtually by definition, the most efficient method of allocating resources. Attempts to bypass the market will therefore be discouraged by a legal system bent on promoting efficiency. . . . The market transaction that he [the offender] bypasses is the exchange of his labor for money in a lawful occupation. . . . Criminal law is designed primarily for the nonaffluent; the affluent are kept in line, for the most part, by tort law.

—RICHARD A. POSNER, AN ECONOMIC THEORY OF THE CRIMINAL LAW

In the sweat of thy face shalt thou eat bread, till thou return unto the ground.

—GENESIS 3:19

Welfare and punishment vary widely in time and space. Equally prosperous countries have markedly different social and penal policies. What determines a given society's mix of welfare and punishment? Comparative studies have led to typological efforts, with countries labeled as inclusive or exclusionary; neoliberal, corporatist, or social democratic; coordinated or liberal.[1] As the saying goes, any typology is better than none, but typologies are not explanations. Others have compared Nordic countries with Anglophone ones in a search for explanations of the latter's "penal excess" and have proposed explanations based on cultural differences.[2] The core problem of cultural explanations is their difficulty in accounting for the fact that in the mid-twentieth century, from the New Deal to the Great Society, the United States was a world leader in both penal reform and social policy, ahead of its Western European counterparts, before becoming the world leader of mass incarceration. Consider two alternative accounts.

The first one is a story of institutions. Legal scholar Nicola Lacey and economist David Soskice have explained American patterns of punishment and welfare using the structure of electoral competition. Decentralization and small voting units make for median voters "who are reluctant to vote for costly public goods whose benefits are not so restricted."[3] The argument draws on Joachim Savelsberg's work on certain specifically American institutions that make criminal justice more responsive to popular emotions: the popular election of prosecutors and judges, and the involvement of popular juries at all levels of sentencing.[4] Lacey and Soskice offer an explanation for American welfare and punishment that is grounded on the concrete institutional mechanisms through which policies are produced—but which does not account for changing patterns of welfare and punishment over the twentieth century.

The second explanation is more structural. Sociologist Loïc Wacquant observes that punishment and welfare are inversely related and that countries where neoliberalism is hegemonic experience a downgrade of their welfare state and an expansion of the carceral state.[5] He therefore proposes a theory of the neoliberal state. Wacquant's neoliberal state implements workfare and mass incarceration to discipline the poor and force them into labor markets. The plight of the poor, and of Durkheimian deviants such as sex offenders, serves to soothe the status anxiety of the economically declining middle classes, who vote in support of less welfare and more punishment. It is an explanation that seeks to reconcile instrumental approaches to punishment (the link to the labor market) and Durkheimian approaches (the making of solidarity at the expense of deviants).

In this chapter I present my theory of the relationship of welfare, punishment, and labor markets. This is a theory of social order based on the principle of less eligibility.

The principle of less eligibility exists in two versions. One says that poor relief cannot be more generous than low-wage work (otherwise, the poor will tend to choose welfare over work). The second version says that punishment should make crime less desirable than low-wage work (otherwise, the poor will commit more crime). I argue that we can combine both ideas: that is, for society to be basically functional, punishment has to make crime less attractive than welfare, and welfare has to be less attractive than low-wage work. In other words, the living standards offered by low-wage work determine the upper limit of both social and penal policy.[6] High living standards for the poor means that Scandinavian countries can afford generous welfare and humane punishment. Lower living standards means that Brazil has meager relief and death squads.

To make my case, I will begin by presenting the historical context of the formulation of the first principle of less eligibility—that welfare has to be less desirable than work. I go back in time because poverty has threatened the quality of life enjoyed by more affluent classes for centuries. Misery has consistently thrust the poor into begging, prostitution, vagrancy, and crime.[7] The problem has remained much the same. On one hand, the poor provide low-wage labor and are thus essential to the economy (they can't all be killed); on the other hand, they make for social problems, which require costly interventions in terms of welfare and punishment. I am interested in the various mixes of welfare and punishment that societies have implemented throughout history to engineer a measure of social order.

LESS ELIGIBILITY AND ENGLAND'S NEW POOR LAW OF 1834

Medieval society in Europe was not complex enough to require organized relief systems. There was not enough stratification for a concept of poverty to make sense, and most economic life revolved around quasi-autonomous rural parishes. The Black Death (1346–53) introduced a breakdown. It disrupted feudal economic relations, discredited established authorities, and favored the bargaining power of workers. Political authorities across Europe responded by prohibiting wage increases. In the decades that followed the Black Death, population grew rapidly, resulting in underemployment, rising food prices, and urban growth.[8] Mendicancy and vagrancy appeared on a large scale. In the rural country of Picardy (now northern France), 13 percent of the population begged for a living.[9] Food shortages and starvation became common events. Throughout the Late Middle Ages (1300–1500), relief was residual and loosely distributed by the church or private institutions. Economic transformations prompted elites to take measures.

Medieval authorities did not want a labor market where wages could increase and expressly forbade their poor to look for better opportunities elsewhere, but they did not know what to do about the excess population. Many vagrants were executed for the mere crime of being on the road.[10] Spanish scholar Juan Luis Vives (1493–1540) thus theorized in *De Subventione Pauperum* (1526) that it was better to extend poor relief, provided that the poor work. Vives's ideas proved influential across Europe. Cities promulgated interdictions against begging and not working, and they proceeded to regulate early forms of poor relief. In Ypres (modern day Belgium) there was a special provision in the law for professional panhandlers and for people pretending to be poor.[11] During unemployment and starvation crises in the sixteenth century, the poor were rounded up and coerced to work so as to prevent them from begging and fomenting protest.

De Subventione Pauperum's focus on labor markets shaped poor law in England.[12] In a first step, the Statute of Artificers of 1562 forbade English workers to look for better jobs elsewhere or to bargain for better wages. Attempts to leave one's job were met with a fine, corporal punishment, and a return to work. Organizing workers toward better conditions was a crime.[13] In a second step, Elizabeth I authorized in 1572 compulsory taxation to provide poor relief and promulgated in 1597–1601 the Elizabethan Poor Law. The (Old) Poor Law's principles were simple:

> In general, begging was forbidden. Employable poor were to be put to work in manufacturing projects organized by overseers of the poor. The able-bodied refusing to work were to be sent to houses of correction. Rogues, vagabonds, and vagrants were to be punished. Poor children were to be put to work or apprenticed. Relatives were made responsible for the maintenance of their destitute kinsmen. Only those who had settlement in a community were entitled to its aid, and what constituted settlement and the methods of its acquisition were carefully circumscribed. Paupers and potential paupers without settlement were to be excluded or expelled from the community.[14]

The Old Poor Law retained all the criminal control over labor that previously existed, including the fixity, but it established a system of relief (and punishment) that "helped break the historical link between harvest failure and mortality."[15] The relief offered was meager but enough to keep the workers alive and, all in all, economically rational.[16] Farmers paid for poor relief between harvests to maintain a supply of workers when needed.[17] Relief was conditional on nonthreatening behavior: "accepting charity meant abstaining from illegal survival strategies and accepting forms of social control. To deserve help, one had to behave deferentially and 'decently,' could not migrate, nor openly resort to begging, prostitution, crime, or looting."[18] The system worked for two hundred years and is credited with enabling England's early economic development.[19]

After 1750, English elites began to think that the Elizabethan Poor Law was becoming expensive.[20] In the first decades of the Industrial Revolution (late eighteenth to early nineteenth century), the Poor Law went into crisis. Real wages fell across Europe. The situation was aggravated by the Napoleonic Wars and bad harvests. The English system of poor relief was inadequate for the extent of poverty that had arisen. Relief spending continued to grow, increasing from £2 million in 1784 to £7 million in 1832. Relief benefited 10 percent of the English population and in the winter of 1832–33 was equivalent for a family to 93 percent of the winter wage.[21] The growth of relief spending forced Victorian elites to rethink social policy.[22] They were guided by a few core ideas: Malthus's concern for unchecked population growth, Bentham's utilitarianism, and Ricardo's iron law of wages. The commissioners of the time concluded that relief had to be made less desirable than work. It was called the "principle of less eligibility":

> A compulsory provision for the relief of the indigent can be generally administered on a sound and well-defined principle; and that under the operation of this principle, the assurance that no one need perish from want may be rendered more complete than at present, and the mendicant and vagrant repressed by disarming them of their weapon,—the plea of impending starvation. . . . The first and most essential of all conditions, a principle which we find universally admitted, even by those whose practice is at variance with it, is, that his situation on the whole shall not be made really or apparently so eligible as the situation of the independent labourer of the lowest class.[23]

The New Poor Law was passed in 1834, and within a few years, social spending fell from 2.5 percent of the national income to below 1 percent.[24] Real relief benefits per capita dropped 50 percent between 1833 and 1838.[25] The earnings of the working class were reduced by two percentage points.[26] The New Poor Law removed the fixity of labor, thus enabling the creation of a proper labor market, but criminal sanctions backing labor contracts lasted until 1875.[27]

Under this law, relief was organized in terms of the workhouse, where the destitute were to be incarcerated and forced to work to deserve relief. Workhouses already existed from the sixteenth century, were used all over Europe, and had spread to Japan in the late seventeenth century and Russia in the late eighteenth century.[28] With the introduction of the New Poor Law of 1834, poor relief was to be made so odious—by way of the workhouse—that only those at risk of starving to death would consider claiming "benefits." Families were separated, and conditions were abject. The idea was to nudge rational individuals into choosing work (outside the workhouse) over welfare and thus to reengineer less eligibility. The effects were straightforward. By 1860, only 5 percent of workhouse inmates were fit to work.[29] To this day the workhouse is a dreadful symbol because it separates completely the issue of relief from ideas of compassion or solidarity.

Toward the end of the nineteenth century the workhouse was progressively abandoned, and the principle of less eligibility appeared to social policy analysts as belonging to a barbaric past. Because less eligibility was theorized to justify the 1834 Poor Law, scholars have reasoned that it is a cruel doctrine, a reactionary ideology. Yet there is nothing intrinsically cruel or reactionary about less eligibility in itself. Less eligibility in Victorian England was harsh because living standards at the time were atrocious. In 1816, the Year Without a Summer, people starved to death throughout Europe. Real wages had fallen in the first decades of the Industrial Revolution.[30] Low-wage workers endured twelve-hour days, sometimes seven days a week; five-year-olds were sent to coal mines; mothers were forced into prostitution after their work shifts. Obviously, poor relief could not be generous in the face of such working conditions. "Any final judgement of the cruelty of the New Poor Law must take into account the conditions of the time," wrote historian David Roberts:

> It was after all an age full of harshness, drunkenness, vagrancy, cruelty, and suffering. . . . None of the critics who denounced the corporal punishment of ill-behaved boys in the workhouses mentioned that such a punishment was a widespread practice in families and schools. In its care of the insane and criminals and its use of child labour the age was a hard age, and crowded workhouses, so appalling to the Webbs, were not so appalling to the destitute of the 1830's. Compared to Liverpool cellar dwellings the commissioners' improved workhouse must not have seemed unusually cruel; and in relation to rural poverty the workhouse test had some justification.[31]

There is broad consensus that real wages and purchasing power only began to increase from the 1820s and less so for the poorest workers;[32] and the cohorts born before the 1830s suffered higher infant mortality and reductions in height, especially in the lowest class of workers.[33] The New Poor Law of 1834 was, then, a consequence of the declining living standards of the lowest class of workers at the onset of the Industrial Revolution.

Despite the association with the reviled New Poor Law, the principle of less eligibility was not an aberration. Less eligibility has always been the principle delimiting the upper limit of social policy, as a discussion of the welfare state literature will show.

WORKFARE AND THE UPPER LIMIT OF SOCIAL POLICY

At the end of the nineteenth century, states in industrial countries seized the responsibility to organize poor relief and developed (more or less) fully fledged welfare states, which became major instruments in legitimizing authority and creating national unity. Modern welfare states do not simply provide relief for the poor: they implement compulsory insurance systems that prevent people from falling into poverty. This is a revolutionary development. Welfare states are able to solve the free-rider problems that had plagued earlier, charity-based relief systems,[34] and they allow for considerably more sophisticated forms of intervention in society and the economy. The insurance mechanism functions as "ex-ante redistribution": the more universal and generalized the insurance against the risks of old age, bad health, disability, and unemployment, the less the need for assistance (poor relief).[35] Modern welfare states best respect the dignity of people at risk of poverty: "such [insurance-based] programs are rarely means tested, entail minimal surveillance, and in some cases obscure —often to the point of invisibility—any notion of dependence on the state."[36]

It is thus necessary to distinguish the welfare state from poor relief. States are now usually a country's biggest employer, and they shape the economy through trade, budgetary and monetary policy, labor regulations, tax structure, education policy, and so forth. There is clear and overwhelming evidence that large, universal welfare states best reduce poverty.[37] Intervention by welfare programs into the economy has become so pervasive that social policy has ceased to concern only the poor. The greater part of welfare expenses today—in education, health, housing, and so forth—is either universal or benefits the middle classes, and only a small component has a narrower focus on the working poor and the structurally unemployed. For the purposes of this study, when I refer to welfare or social policy, I mean relief for the poor specifically.

Welfare states have been major forces in the making of contemporary societies, and a considerable literature has been devoted to explaining why they came about in the first place. An important part of the answer is that states needed fit soldiers to wage the large-scale wars of the first half of the twentieth century.[38] For decades welfare states only grew in size and scope, but since the 1980s, welfare retrenchment in the Anglophone world has sparked a new interest in why welfare states expand or contract.

Since the beginning of welfare retrenchment, most influential accounts in political science and economics have considered the *political* conditions for variations in welfare generosity. We can divide these accounts into two strands: contingent and structural. Contingent theories emphasize the complexity of each particular case. Things happen for historically situated reasons. Take, for instance, the idea that welfare states are an elite project.[39] The evolution of welfare states depends on elites' "shifts in thinking." Another contingent theory is grounded in electoral politics: the historical-institutionalist account ("power resources theory") holds that welfare states are pushed by left-wing coalitions representing the working class and unions.[40]

Structural theories are more ambitious: they look for general explanatory principles. In the rational-choice explanation for welfare evolution (the "selfish voter"), median voters will vote for redistribution if median income is below mean income.[41] In another genre, Durkheimian theories hold that in ethnically or religiously polarized societies, there is less redistribution because voters do not accept that the other group should get subsidies at their expense. This would help explain why European welfare states are under pressure to retrench when migrants come, or why European voters do not want migrants, and why Americans are reluctant to fund a meaningful welfare state—because African Americans will benefit.[42]

This theorizing is helpful, but it assumes that welfare is a benefit that poor voters grant themselves or that elites generously dispense. Political science has conceptualized the volume of social policy as the outcome of a bargain between classes and, in democracies, as a self-gift voted for by the masses for the masses. According to these accounts, the key reason for welfare retrenchment is the inability of working classes to impose better terms, either because the elites have changed their minds, because the working classes have been unable to forge new coalitions, or because they have become divided by ethnic resentment. In other words, political science has neglected the historical link between relief for the poor and labor markets. A major exception has been Piven and Cloward's *Regulating the Poor,* which is a history of poor relief in the United States from the Depression to the urban riots of the 1960s.[43]

Piven and Cloward argue that poor relief serves to soothe the revolutionary grievances of the working classes and that it is a function of unemployment. I focus on the latter claim. When there are jobs, welfare has to be meager, and eligibility rules have to be strict, to make sure people look for jobs and work for capitalists. When jobs disappear, welfare has to expand to prevent people from starving, thus avoiding protest and making workers available for the next economic expansion. Since its first edition in 1971, *Regulating the Poor* has been perceived as cartoonish leftism and its welfare-as-social-control thesis a conspiracy theory. But recent developments in social policy have vindicated their analysis. The 1996 welfare reform in the United States was explicitly designed to get the poor out of welfare and into labor markets, either by limiting cash welfare in time or by subsidizing the earnings of the working poor through the Earned Income Tax Credit (EITC).

These developments represent a shift toward *workfare,* a theme that has become mainstream. Under workfare, recipients have to work or undergo training to be eligible for aid. The function of workfare is straightforward: it is "to subordinate social policy to the needs of labour market flexibility and/or the constraints of international competition."[44] Studies have documented how local welfare systems are designed to maintain a supply of disposable labor. Political scientist Joe Soss and his colleagues have for instance shown how welfare sanctions in Florida were highly correlated with tourism tax revenues: when the Florida tourism industry needs seasonal workers, welfare offices make sure that recipients become available.[45] The only controversial element of the *function* of workfare is whether labor market flexibility is desirable in the first place.

There is more to say about the reason for the existence of workfare. Economists Timothy Besley and Stephen Coate have distinguished between the deterrent and the screening argument.[46] The deterrent argument speaks to the conception that welfare is wrong in itself, that it leads to skill loss or encourages vice and indolence.[47] In this line of argument, workfare makes sure that relief does not attract the lazy. The deterrent logic originates in societies where wages are so low and work conditions so bad that the idea of relief for the able-bodied is nonsensical; the historical solution is to coerce people into work along the continuum of slavery, serfdom, and forced labor.[48] It is otherwise a staple idea of reactionary approaches to social policy.

The screening argument has far more theoretical leverage. In abstract terms, one logic of providing relief is universal benefits, where eligibility requirements are only conditioned by citizenship. The most radical form of universal benefit is basic income, where everyone gets an income above the poverty line. This, by definition, eliminates poverty. For various reasons, basic income is not an option in current conditions, but the logic of universal benefits animates Scandinavian social policy. It is generally argued that universal social policy gets more popular support and is better suited to reducing poverty.[49] The other logic of providing relief is targeting, meaning that relief depends on stricter conditions of eligibility (for instance, only unemployed, single mothers may get cash aid). Targeting allows in theory for an optimal allocation of resources and a maximum impact of relief. Targeting means that only the really needy should receive help.

But to decide who is really in need is costly. Eligibility needs to be determined on a case-by-case basis by an apparatus of specialized workers who resolve asymmetries of information between the claimant and the provider. The screening argument is that workfare is a solution to the problem of targeting because it involves self-targeting. As such, and as Martin Ravallion argues, workfare schemes reproduce the logic of the workhouse:

> The workhouses that emerged in Europe around 1600 can be interpreted as a means of getting around the information and incentive problems of targeting. This was done by design features that only encouraged those truly in need of help to turn to the workhouse and encouraged them to drop out of it when help is no longer needed, given better options in the rest of the economy.[50]

In the unequaled prose of the *Poor Law Commissioners' Report of 1834:*

> If the claimant does not comply with the terms on which relief is given to the destitute, he gets nothing; and if he does comply, the compliance proves the truth of his claim—namely his destitution.[51]

Because workfare forces recipients to work to receive (meager) aid, it incentivizes them to choose regular paid work over meagerly aid conditioned on work. It also prevents them from claiming benefits and using their free time to work in the informal or criminal economy.[52] In other words, the screening argument for workfare dovetails with the logic of less eligibility: policy makers have to set the right incentives so that the poor prefer work over welfare, and they must do so at minimal administrative cost. In labor markets where the minimum wage is high, social policy can afford to be less discriminating, since high wages and the status benefits to working drive the poor into choosing work. Where the living standards offered by minimum wage are low, targeting is more necessary and costlier.

Today, the main trend in the evolution of social policy is targeting,[53] and because workfare is one solution to targeting costs, "targeted systems nowadays have been remodeled not only to be more work friendly, but even to encourage and reward work."[54] The shift of social policy from redistribution to prowork policies typically leads to lowered social protection through the following mechanism: positive incentives to encourage work usually benefit already employed households, and negative incentives punish the unemployed, thus accentuating inequalities.[55]

To many, the "Schumpeterian workfare state" is a perversion of the noble idea of the "Keynesian welfare state,"[56] a counterhistorical development of the neoliberal reaction that occurred in the 1980s. In retrospect, subordination to labor markets always has the organizing principle of poor relief, with less eligibility being the principle delimiting the upper limit of social policy. It was only possible to massively expand the welfare state in general and poor relief in particular in the postwar West because living standards were rising and inequalities were low. The most generous forms of welfare state have been the product of both historically aberrant postwar growth and a massive flattening of inequalities because of world wars, mass destructions, and genocide.[57] Universal welfare states correspond to societies with high living standards for the working class; workfare is less eligibility at work in a situation where living conditions at minimum wage are inadequate for more generous forms of relief. It is the new solution to getting the poor to work in an age when simply forcing them to do so under criminal penalty, as it used to be the case for centuries, is not (yet) an option.

In the context of welfare retrenchment and the shift to workfare, we may do well to get back to studying social policy as labor market regulation. Thanks to the principle of less eligibility, we understand why poor relief contracts when labor market prospects deteriorate. Welfare cannot be more desirable than work; a decline of living standards at the bottom of the labor market will lower the upper limit of social policy.

I now turn to discussing punishment, because less eligibility, as theorized in the *Poor Law Commissioners' Report of 1834* (welfare has to be made less desirable than work), is an incomplete formulation. Since the 1970s, scholars have theorized that punishment and welfare are not distinct policy realms. Foucaldians have emphasized how social policy is not an irenic, benevolent intervention.[58] Marxists have underlined the role played by welfare institutions in maintaining social order and enforcing capitalist work norms.[59] Managing the poor has historically involved a mix of welfare and punishment.

CRIME, PUNISHMENT, AND THE LABOR MARKET

When I speak of punishment, I refer to a theoretical construct that encompasses police work, criminal justice, prison, and so forth—the big stick carried by states to keep people in line. Punishment, at its simplest, is a reaction to crime, but this definition is misleading. On one hand, defined abstractly, crime is ubiquitous. We all have stolen something at work, been verbally violent, or done something illegal with our computer. Punishment, on the other hand, is extraordinarily specific. Punishment focuses on a select number of crimes: physical (including sexual) violence, theft, drug trafficking, all crimes overwhelmingly committed by lower-class young men. These are fairly general truths. What remains to explain is the astounding variance in the severity of punishment. Just as social policy is more or less generous in different countries, penal policy varies considerably over time and space in severity. Some societies provide restorative justice seminars; others cut off hands. However severe, punishment depends on certainty—the administrative capacity to maximize the probability of arrest and sentencing. Medieval societies, for instance, relished public torture, but their states were unable to catch most criminals. Today, incarceration rates in many countries are capped by prison capacity.

Critics of punishment often point out that variations in crime rates are empirically uncorrelated with variations in punishment.[60] In the Durkheimian tradition, for instance, punishment serves to express and worship social norms by sanctioning deviants. This may lead to dysfunctional overshooting, such as moral panics.[61] In this approach, punishment has little to do with crime control. For the purposes of my argument, I adopt a more instrumental perspective. Many empirical studies have demonstrated conclusively an effect, not so much of crime on punishment, but of *punishment on crime,* through two main mechanisms: incapacitation and deterrence.[62]

Incapacitation is the specific effect of incarceration. People "inside" cannot commit crime on the outside. Incapacitation rests on the principle of "stochastic selectivity":[63] there are high-rate and low-rate offenders, and incapacitation works best when high-rate offenders are incarcerated. We don't know who high-rate offenders are, but maximizing incarceration rates helps in solving this problem because it puts a lot of people behind bars, among them high-rate offenders. There is evidence that since the 2000s, American incarceration rates have climbed so high that the marginal benefit of additional prisoners is decreasing; that is, incarceration is now counterproductive.[64]

Deterrence is the other mechanism through which punishment influences crime rates. Deterrence refers to two mechanisms: how the threat of punishment prevents crime ("general deterrence") and how the experience of punishment prevents crime ("specific deterrence"). There is now a lot of research backing up the deterrent capacity of punishment.[65] Prison exerts some deterrence. For instance, under California's "three strikes" law, people with "two strikes" are 20 percent less likely to commit a third "strikable" offense.[66] In general, it seems that longer sentences have little additional deterrent power over shorter sentences, and the certainty of punishment is far more of a deterrent than the punishment's severity. Research shows that police play a strong deterrent role (typically observed when the number of police officers is increased or reduced) and that long prison sentences have little to no deterrent power. Research is inconclusive about the deterrent effect of the death penalty.

The simplest theoretical model based on the reality of deterrence is economic theory. To make sense of the variations of punishment, Gary Becker has devised a thermostatic model: when crime is up, people are willing to pay for more punishment, which lowers crime; as crime goes down, people demand lower taxes, therefore less punishment, and crime goes up again.[67] But the model doesn't reflect how punishment is organized in actual societies. There is not much evidence to back the idea that criminal justice is a direct function of crime rates, either at the comparative-historical level or for the specific country and period that concerns us (the contemporary United States).[68] But this doesn't mean that economic insights are false.

Isaac Ehrlich has devised a more sophisticated model.[69] According to Ehrlich, the supply of crime depends on two variables: the price exacted by punishment on crime and legitimate labor market earnings. In essence, the potential criminal is confronted with a trade-off between, on one hand, criminal opportunities discounted by the fear of getting caught and, on the other, low-wage work opportunities. Ehrlich emphasizes that an optimal penal policy is not just about getting the certainty and severity of punishment right but also to promote educational and employment opportunities, so as to offer unskilled persons a viable alternative to criminal life.

Scholars have long had a hard time establishing a strong and conclusive relation between crime and unemployment.[70] Since the late 1990s, a number of studies have narrowed their scope toward associations between crime and low-wage labor markets. The results are spectacular. Economists now find that crime is strongly correlated with increases in youth unemployment and falling wages for unskilled labor, whether in the United States, Germany, England and Wales, France, or Sweden.[71] All other things being equal, people who enter labor markets during a period of high unemployment are more likely to be arrested and incarcerated in the United States and the United Kingdom.[72]

The neoclassical model is a magnificent achievement: both the deterrence and the labor market components are vindicated by empirical studies. Yet economists are routinely underwhelmed by penal policy. They have built a model to design optimal crime-control policy, and policy keeps being irrational. Ehrlich complains that punishment is a "lottery."[73] Utilitarian criminologist Daniel Nagin regrets that crime-control policy's benefits are not judged against costs.[74] Amazingly, this exact criticism is shared by scholars at the other end of the theoretical spectrum. Like Ehrlich, radical political scientist Frances Fox Piven thinks that mass incarceration is detrimental to capitalism.[75] Like Nagin, Garland analyzes the American state as "weak" and unable to design more rational penal policies.[76] In other words, criminals behave like fairly cooperative subjects with economists (they follow plausible incentives), but policy makers seem more difficult to understand. There is thus a flaw in the model, which I correct thanks to early twentieth-century Marxist Georg Rusche.

Rusche was a German sociologist loosely affiliated with the Frankfurt School. In the early 1930s he cowrote with Otto Kirchheimer the great book exploring the relation between punishment and labor markets, *Punishment and Social Structure.*[77] The book is a history of punishment in medieval Europe and argues that punishment methods functionally adapt to the needs of labor markets. The account begins in the thirteenth century. The Black Death in the fourteenth century killed off one-third of the European population, precipitating severe labor shortages. Punishment became more lenient, less lethal, and thus less wasteful of the labor force. In the sixteenth century, when the labor stock was reconstituted, and "useless" men began to abound (vagrants, beggars, etc.), executions returned in spectacularly imaginative ways. Vagrants and criminals were burnt at the stake, dismembered, disemboweled, immured, buried alive, boiled to death, and so on. But after the Thirty Years' War left about eight million dead in the seventeenth century, labor shortages made for dangerously rising wages. Executions receded, yielding to forced labor (galleys, workhouses, etc.). In short, punishment was historically a tool to manage the labor force.

This argument about methods per se obscures a more interesting point: punishment is directed toward men who cannot or refuse to be wage laborers, and it varies in volume according to the quantity of idle or criminal men. When there is a large surplus in the reserve army of labor, and therefore an excess of potential criminals and troublemakers, punishment becomes more punitive to ensure social order. The connection with neoclassical economists evidencing the relation between crime and low-wage labor markets is obvious. The difference between economic theory and Rusche's argument lies in their assumptions about what can happen in the real world. Economic theory assumes that rational policy makers will seek optimal levels of punishment and of low-wage earnings to set incentives right and get the lowest crime for the cheapest penal policy and the lowest wages. Rusche's historical insight makes his theorizing more plausible.

Because employers have historically been unable or reluctant to offer better wages, punishment is the only adjustment variable. If criminal life (after factoring in the probability and severity of punishment) is more rewarding than work, the poor will choose crime over conformity, and society will fall apart. Punishment has to provide the necessary incentives. Punishment's purpose is not (just) crime control; it is (also) to force the poor into labor markets or suffer the consequences. Because punishment, not wages, is the main adjustment variable, it can be wasteful, irrational, and overly punitive. Rusche's insights allow us to understand why criminal justice systems spend money on undermining the life chances of prisoners, despite the expected outcomes of maximizing recidivism, intergenerational misery, and so on. Usually, such endeavors are understood as "retribution" and other irrational aims. In fact, in societies where labor market prospects are dismal and welfare meager, it is inevitable that punishment will seem wasteful.[78] Rusche's argument resolves the paradox that American mass incarceration is dysfunctional to capitalism and the symptom of a weak state.

Thus, the principle driving punishment levels is a variation on less eligibility. Less eligibility in *Punishment and Social Structure* refers to the desirability of punishment versus work. I quote from an article Rusche wrote in 1930:

> Although experience shows the rich to occasionally break the law too, the fact remains that a substantial majority of those who fill the prisons come from the lower strata of the proletariat. Therefore, if it is not to contradict its goals, the penal system must be such that the most criminally predisposed groups will prefer a minimal existence in freedom, even under the most miserable conditions, to a life under the pressure of the penal system.[79]

In other words, the principle of less eligibility applied to punishment means that the living standards of the lowest class of workers are the upper limit of penal policy. High living standards imply less invasive and less severe punishment; lower standards mean more punitive arrangements. This is a powerful argument, and the reader may wonder why Rusche's work is not better known or taken more seriously. The reason is because the correlation that Rusche evidenced between punishment methods and labor markets disappeared in the nineteenth century. The eminent British sociologist T. H. Marshall dismissed *Punishment and Social Structure* on such grounds in a brutal review in 1940.[80]

I propose that punishment ceased to be directly correlated with the labor markets because welfare became the intermediary variable. Before the nineteenth century, poor relief was so meager that destitution and criminality were, for able-bodied men, virtually synonymous. Merely being a vagabond was a serious crime, sometimes punishable by death, for most of recorded history; for example, 12,000 vagrants were hanged under Henry VIII.[81] Men were either working poor or criminals, hence the penal version of the principle of less eligibility, as stipulated by Rusche: punishment had to make crime less desirable than work. During the nineteenth century, rising living standards for workers and increasing state power in the realm of social policy transformed the equation. This is precisely the problem that the early Victorians, benefiting from the hindsight of a more advanced aid system, saw coming when they formulated the New Poor Law: relief administration had to make sure that relief would not pay more than work. Progressively, wage work ceased to be heavily regulated under criminal penalties, and poor relief systems grew in scope and generosity, eventually becoming part of sophisticated insurance-based welfare systems. The alternative was not simply work versus crime but also work versus relief.

THE UPPER LIMIT

Now we can state the correct formulation of the general principle of less eligibility. For people to accept demeaning working conditions, welfare has to be less attractive than low-wage work, and punishment has to make criminal life less attractive than welfare. The living standards of the lowest class of workers determine the upper limit of social policy and, transitively, of penal policy. Less eligibility is the principle governing social order. This principle says nothing about the desirability of order and collapse. It merely states the policy constraints under which order is maintained. It leaves open the political and cultural contingencies that affect what happens below the upper limit. Our object of study therefore is the mix of welfare and punishment as determined by the principle of less eligibility, which is implemented to govern and manage poverty in a given society.

I cannot offer systematic empirical validation of the theory in this book. Still, if I am correct about the reformulation of the principle of less eligibility, then five falsifiable empirical relations are true:

- Punishment should have an effect of crime. We know this is the case thanks to the deterrence and incapacitation literature, as discussed above.[82]
- Because the theory assumes a fundamental trade-off between work and crime, lower wages and higher unemployment in low-wage labor markets should result in higher crime. We know this is the case in several countries, as discussed above.[83]
- Because the theory assumes a trade-off between work and welfare, higher welfare benefits should reduce the labor supply. This has been consistently shown since the late 1970s in the United States by welfare economists.[84]
- Welfare should decrease crime. This is a consistent finding in the United States, in developing countries where welfare programs are introduced, and in cross-national research.[85]
- There should be an inverse correlation between the generosity of welfare and the extent of punishment, typically measured by incarceration rates. Again, this is a consistent finding in both the United States and in cross-national research.[86]

In other words, the principle of less eligibility is backed by a wealth of indirect quantitative confirmation.

I understand less eligibility to be a structural fact —that is, something that constrains policy, regardless of people's belief in it. This sets me apart from many prominent authors in the field, who see less eligibility as "old tropes" or as a Victorian ideology.[87] I argue that less eligibility only makes sense as a structural fact of social organization, not a mere ideology. The key propriety of the principle of less eligibility is that generous welfare and humane imprisonment are only possible in societies where the minimum wage is decent. Less eligibility does not mean that we have to make relief stingy or prison cruel but that an appealing minimum wage can drive social and penal standards up, because the minimum wage sets the upper limit for welfare and punishment. Societies with the most generous welfare states and the most humane prisons are the contemporary Nordic social democracies (Finland, Denmark, Sweden, Norway, and Iceland), where penal policy is the most progressive in the world.[88]

Finland is the perfect example for how less eligibility can drive up penal standards. Before World War II, Finland was a dirt-poor country under Russian domination. Finns had the highest incarceration rate in Europe, with about 200 prisoners per 100,000 inhabitants, and a criminal justice system influenced by tsarist penal ideas. Postwar Finland became a prosperous country and developed a generous welfare state. In the 1950s the penal policy-making elite were torn about what direction to take. Hardliners argued in favor of keeping Russian punishment, fearing that leniency would trigger a crime wave. Reformers eventually won the day, and by the 1960s the incarceration rate went down to about 60 prisoners per 100,000, among the lowest rates in Europe and within the Nordic average.[89] Nordic countries, for instance Sweden, did experience a crime boom in the late 1960s,[90] but their rising living standards allowed for different policy choices from in the United States. Today, there is no plea bargaining in the Nordic countries, mediation practices are widespread, and all prisoners are eligible for early release. About 20 percent (Sweden) to 40 percent (Denmark) of inmates do time in *open* prisons, and there are saunas in Finnish prisons.[91] In Finland, about 3.1 percent of criminals convicted of a felony go to prison; in the United States, 73 percent do.[92] Recidivism rates in Finland are far below those in the United States.

There are certainly cultural or political reasons for the Scandinavian mix of welfare and punishment. My argument is that in these societies the living standard of the lowest class of workers is so high that it is possible to set generous relief systems for the poor, which in turn enables high penal standards. As Edward Sieh argues, just because Swedish prisons are lavish by American standards doesn't mean that Swedish criminals enjoy incarceration, for they know life is better on generous Swedish welfare and better still on minimum wage.[93] In fact, in 1971 sociologist David A. Ward interviewed Swedish inmates from a maximum-security prison outside Stockholm. They had gone on hunger strike to protest their incarceration conditions. Ward discussed with them the demands of the Attica prisoners, who had staged a major uprising the same year (33 prisoners and 10 guards killed). For instance, Attica prisoners demanded that solitary confinement not exceed 30 days. But in Sweden, solitary confinement "was regarded as rather uncommon by the inmates, but when it did occur, it was usually limited to seven days and generally lasted two or three days." The leaders of the Swedish prisoners concluded: "I'm ashamed of the kinds of problems we have to discuss here compared to the problems the American inmates have."[94] Yet their grievances were real; they just belonged to a better structure of less eligibility. Still, it is nonsensical to implement Scandinavian standards of imprisonment in today's United States, because this would mean that prison would be much more appealing than, say, homeless shelters. This would cause a breakdown of less eligibility.

The key to understanding the evolution and variation of welfare and punishment, therefore, is the living standards of the lowest class of workers. These living standards are usually defined by market earnings, to which is added monetary public redistribution (if any) and a wide range of factors, such as working conditions, housing and commuting costs, cost of living in general, and also (among others) access or not to subsidized education, daycare, and health care. The pressing question is, of course, what determines the upper limit.

Market earnings, for instance, are largely determined by minimum-wage laws and collective bargaining. This underlines the role of labor unions in setting the living standards for the lowest class of workers. Public redistribution and other amenities related to the welfare state (public housing, free education, health care, etc.) depend largely on party politics: electoral victories and defeats play a crucial role in shaping the economic policies that will determine labor laws and the scope of the welfare state. But labor activism and party politics interact with other powerful factors, such as history and geopolitics. The contingencies of world history, and the historical trajectories in nation- or institution-building, weigh heavily on the range of available options. If a country like Albania likely has the lowest upper limit in Western Europe, it is not for lack of tenacious trade unionists and is probably related to centuries of Ottoman colonial rule followed by decades of communism. If Greece has recently seen a steep decline of its lower-end wages, it is not because the Left has lost elections but is probably related to the aftermath of the financial crisis and the balance of power within the European Union. Nation-states are rarely free to do whatever their elites want. Most national economic policy across the world is determined by international relations (which is why it is fitting to study the United States, since it is not a client state). In addition, economic growth is not decided by states. Economic growth (or depression) determines the quantity of income available in a given polity. Growth is in part related to technological change—from specific inventions revolutionizing economic and social relations to epochal shifts in the structure of the economy—which typically impacts economies in ways that extend beyond the reach of labor activists or the ruling party. In other words, what determines the upper limit in a given place at a given time is a difficult empirical question.

In virtually all societies almost all of violent crime, and an overwhelming share of nonviolent crime, is committed by men, *de facto* placing women in a simplified incentive structure where mostly welfare and work are at play. Many societies restrict welfare to poor women, as poor men are expected to work, thus leaving men the options of work and crime. If one holds a strictly individualistic understanding of less eligibility, then it is a theory that applies mostly to (young) men. But men have mothers and wives, and the principe of less eligibility is perhaps best understood in terms of society-level patterns where female income is key to male decision-making.

Questions of race, religion, gender, or legal status systematically affect the position of people in labor markets and in systems of welfare and punishment. For instance, it is well documented that systematic discrimination undermines the economic situation of racial minorities in Europe and North America. The practical consequence is that racial minorities are more likely to be at the bottom of the labor market. But whatever the race of this lowest class of workers, their living standards determine the upper limit for welfare and punishment. Also, because societies are not closed systems, there is a way for individuals out of a given structure of less eligibility: migration. Italian scholars have theorized the concept of "transnational less eligibility" to refer to the idea that states criminalize migrants and deny them welfare to force them into untaxed, lower-paid work.[95]

Less eligibility means that welfare and punishment vary according to the condition of the lowest class of workers in the labor market. Welfare and punishment are concepts, but they refer to empirical realities: social and penal policies. Real, historical policies are the product of contingent policy making.

LESS ELIGIBILITY AND CONTINGENT POLICY MAKING

In general, we know there are restrictions to rational policy making: politics, problems of coordination among different agencies dealing with different problems, imperfect information and bounded rationality, and so on. How does contingent policy making adjust to structural change? This question, admittedly fundamental, refers to two subproblems.

Subproblem 1 refers to how policy makers assess the workings of less eligibility at a given historical moment: how they judge welfare to be too generous or too meager, or punishment to be excessive or insufficient.

This involves comparing living conditions under minimum wage, welfare, and criminal life. Before modern statistics (crime rates, welfare enrollment, labor-force participation, unemployment, inflation, etc.) became available, assessment must have been more qualitative and possibly more reliant on class prejudice, perhaps more prone to mistakes, and certainly more conservative: "In what age would it not be possible to collect complaints from the upper classes about the laziness of workers?"[96] When systematic data started to be collected, more sophisticated policies could be implemented. For instance, Victorian prison administrators tried to scientifically calculate the food provided to prisoners so that they received less than they would outside.[97]

Even so, they made colossal mistakes. The most famous one is "transportation," the English policy of deporting convicts to Australia. More than 160,000 convicts were deported between 1788 and 1868. According to both Mannheim and Rusche, life in Australia became much better than in England, punishment became reward, and the policy probably incentivized some to commit crime.[98] The same could be said for the French policy of deportation to New Caledonia. In more recent times an Alaska prison was apparently closed down because the conditions were too good.[99] In other words, there are mistakes related to less eligibility. When these mistakes occur, problems arise in the form of more crime or not enough workers, which prompts powerful interests to urge action.

Because penal policy is usually a deterrent in its own right—being imprisoned is a disutility, regardless of prison conditions—miscalculations such as penal transportation are rare. Variations in crime rates provide sufficient information as to the basic soundness of a given punishment apparatus. Social policy is in theory more prone to perverse effects, which are sometimes called "welfare traps": the idea that welfare is too attractive compared to minimum-wage work. Many social scientists take offense when welfare traps are mentioned because , in practice, relief is always so meager that welfare traps are unlikely to occur.[100] In fact, people are much more likely not to take up the social benefits to which they are entitled.[101] Regardless, the fact that welfare traps are rarely documented demonstrates the principle of less eligibility's validity: relief is almost always less generous than wages.

Subproblem 2 refers to the political contingency of policy making. How do contradictory ideals and interests coalesce into decisions that end up falling in line with the demands of less eligibility?

Here we may take comfort in learning that debates on the optimal amount of punishment and welfare have a long history. Policy making has always been an arena for competing interests to influence final decisions. Medieval indigent relief was a controversial subject among different elites.[102] In the sixteenth century a dispute opposed two famous theologians, Domingo de Soto (1494–1560) and Juan de Medina (1490–1547). Domingo was a religious conservative and benevolently inclined toward the poor. He defended a structural analysis of poverty, based on the movements of the economy, as opposed to the laziness or morality of the poor. Juan, a modernist reformer, argued that the organization of poor relief should hunt for malingerers and false beggars to maximize the number of available workers, so as to limit wage inflation.[103] Their dispute, and its echoes in contemporary conversations about the poor, shows how every society has its internal debates about what to do about poverty and crime and how to balance compassion for the poor with the interests of capitalists. Historical circumstances drove different countries to focus on different aspects of the mix of welfare and punishment. For instance, in the eighteenth century, British elites were more concerned about labor-market regulation than were the French, who cared more for peasant revolts and crushing political agitation.[104] In the late nineteenth century, English ideas about punishment were the subject of fierce debate between deterrence-obsessed Victorians and penal-welfarist reformers.[105]

Below the same upper limit, different societies will vary in how they arrange the particulars of welfare and punishment. What happens below the upper limit is open to political, cultural, and historical particularities. From the standpoint of historical contingency the outcome of a social-penal policy mix always depends on the balance of power between hawks and doves at a given time, which is why countries with similar living standards for the lowest class of workers have different policy mixes. In democracies, popular opinion obviously plays an important role. In fact, the greater sensitivity of the criminal justice system to popular pressure in the United States has been a determinant of more punitive policies, while the bureaucratic insulation of German policy makers and judges has resulted in penal restraint.[106]

The point is not to make a theory of everything.[107] My claim is that these other factors—culture, politics, history—play below the living standards of the lowest class of workers. No amount of "changing sensibilities" will durably set welfare benefits above minimum wage, and "symbolic power" will not be strong enough to make prison more amenable when poor relief is dismal. If contingent policy making does not make punishment deterrent enough, or if it makes welfare too attractive relative to low-wage work, the consequences will quickly be manifest (more crime, a shortage of workers) and will trigger adjustment. An adjustment is itself a contingent policy process: there will be debates, politics, triggering events, and more or less favorable conditions. The adjustment process will take more or less time to achieve a new sustainable mix of welfare and punishment. My argument is that this adjustment is bound to happen.

LESS ELIGIBILITY AND MORALITY

For clarity's sake I have framed the theory of the upper limit in the language of trade-offs, of deterrence, welfare traps, and structural incentives. I do not mean to argue rigidly that every actual human calculates, but I do assume that in the long run, and probabilistically speaking, incentives tend to create observable macroregularities. Such perspective is often accused of neglecting the importance of morality and meaning. Wacquant has aimed to reconcile these two facets of the issue by arguing that contemporary penal excess fulfills the function of easing the economic anxieties of the declining middle class.[108] I might adapt it to a less-eligibility argument as follows: less eligibility carries an intrinsic morality that makes its enforcement seem unquestionable. The vast majority of the general population, and the working poor in particular, believe it would be wrong for people on welfare to make more than people who work or that prison amenities should be adapted to living standards on the outside.

This widespread morality has survived very different times. Let it be remembered that, for centuries, poverty was seen as a good thing. It was obvious to social thinkers in the early stages of the Industrial Revolution that "poverty was deemed essential to incentivize workers and keep their wages low, so as to create a strong, globally competitive, economy."[109] Hunger ensured a steady supply of willing workers. As Patrick Colquhoun (1745–1820), the founder of the modern police force, dryly observed:

> Poverty . . . is a most necessary and indispensable ingredient in society, without which nations and communities could not exist in a state of civilization. It is the lot of man—it is the source of wealth, since without poverty there would be no labour, and without labour there could be no riches, no refinement, no comfort, and no benefit to those who may be possessed of wealth.[110]

This is because wage work was long considered (and treated as) a dignified form of slavery.[111] To force people into wage work was a central concern for early capitalists.[112] In the nineteenth century, English wage-workers were subjected to regulations not significantly different from that of Russian serfs.[113] Only with the gradual elevation of workers' living standards toward the end of the nineteenth century did *worker* cease to be synonymous with *poor.*[114] It is only since then that economic thought began to conceptualize poverty as an impediment to growth and encouraged antipoverty initiatives and efforts toward education.[115] This was one of the most important shifts in thinking in the history of humankind. It has not changed a thing about the structural logic of the relationships between labor markets, welfare, and punishment. This suggests that the principle of less eligibility is not a moral artifact of Anglo-Saxon capitalism.

This is not to say that I claim universal validity for the principle of less eligibility. While the principle of less eligibility is most useful for making sense of historical variations, it has nothing to say about change in enduring patterns of welfare and punishment. It cannot explain why imprisonment became the modern form of punishment or why the modern welfare state came to be the way it is. I also suspect that societies where the labor market is not the overwhelming supplier of livelihood (subsistence economies and societies with high degrees of kin solidarity) are impervious to the logic of the upper limit. In any case this is an empirical question, and claiming theoretical relevance for six centuries of Western history is ambitious enough.

CONCLUSION

In most societies there is a segment of the population that is not integrated into labor markets. These are the people who are the most likely to constitute a threat to social order and to exhibit unpleasant behaviors—crime, vagrancy, and so forth. Such people are dealt with using a mix of welfare and punishment. We know welfare and punishment to vary wildly across time and space, with social policy being more or less stingy, punishment more or less barbaric. My question is, what determines the generosity of social policies and the humanity of penal policies? The principle of less eligibility holds that in every society welfare will be made less attractive than lower-wage work, and punishment will make crime less attractive than welfare. It explains why relief for English poor became meager in 1834, and why Finnish prisons have saunas today. Punishment and welfare are capped by the situation of the lowest class of workers in the labor market—the upper limit of social and penal policy. In the next chapter I review the evolution of this upper limit in the contemporary United States and propose an interpretation of the evolution of welfare and punishment based on the declining situation of low-wage workers.

2

The Great Adjustment

Punishment and Welfare in Postwar America

The standard of living of the average American has to decline. . . . I don't think you can escape that.
—FEDERAL RESERVE CHAIRMAN PAUL VOLCKER

The minimum wage has caused more misery and unemployment than anything since the Great Depression.
—RONALD REAGAN

America's real safety net is drugs, alcohol, cheap food and free porn.
—AMERICAN SINGER HENRY ROLLINS

In this chapter I explain the evolution of welfare and punishment in the United States since the 1960s. According to the principle of less eligibility, the living standards of the lowest class of workers determine the upper limit for the generosity of welfare and the humanity of punishment. I apply this framework to the American case since the 1960s and ground my story in two main facts. First, before the 1960s there were two separate societies in the United States, one white and one black, with distinct patterns in living standards, welfare, and punishment. The Great Migration of African Americans from the South unified the two structures of less eligibility. Crime and welfare rolls increased sharply, revealing a breakdown of less eligibility. Second, the range of options to solve this breakdown in less eligibility was restricted by economic transformations. Since the 1970s, structural change has caused a decline of the living standards of low-income Americans. The lower limit for welfare and punishment was being brought down at a moment of crisis. The consequence was a great adjustment, a reengineering of less eligibility with a less generous welfare state and a more punitive penal state.

THE BREAKDOWN OF LESS ELIGIBILITY

Before the 1960s there were two separate structures of less eligibility in America, one white in the North and one black in the South. The northern white society was a world leader in social progressivism already in the nineteenth century. Farmers pushed for "agrarian statism" and obtained the income tax, central banking, antitrust policy, federal construction of roads, federal control of railroads and telecommunications, and so forth.[1] American veterans' and mothers' pensions existed long before their European counterparts.[2] Americans boasted a punitive top marginal income tax rate (79–87 percent) between 1936 and 1962, higher than in France and Germany. The social policies developed between the New Deal and the War on Poverty inspired postwar European policy makers. The United States started a minimal income scheme (Aid to Dependent Children) in 1935, much before the United Kingdom's National Assistance Act (1948). Sweden started its program in 1957, Denmark, Germany, the Netherlands, and Norway between 1961 and 1964.[3] In 1964 the US passed the Economic Opportunity Act, further extending the safety net.[4] President Richard Nixon seriously considered passing a quasi-basic income bill in 1970.[5] Americans were also leaders in penal reform. Michigan, Minnesota, and Maine had abolished the death penalty as early as the mid–nineteenth century; France was still chopping off heads in 1977. All in all, until the early 1970s northern white America was on the same trajectory as Western European social democracies, actively working to integrate the working classes into the "affluent society" and using the full power of taxation, antitrust laws, and the welfare state to this end. All this shows that the United States is not culturally inclined toward restrictive welfare and harsh punishment.

The main force resisting the expansion of the welfare state was southern Democrats.[6] In the South, African Americans lived in a completely different society, one shaped by slavery's legacy. Before its abolition in 1865, American slave owners had relied on the most horrific forms of punishment (torture, mutilation, etc.) to force slaves into work. Even when slavery was abolished, work conditions did not improve greatly, and the connection between labor and punishment was quickly reestablished:

> The Thirteenth Amendment, which abolished slavery and involuntary servitude "except as a punishment for crime" enabled the widespread use of debt peonage and convict leasing. This resulted in the deaths of tens of thousands of African Americans between the 1870s and the 1940s, exceeding by a significant magnitude the number who died from lynching. At its worst, more than one in four leased convicts died in under two years from a mix of overwork, malnutrition, and unsafe working conditions. . . . Criminalization of vagrancy, loitering, quitting a job, petty theft, and even talking loudly in public could result in incarceration for blacks, accompanied by exorbitant fines and court costs. White employers paid off these debts and in return forced victims to work for years without pay under horrendous conditions. . . . This extractive system was central to the southern

> economy under "Redemption" and Jim Crow. Indeed, debt peonage, chain gangs, and convict leasing enabled the economic resurrection of the region and continued well into the Progressive Era.[7]

In the first half of the twentieth century most southern blacks worked as sharecroppers in abject poverty. Their standards of living were far below those of poor whites. As farmworkers they lived in perpetual debt, were malnourished, and had little or no access to running water. Because of Jim Crow laws, their eligibility for relief was minimal to nonexistent. After the 1930s they were technically eligible for New Deal federal programs but were seldom able to actually get relief or avail themselves of benefits under the GI Bill.[8] They had minimal access to health care, no pensions, and no unemployment insurance, even though work was highly uncertain. When they tried to unionize and demand better wages, they were often met with police brutality, murder, and lynching.[9] Approximately 3,500 blacks were lynched in the South between 1880 and 1950.

In short, whites and blacks lived in two different structures of less eligibility. Poor whites and poor blacks had different standards of living, different access to welfare, and different severities of punishment. The two societies lived separate and unequal.

The mechanization of agriculture from the 1940s on transformed southern labor markets. Sharecroppers were no longer needed; meanwhile, northern industries needed workers who were becoming scarce with the combination of restrictive immigration policies and World War II. This accelerated the Great Migration, which had started in the 1910s. By the 1960s, six million African Americans had moved to the cities of the northern East Coast, the Great Lakes, and California.[10]

Most African Americans from the South were farm laborers with little education. They competed for unskilled jobs in manufacturing but faced intense discrimination in labor markets. The black unemployment rate was twice that of whites, and the AFL-CIO estimated at the time that 36 percent of all long-term unemployed Americans were black.[11] Not only were blacks disadvantaged to begin with, but the sectors in which they were employed began to shrink. Black industrial employment started to drop in the 1960s as American manufacturing began its relative decline within the overall economy. In addition to employment discrimination, black migrants suffered extreme residential segregation. They could only find housing in a few dilapidated neighborhoods in each city they went to. The population density of Watts in Los Angeles was thrice that of white neighborhoods in the same city.[12] Rents were artificially inflated as multiple families squeezed into small houses. As a consequence, the Great Migration did not result in an equalizing of living standards between the lowest classes of white and black workers.

Meanwhile, in the 1960s President Johnson launched the Great Society. The Economic Opportunity Act of 1964, which started the War on Poverty, came with a $1 billion investment. The Office for Economic Opportunity, the agency that oversaw programs such as the Job Corps, Head Start, and the Community Action Program, spent $200 million in its first three months of operation.[13] In spite of these efforts urban poverty grew. Between 1959 and 1968, while the national (relative) poverty rate dropped from 22 to 12.8 percent, the absolute number of poor in cities increased 62 percent.[14]

The combination of an increased presence of poor African Americans, dire labor market prospects, and an increased availability of poor relief created what Piven and Cloward have called a "welfare explosion."[15] As part of the Community Action Programs of the War on Poverty, the (Democratic) federal government subsidized activists throughout the country to force local welfare bureaucrats—usually controlled by the Democratic Party machine—to finally grant African Americans what they had long been eligible for.[16] In other words, while working-class blacks suffered lower living standards than their white counterparts, they were placed in the same welfare incentive structure. Unsurprisingly, welfare enrollment among African Americans soared. Between 1960 and 1968 the number of applications grew 85 percent, and the approval rate rose from 55 to 70 percent.[17] The number of food stamps recipients grew from about 500,000 in 1965 to 22.4 million in 1981 (USDA), and changing eligibility rules increased the number of disability benefit recipients threefold between 1960 and 1975.[18] Meanwhile, the Supreme Court transformed the legal meaning of benefits. Welfare benefits had long been seen as a gratuity, not an entitlement. This meant it was easier for bureaucrats to deny or revoke benefits. With *Goldberg v. Kelly* (1970), the Court decided to treat benefits as entitlements, worthy of procedural rights and subject to due process.[19]

In the following years economic conditions deteriorated. Deindustrialization and oil shocks increased unemployment and inflation, cutting real wages. On the lower rungs of the labor markets African Americans suffered pervasive racial discrimination and competition from incoming migrants, all while public sector jobs were shrinking. During the Carter recession in the 1970s, the unemployment rate for black youths reached 60 percent.[20] The ruthless residential apartheid that had prevailed where African Americans had moved in was relaxed, and middle-class blacks were able to move out to richer and whiter neighborhoods. Poor, minority neighborhoods became pockets of concentrated poverty, leading to more crime.[21] The dearth of jobs for black men made them unappealing marriage prospects, and black women had more children out of wedlock.[22] Between 1960 and 1982 the proportion of women-headed families in the black community rose from 22 percent to 42 percent.[23] The combination of low wages and high costs of childcare and transportation incentivized single mothers to rely on a combination of welfare and informal work.[24]

In addition to increased welfare availability, the United States decreased the intensity and severity of punishment in the 1960s. The general belief that crime was a problem that would be solved by an affluent society, and that prison only made people worse, led policy makers to decide against building new prisons in the 1960s and 1970s, while the population was growing rapidly. The ratio of incarceration rate to crime rate (the "punitiveness ratio," created by public policy scholar Mark Kleiman) fell precipitously in the 1960s, and in spite of the explosion of the prison population in the 1980s, the punitiveness ratio of 1962 was only recovered in 1997, as crime started to fall.[25] This means that accounting for crime levels, even though 1997 America imprisoned its residents at a rate four times that of 1962 America, 1962

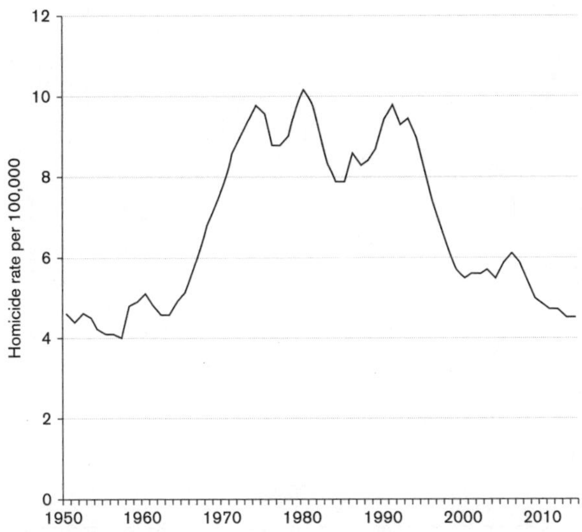

FIGURE 1. Homicide rate in the United States, per 100,000, 1950–2014. Source: FBI UCR reports, https://ucr.fbi.gov/crime-in-the-u.s.

America was as punitive as 1997 America. This decreased severity is best exemplified by the average punishment for burglaries. Comparing the total number of burglaries with the total time of prison served for burglary, Kleiman found the "price" of the average burglary to be fourteen days of prison in 1962, four days in 1974, and back to sixteen days in 2007. Computing the days served in prison with proceeds from the average burglary, Kleiman found that thieves earned less than $200 per day incarcerated in 1962, against $800 in 1974.[26]

In the 1960s, northern African Americans joined the less eligibility structure of their white counterparts when punishment severity loosened. The Warren Supreme Court ruled against police brutality and in favor of increasing the civil rights of police suspects: for instance, *Brady v. Maryland* (1963, prosecutors have to disclose exculpatory evidence), *Escobedo v. Illinois* (1963, suspects have a right to counsel), *Gideon v. Wainwright* (1963, a public defender must be assigned for defendants who cannot afford a lawyer), *Miranda v. Arizona* (1966, police officers have to inform defendants of their rights). Whites still enjoyed vastly greater civil rights protections and more lenient policing and sentencing, but the situation of blacks regarding punishment in the North was incomparably favorable compared to the medieval brutality in the South.

The declining severity of punishment affected all Americans. At the same time, crime soared across racial groups. Between 1963 and 1974 the homicide rate more than doubled, from 4.6 per 100,000 to 9.8 per 100,000 (fig. 1).

Crime rates increased across racial groups but likely rose faster among blacks. However, I have only found race-specific data for homicides since 1976, thus missing the critical time frame of the 1960s (fig. 2).

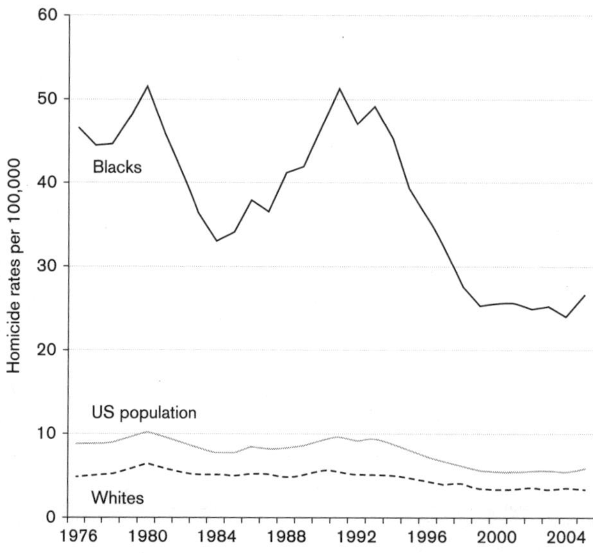

FIGURE 2. Homicide rates for blacks, whites, and the US population, per 100,000, 1976–2005. Source: FBI UCR reports, https://ucr.fbi.gov/crime-in-the-u.s; Fox and Zawitz, *Homicide trends in the US.*

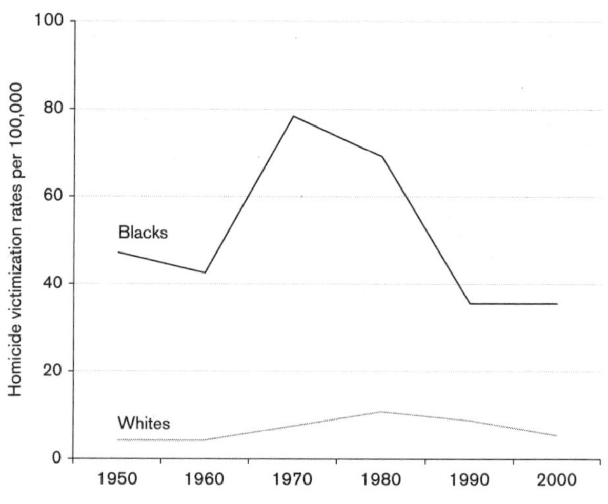

FIGURE 3. Homicide victimization rates for blacks and whites, per 100,000, 1950–2000. Source: O'Flaherty and Sethi, Homicide in black and white.

Because we know that homicide is consistently committed within racial groups, data about victims (not perpetrators) may provide indirect evidence of rising crime among blacks (fig. 3).

Crime-rate patterns among African Americans are consistent with the hypothesis that young black men in the North faced dire work opportunities because of deindustrialization and racism, in parallel with increasing rewards for criminal activity, which resulted in an increase in black crime. I am not trying to argue that blacks were "responsible" for the crime boom. Blacks were and are a small minority of the American population (10–14 percent between 1960 and 2015), and minor variations in the white homicide rate create big overall effects. The crime boom of the 1960s and 1970s was stronger in the United States than in other Western countries. The causes of this increase are still difficult to ascertain.[27]

In addition to rising crime rates, Americans in the 1960s experienced deadly riots. The riots were almost all triggered by incidents of police brutality. The confrontation between predominantly working-class white officers with poor blacks, combined with an overreliance on car patrol and rapid response at the expense of fostering police-community relations,[28] resulted in massive misconduct and abuse that, combined with segregation, job discrimination, poverty, and the struggle for civil rights, precipitated large-scale urban riots in Harlem, Philadelphia, and Rochester (1964), Watts (1965), and Chicago (1966). During the "long hot summer" of 1967, 159 riots took place, and 41 percent of cities with populations of more than 100,000 were involved, including Newark and Detroit. In a context of growing black militancy, many whites were terrified by the looting, the burning of white-owned businesses, the escalation from Molotov cocktails to sniper fire, and what they saw as black hatred for whites, especially after the 1967 Detroit riot left 43 dead. Detroit was the city where blacks had been relatively more prosperous, and the riot there killed any remaining support for the War on Poverty.[29] More than a hundred riots followed the assassination of Martin Luther King Jr. in 1968. In Washington, DC, "Johnson ordered the U.S. Army into position after the burning and looting had come within two blocks of the White House."[30] At least 191 people died during the riots of 1964 to 1968.[31]

In the context of the civil rights movement, riots, rising crime rates, and increasing welfare caseloads aggravated racial tensions. The backlash (or "frontlash") began in the late 1960s[32] and is perhaps best described in the ethnography of a Brooklyn neighborhood, Canarsie.[33] Canarsians were working-class Jews and Italians who had fled their old neighborhoods when African Americans arrived there in the 1960s. They lost a lot of money in the process and were financially punished by high interest rates. Their main concerns were black muggers, urban riots, and their combined effect on the value of their homes. They resented social explanations for crime and saw the proper role of welfare as "a dignified alternative to starvation." They viewed "rioting not as an outcry against grievous wrong but as a manifestation of the ghetto dwellers' tendency to scream for benefits, to wallow in self-pity about exploitation long past, and to use lofty ideals to mask thuggery."[34] Once Democratic Party voters, by the 1980s they had entirely switched to thinly veiled racism, law and order, and antiwelfare politics. Support for the Democratic Party among working-class whites across America dropped twenty percentage points between the periods of 1960 to 1964 and 1968 to 1972, from 55 percent to 35 percent.[35]

These events and their racial undertones help us to understand, from a contingent-historical standpoint, why welfare and punishment changed so quickly and so radically from the 1970s on.[36] From a structural point of view there has been a decline, since the 1970s, in the living standards of the lowest class of workers in the United States.

THE STRUCTURAL CONTEXT: THE LOWERING OF THE UPPER LIMIT SINCE THE 1970S

Between 1967 and 2006 there was a decline in the relative earnings of low-income American households. The 10 percent poorest households saw almost no increase in earnings, while the rest of American society, and the richest in particular, became comparatively richer.[37] There was even an *absolute* decline in the earnings of lowest-income male American workers.[38] These are figures for 1967 to 2006, that is, just before the 2008 financial crisis. Ironically, economist Jonathan Heathcote and his coauthors note that "access to financial markets has limited both the level and growth of consumption inequality."[39] We can therefore safely assume that the situation of low-income workers worsened after the crisis, as such households suffered most from the Great Recession.[40]

A decline in relative living standards is probably as consequential as an absolute one. Unless absolute poverty refers to impending death from starvation, poverty is always relative to society-specific expectations. "Being poor" is not the same in Niger and in Norway. In Scandinavian welfare capitalism, "not starving" is not an appropriate threshold for absolute poverty. Instead, the threshold there should include shelter, heating, access to health care, and so forth—all of which constitute luxuries in poorer societies.[41]

Among the direct factors to declining low-wage earnings, rising unemployment in the 1970s resulted in a sharp decline in the number of hours worked by lower-skilled men, which aggravated earnings inequality.[42] Another direct factor was the declining minimum wage. Between 1968 and 2013, the (real) federal minimum wage shrank by 24 percent, and "since the 1970s, the statutory federal minimum wage has not been high enough for a person employed full-time year-round to bring a family of three or more above the official poverty line."[43] Labor economists have shown that the declining minimum wage contributed to income inequality.[44]

It is tricky to infer declining *living standards* from declining *earnings* because it is difficult to compare the costs of primary goods over time, just as it is impossible to decide what constitutes a primary good in the first place. Still, declining earnings usually do not result in rising living standards, and, during the period under study, low-income workers did not benefit from lower housing costs. Between 1960 and 2010 the share of cost-burdened renter households rose from under 25 percent to 50 percent.[45]

Earnings declined, and so did the quality of work. Low-wage work was no longer a transitional phase from youth to adulthood. In 1979 teenagers made up 27 percent of low-wage workers; in 2013 their share dropped to 12 percent.[46] The employment stability of men declined, especially at the bottom of the income distribution: workers began to change occupations more often, and nonstandard employment (temp agency workers, on-call workers, contract workers, and independent contractors or freelancers) rose.[47] With nonstandard employment practices, the health insurance coverage of high school dropouts declined from 67 to 50 percent between 1979 and 1997.[48]

As a consequence of increased nonstandard employment practices and structural changes in the economy, earnings volatility increased. "Transitory variance" (the instability of earnings over time, typically because of temporary unemployment) doubled between 1974 and 2000.[49] This affected low-wage workers more than anyone else, as a spell of hard luck could propel them into poverty. With increased income volatility "among men and women under age 30, nearly 40 percent experienced poverty in the 1990s, compared with just 25 percent in the 1970s."[50]

To explain these transformations, sociologist Matissa Hollister has assembled the "new employment narrative," synthesizing the work of labor economists such as Michael Piore, David Autor, and Peter Cappelli.[51] Postwar employment was organized along two pillars: strong labor unions for blue-collar workers and "internal labor markets" for white-collar workers (long-term employment in big corporations with opportunities for promotions). Since the 1970s, a number of phenomena have combined to weaken the position of low-wage workers, starting with increased foreign competition, as Europe and Asia caught up with America's industrial sector. Technological change has been "skill-biased," increasing the relative productivity of and demand for skilled workers over unskilled ones.[52] The shift to a service economy, and the decline in manufacturing, has weakened union power. Male private union membership dropped from 34 percent in 1973 to 8 percent in 2007, while inequality in hourly wages increased by over 40 percent.[53] Well-publicized layoffs in the 1980s contributed to further taming the labor movement.

In manufacturing, a shift from mass to specialized production resulted in shorter business cycles and a need for more flexibility. The great corporations, which used to employ a large workforce with internal promotion opportunities, became a thing of the past. Since 1997, the number of public corporations in the US has declined by 55 percent, as companies have been sold, bought, sliced up into smaller entities, and reorganized as chains of subcontractors.[54] The shareholder turn has focused firms on short-term profits. Firms have implemented high-performance work systems to pressurize their employees, while the business models of labor-intensive employers increasingly rest on low-wage work:

> Most have slim profit margins: Walmart and Target earn between three and four cents on the dollar; a typical McDonald's franchise restaurant earns around six cents on the dollar before taxes, according to an analysis from Janney Capital Markets. In fact, the combined profits of all the major retailers, restaurant chains,

> and supermarkets in the Fortune 500 are smaller than the profits of Apple alone. Yet Apple employs just seventy-six thousand people, while the retailers, supermarkets, and restaurant chains employ 5.6 million. The grim truth of those numbers is that low wages are a big part of why these companies are able to stay profitable while offering low prices.[55]

In the new employment landscape, flexible labor markets have meant that employers do not have to retain people, nor do they have to train them to keep them productive in the long run; they can fire employees and replace them with new ones with more desirable skills.[56]

The transformation of the economy has had disparate consequences for men and women. While men have been most affected by industrial decline and weaker labor unions, women have joined the labor force in great numbers. Couples have thus become more homogenous in terms of social status, combining two matching incomes and thus maximizing inequalities.[57] A further contributor to job polarization has been the rise of the "care economy," as highly skilled, high-income women have increasingly paid unskilled workers to clean, cook, and babysit. This domestic work was formerly provided by the stay-at-home wife of the male breadwinner and is now typically performed by immigrant women, opening new avenues for low-wage labor and increasing inequality.[58] Because of the decline in manufacturing, low-income men have suffered most from the transformation of the economy—an important point, as crime is mostly committed by men. Although high-income women have gained the most, the fate of low-income women has been influenced by another major transformation—that of the family. Between 1960 and 1980, divorces doubled, with economic consequences that have been especially adverse for lower-educated women.[59]

The key marker of aggravated inequality and declining relative living standards for the lowest class of workers remains life expectancy. We know that rich people live longer. For men who were born in 1920, and who retired in the 1980s, there was a six-year difference in life expectancy between the top 10 percent of earners and the bottom 10 percent. But for the generation of men born in 1950, and who retired in the 2010s, having joined the labor markets circa 1975, that difference has more than doubled, to fourteen years.[60]

Since the 1970s, therefore, the living standards of the lowest class of American workers have declined. The upper limit of social and penal policy was lowered at a time of crisis. Because of these declining living standards, the reengineering of less eligibility that occurred, which I describe below as increased punishment and reduced welfare generosity, was a structural necessity. The most spectacular transformation occurred in the changing landscape of punishment.

REENGINEERING LESS ELIGIBILITY

In 1968 Richard Nixon won the presidency on a law-and-order platform (the slogan was "Freedom from fear") and quickly proceeded to fund crime-control efforts. Between 1969 and 1974 the Law Enforcement Assistance Administration's budget increased from $63 million to $871 million.[61] The rise of juvenile crime—robbery in particular—prompted states to pass legislation allowing the prosecution of minors as adults. This was achieved in all 50 states by 1997.[62] Elected officials and policy makers embraced punitive practices at the expense of rehabilitative missions as early as the 1970s—before the rise in incarceration in the mid-1980s and before the 1996 welfare reform.[63] Legislators at the local and federal levels enacted a number of measures from the 1970s that drove up incarceration rates: the Rockefeller drug laws and the War on Drugs (especially on crack cocaine), truth-in-sentencing, three-strikes-and-you're-out, mandatory minimums, and a boom in "life without parole" sentences.[64] These reforms came to full effect in the mid-1980s.[65]

Once new prisons were built and sentencing reform passed, incarceration started to rise in the 1980s, from about 150 prisoners per 100,000 Americans to more than 700 per 100,000 in the 2000s, to stabilize around 660 per 100,000 in the mid-2010s. American prisons shifted from two-thirds white in 1970 to two-thirds black and Latino in 2000.[66] The social characteristics of this incarcerated population were perfectly in line with the principle of less eligibility. Between 1976 and 1995, states which experienced declines in low-skilled wages saw larger increases in incarceration.[67] The incarcerated massively came from the poorest segments of society. According to a mid-1990s survey of jail inmates, two-thirds lived below the poverty line at the time of arrest, half were high school dropouts, and half were either unemployed, economically inactive, or only occasionally employed.[68]

The punitive adjustment extended after incarceration. Between 1960 and 1980 the share of unconditional parole release dropped from about 40 percent to almost 15 percent.[69] It also concerned other areas of punishment, such as policing, which I'll discuss in detail in chapter 4. The general idea is that following the 1960s and early 1970s, punishment has become more severe. This transformation in punishment and welfare was supported by electoral majorities and the policy-making elite alike.

In the realm of social policy, measures were taken in the 1970s to limit the generosity of welfare. To counter Supreme Court efforts to protect welfare recipients, elected officials voted to restrict benefits and their eligibility parameters.[70] The Nixon plan for a guaranteed income for families with children was buried by the Senate.[71] Policy makers cut benefits to make work more desirable than welfare. The real value of AFDC (Aid to Families with Dependent Children, "welfare") dropped 42 percent between 1970 and 1996:[72] "no other group in American society experienced such a sharp decline in real income since 1970 as did AFDC mothers and their children," wrote policy scholar Robert Greenstein.[73] In addition to reducing the benefits' monetary value, "the federal government increased the amount of information and paperwork required to determine welfare eligibility, and denied benefits to low-income families who failed to keep up with the paperwork"—a process called "churning."[74]

In the 1980s the Reagan administration took a number of steps to reduce the generosity of the American welfare state. The Omnibus Reconciliation Act of 1981 put limitations on cash aid, and states that overpaid food stamps to the poor were penalized. States whose "error rate" exceeded 5 percent lost federal funding, which strongly incentivized them to be much stricter in determining eligibility.[75] Fraud investigation units were formed throughout the country to detect "welfare cheats," sometimes run by law enforcement rather than social workers.[76] Between 1979 and 1988 the number of people under the poverty line increased from 26 million to 33 million, and homelessness resurfaced.[77] Efforts to curb benefits culminated in the 1996 welfare reform.

From 1996 onward welfare benefits (renamed Temporary Assistance for Needy Families, TANF) were limited to 60 months over a lifetime. The idea was to end welfare dependency and to force poor people into low-wage work. The conditions under which welfare is allocated were further restricted. Under "family cap" policies, once a mother got welfare, the amount she received could not increase with newborn children. "Family cap" was thus designed to block the fertility of poor women.[78] The 1996 welfare reform made fraud liable to criminal (as opposed to civil) penalties. Recipients became constantly suspected of fraud and frequently investigated. An estimated 33–52 percent of TANF recipients have been sanctioned at least once, usually for missing appointments.[79] With ever less generous benefits, welfare recipients have become forced to find other sources of income, which almost always constitute fraud, either because the income is unreported (as it would decrease benefits) or because the source of income is illegitimate (off the books or illegal).[80] The computerization of files from different administrations allows investigators to quickly find unreported income. Another common fraud is not reporting a new income-generating partner living at home or not reporting the departure of a child. Because of the tangled nature of family arrangements, many fraud investigations originate in anonymous denunciations from bitter ex-partners.[81] Research suggests that the rules are so arcane that in half of cases, recipients do not know the precise reason why they have been sanctioned or lost their benefits.[82]

The general movement was thus a shift of federal expenditures away from the poorest and toward workers,[83] as well as a decline in cash welfare: "in 1979 25.4 percent of [the] post-tax income [of one-parent families] came from government sources including cash welfare, food stamps, disability, and the Earned Income Tax Credit (EITC). This fell to 13 percent by 2006."[84]

The reduced generosity of American relief followed the principle of less eligibility. States where benefits were the highest compared to local wages in 1976 were the most likely to cut them by 1995, and conversely states with high minimum wages were less likely to terminate a program called General Assistance.[85] There is also indirect evidence of the adjustment between the 1970s and 1990s in the work of Katherine Beckett and Bruce Western on imprisonment and welfare spending across the 50 states. These authors find that in 1995, "welfare and incarceration were strongly negatively related," meaning that "states with less generous welfare programs incarcerated at a significantly higher level."[86] This is consistent with the principle of less eligibility. But more interestingly, Beckett and Western do not find the same relation for 1975 and 1985, which suggests that the adjustment was still under way and not yet complete.

There has thus been a drastic policy response in both penal and social policy to realign the rewards of welfare and crime below the rewards of low-wage work. Given the gap between black and white standards of living when the Great Migration occurred, the merging of two structures of less eligibility caused a breakdown. At the same time, declining living standards for low-income workers lowered the upper limit. What could have happened, and would have changed the face of the United States, would have been a major plan to transform the economy in favor of the poor. This would have prevented the joblessness that ultimately resulted in more crime and welfare dependency and led to the adjustment that did happen: mass incarceration and welfare reform.

At the same time, from the mid–1990s onward, crime fell in historic proportions. By 2010, homicide rates were halved. There is no consensus on what caused the crime drop. Many explanations have been discussed. The abortion theory (unborn unwanted babies after 1973 didn't become teenagers in the late 1980s, therefore couldn't commit crime) is now regarded with skepticism.[87] Similarly, the reduction in lead exposure theory (lead exposure reduces children's IQ and makes them more impulsive, therefore more criminal) is not as promising as it once seemed.[88] The lowering effect of immigration on crime in the United States is at best weak.[89] Crime fell in most Western countries at the same time, suggesting global causes at play, such as population ageing and the improvement of passive security (houses that are more difficult to burglarize and cars more difficult to steal). Teenagers today spend much more time on internet and video games, away from the streets, than in the recent past.[90] Decreased alcohol consumption also played its role.[91] But each country has its specificities, and the United States experienced a higher-than-average crime boom in the 1960s and 1970s. There is evidence that the crime drop began in the 1980s but was interrupted by a sudden and short-lived crime boom related to the crack cocaine epidemics.[92] The most persuasive sources I can find suggest that changes in policing, increased incarceration, and better economic prospects did contribute to declining crime trends in the United States in the 1990s.[93] The punitive adjustment—in my view a consequence of the lowering of the upper limit documented above—thus likely was a contributing factor to the crime drop,[94] and falling crime brought legitimacy to the new mix of welfare and punishment.

THE CONSEQUENCES OF DEINDUSTRIALIZATION IN THE 2000S

In 2001, China joined the World Trade Organization, ending the yearly negotiation of tariffs on Chinese imports in the United States Congress. This removed the uncertainty over possible tariff increases and Chinese goods starting to flow to the United States. The deindustrialization that occurred between 1965 and 2000 was a relative decline compared to other sectors and general population growth, but employment had held steady at about 18 million workers. Between 2001 and 2007, in pre–Great Recession America, manufacturing employment dropped 18 percent, in large part because of imports from countries such as China, which had cheaper production costs.[95]

The consequences have been particularly negative for the low-skilled, white working class. The counties most exposed to Chinese competition have seen relative declines in housing prices and business activity, leading to reduced tax revenue and less public services where they are more needed.[96] In these counties the decline of manufacturing employment has resulted in men being unable to marry and more children being born out of wedlock, in large part because women earn more and are less likely to marry men who earn less.[97] Nowadays, working-class men, especially white men, who formed the bulk of blue-collar rural communities, are dying at an unusually faster rate:

> From 1978 to 1998, the mortality rate for US whites aged 45–54 fell by 2 percent per year on average, which matched the average rate of decline in . . . all other industrialized countries. After 1998, other rich countries' mortality rates continued to decline by 2 percent a year. In contrast, US white non-Hispanic mortality rose by half a percent a year.[98]

White working-class Americans die of smoking, alcoholism, suicide, and drug overdose—"deaths of despair."[99] This higher mortality has been in proportion to exposure to foreign competition and "progressively worsening labor market opportunities."[100] Unsurprisingly, the decline in manufacturing employment has also resulted in higher crime.[101] With declining labor market opportunities for working-class males, higher crime, and residual welfare institutions unable to pick up the tab, incarceration rates have risen, this time among the white rural population.

As a consequence, since 2000 (as manufacturing employment started to drop) there has been a steep increase in white rural prison admissions.[102] The *New York Times* reported that "the annual number of new black prison inmates fell by about 25 percent from 2006 to 2013, and the number of Hispanic inmates fell by about 30 percent, while the number of new white inmates fell by only about 8 percent."[103] This white incarceration is highly correlated to poverty and low education.[104] In the 2010s the growth of incarceration in the United States has been driven by poor rural white counties whose local prosecutors and judges have sought harsh sentences for both dealers and users of heroin and meth.[105] About 60,000 people die every year of drug overdose in the United States; it is the leading cause of death for Americans under 50).[106] At 400 per 100,000 people, the rate of incarceration for American whites in the 2010s is still vastly lower than the African American incarceration rate of about 2,300.[107] But the rise in white incarceration in the 2000s following the decline of economic opportunities for its working class shows less eligibility at work.

As of 2017 the conditions on low-wage labor markets leave little chance of increased generosity of benefits or of a reduction in severity of punishment. Granted, unemployment is low. The meagerness of welfare benefits and the availability of low-wage work certainly contribute to this. The "low-wage recovery" following the Great Recession has seen the economy adding 1.8 million low-wage jobs, especially in the fast-food and retail sectors, at the expense of a million high-wage jobs (NELP 2014). But the work rate of adult men has dropped 13 percentage points in the past

50 years. The United States ranks twenty-second in the OECD, ahead of only Italy, in male-labor-force participation among those aged 25 to 54 years.[108] Some of this is due to increased participation by women in the labor force since the 1996 welfare reform.[109] A lot of it seems related to the lasting impact of incarceration. Millions of men have become unemployable, either because they lack skills or because of employer bias against hiring those with a criminal record. The low rate of labor-force participation, in addition to the size of the prison population, artificially lowers the unemployment rate and makes for a population of men who are less likely to get married and more likely to commit crime.[110]

Working conditions and pay for low-wage workers—the upper limit—are still unfavorable. Out of 17 OECD countries, the United States has the highest rate of in-work poverty.[111] American workers at minimum wage earn a net disposable income (after tax and after benefits) that places them in a poverty risk more favorable only than that of Bulgaria.[112] A study in New York, Los Angeles, and Chicago found that 22 to 29 percent of low-wage workers earned less than minimum wage, mostly because of violations of break laws and of wage theft (by employers).[113] Low-wage workers in the United States not only earn little; they enjoy few benefits. Among the 10 percent lowest paid workers, 60 percent have no health insurance *and* no retirement benefits.[114] In many sectors the take-up rate of Obamacare is around 1–2 percent, because health insurance is simply too expensive.[115] In fact, many low-income workers are so poor that government ends up subsidizing their income. For instance, between 2007 and 2011, instead of paying living wages, the fast-food industry cost the taxpayer $7 billion per year in Medicaid, the Children's Health Insurance program, food stamps, and EITC (the Earned Income Tax Credit.)[116]

The EITC is perhaps the most important development in recent American social policy. It supplements the income of *working* families so that they can rise above the poverty line, providing up to $5,300 to families with two children. It is now by far the biggest cash welfare program in the United States. In 2011 the EITC amounted to $55 billion for 26 million households, 5 times more money than TANF and 14 times as many recipients.[117] Between the early 1990s and the mid–2010s, "EITC recipients jumped from 14 percent of the US ulation . . . to 23 percent . . . , and the average EITC benefit level rose by about 50 percent."[118] The rise of EITC (and of the similar Child Tax Credit) and the demise of AFDC/TANF have transformed the structure of the safety net, favoring recipients near the poverty line over the poorest, those with incomes less than half the poverty line.[119] The EITC is sometimes viewed favorably among progressive circles, perhaps because it is better than nothing.[120] The sad reality is that the rise of the EITC did not decrease in-work poverty, which has remained stable since the 1980s. This may appear puzzling, since the EITC was designed to make work pay and has expanded greatly over the years. The explanation is twofold. First, many EITC recipients also used to get traditional welfare benefits (the working poor are not always working).[121] Second, the EITC has had "large negative impacts" on wages, which "offset the increased transfers."[122] In other words, the earned income tax credit has been a giant subsidy to American businesses so that they can pay workers below Ricardo's iron law of wages, and it serves to make low-wage work more attractive.

In fairness, one safety net program has grown in scope and generosity, especially in the aftermath of the Great Recession: the Supplementary Nutrition Assistance Program (SNAP), formerly known as food stamps.[123] But the stinginess of the American welfare state is well documented in international comparisons. The United States and Sweden have the same pretax and transfers poverty rate; it is only after transfers (social benefits) that Sweden boasts a much lower poverty rate.[124] In a recent contribution, sociologist David Brady and his coauthors calculated for 29 countries the chances of being poor in relation to a number of risks (unemployment, single motherhood, etc.).[125] They found a form of American exceptionalism: while the prevalence of each identified risk is below average compared to the other countries (i.e., the unemployment rate is lower, the single motherhood rate is the same, etc.), Americans incur the greatest probability of falling into poverty when they are unemployed, single mothers, and so forth. The reason is the comparative weakness of the American welfare state, especially in regard to unemployment and low education, which are the two likeliest factors of poverty. The absence of a meaningful safety net has given rise in recent years to extreme poverty in the United States—families living on less than two dollars a day.[126]

Incarceration has slightly decreased since 2008, and crime is low, suggesting that a new equilibrium of less eligibility has been reached after the great adjustment of the 1980s and 1990s. But American punishment is not just incarceration and increasingly consists of monetary sanctions such as fines, fees, and restitution payments. Between 1991 and 2004 the proportion of imprisoned people who received an additional monetary sanction has increased from 25 percent to 66 percent. Sanctions average $4,000 and include all sorts of fees (court fees, jail booking fees, urine sample fees, etc.).[127] Most states charge for costs of conditional supervision (probation and parole), and electronic monitoring is often outsourced to private businesses, which charge $300 to $1,500 per month. Most of these "legal financial obligations" are never recovered, because defendants are poor and already in debt, but a small industry of debt collection agencies buys debt and takes people to court.[128] The rise of monetary sanctions shows how punishment in the United States maintains severity even in the face of apparent prison downsizing.

CONCLUSION

Over the past 40 years, the United States has grown richer but also more unequal. The lowest paid 10 percent of the population have seen their earnings decline. The principle of less eligibility states that the living standards of the lowest class of workers set the upper limit for welfare and, transitively, punishment. This means that declining living standards of low-wage workers should translate into a less generous welfare state, and a more punitive penal state. This is what has happened: a process of less eligibility adjustment.

Before the 1960s the United States had devised a dual mix of welfare and punishment, one for whites, which followed the European trajectory, and one for southern blacks, which was horrifically cruel—Jim Crow. The postwar migration of African Americans happened at a time of racism and declining opportunities for low-skilled workers, leaving blacks in a disadvantaged position. At the same time, welfare benefits became more generous and punishment less punitive, and a crime boom ensued. This was a breakdown of less eligibility. The policy response might have been different, but at the same time a historical trend of declining living standards for the lowest class of workers lowered the upper limit for social and penal policy and only allowed for a thorough adjustment of less eligibility. Welfare and punishment have followed an ever less generous, ever more punitive route.

From this, I propose an empirical investigation of the outcome of this punitive reengineering of less eligibility. I propose to look at welfare and punishment in an urban black community where crime has dropped dramatically, at the cost of widespread incarceration. This community is East New York, Brooklyn.

3

The Crime Drop and the East New York Renaissance

I was driven from the Bronx. I know. How much is your home worth if you can't tell your friends to get off at the 105th Street subway station?
—A CANARSIE MAN QUOTED IN RIEDER, CANARSIE

In the 1960s, East New York was transformed by social change. It became a high-crime black neighborhood. By the mid–2000s, crime had fallen dramatically. As a consequence it constitutes an interesting window of observation for the effects of the adjustment of less eligibility described in chapter 2. East New York residents, primarily poor and low-income, suffered most from welfare retrenchment and punitive penal policies. They also benefited from the ensuing crime drop. I focus below on the consequences of the crime drop.

EAST NEW YORK FROM THE 1960S TO THE 1990S

Until the 1950s, East New York was a white working-class neighborhood. It was a rat-infested slum for poor immigrants, but after World War II many residents benefited from GI Bill opportunities to improve their standing in American society, hoping to buy a house in the rapidly developing suburbs. The baby boomers were kids, and there was a general sense that the rising tide was lifting all boats. There were a few black families in East New York who were not made to feel welcome, but there also were socialist activists who defended the principle of working-class unity over racial division.

Meanwhile, the Great Migration was at its height, and millions of African Americans were looking for shelter in northern cities. Because of segregation, blacks and Puerto Ricans could not find apartments in more affluent white neighborhoods. They went to existing ghettoes (like Harlem) or to the poorest white slums (like East New York or neighboring Brownsville). Within years, blacks and Puerto Ricans almost entirely replaced the original white population. Between 1960 and 1966 East New York went from 85 percent white working class to 80 percent black and Puerto Rican.[1]

Most white homeowners left in fear of falling real estate values. The situation was a great opportunity for business. In a practice called blockbusting, real estate brokers scared white homeowners into selling their houses in a hurry, sometimes parading black families up and down the street.[2] White homeowners sold at a loss, and brokers sold the houses to one or several black families at higher than market value (since blacks couldn't buy anywhere else). As the black population grew, it became ever easier to make whites sell. White renters also left, for different reasons. Some were harassed out of their rent-controlled apartments. Once they were gone, their apartments were rented out to several black families in dire need of housing. Real estate agents knew that options were extremely limited for people of color, so they could increase rents by stuffing several families into a single house. One East New York landlord increased his annual rent collection from $107,000 to $296,000.[3] This resulted in severe overcrowding, which led to more kids in the streets.

Some former (black) residents described the early 1960s with a "paradise lost" narrative. A physician who grew up in the neighborhood told Jenn and me that public housing was like a "village." Kids could freely play outside, jump-roping in the courtyards, and the New York City Housing Authority took care of the buildings. He recalled, nostalgically, that tenants were fined $5 for playing darts on wooden doors. A tenant organizer remembered a time when public housing was in good shape, newly built, looking good, well maintained. The Unity building was "beautiful," she said. Because people didn't have air conditioning or televisions, they used to spend a lot of time outside, watching over kids playing in the parks. The Jews and Italians who left Brownsville and East New York at that time did not recall such an idyllic past, but things went much worse soon after.[4]

Poverty, unemployment, school underfunding, and overcrowded housing meant that many kids and young adults were in the streets, and racial tensions quickly appeared. Crime became pervasive. In New York City as a whole, between 1962 and 1972, the number of robberies per year increased from 6,600 to 78,000.[5] In East New York the first riot, in 1966, opposed blacks and Puerto Ricans. A second one that year pitted people of color against Italians. In 1967—the year of the deadly Newark and Detroit riots—an 11-year-old black child was shot dead by a sniper during a week of unrest. The violence that ensued drove many Italians out of the neighborhood.[6]

When white public housing tenants left, the white flight was complete. City authorities had decided to concentrate public housing in the poorest neighborhoods, which was cheaper and politically expedient, since it didn't threaten property values in more affluent neighborhoods. Meanwhile, transitioning neighborhoods were "redlined" by the banks—a practice whereby banks stop granting loans in a given geographic area that they consider too risky. This prevented or disincentivized landlords from maintaining properties, which meant (even) worse housing conditions. Families were moving all the time, "in the generally unfounded hope that conditions couldn't be as bad in the house on the next block."[7]

East New York was also burning. In 1965 there were four arsons per day,[8] and the burning continued well into the 1970s. One man interviewed by sociologist

Jonathan Rieder told him: "I am amazed what happened to Brownsville. It's like it was bombed out. It looks like Dresden after the war."[9] Some of the fires were accidental and related to the poverty of public services. Some were "transparent arson-for-insurance schemes." Firefighters would arrive in the middle of the night to find the entire family outside a burning house, fully dressed, with their belongings carefully packed;[10] and "despairing residents . . . set most of the fires themselves, seeking thrills, relocation, and metal to sell."[11]

In the 1970s the situation worsened. There were 27 doctors for 100,000 residents in the neighborhood. The city average was 250.[12] Middle-income blacks fled the neighborhood as they found opportunities in suburbs where segregation was less strictly enforced. The homeownership rate fell below 25 percent.[13] Predatory real estate schemes continued, this time involving corrupt officials from the Federal Housing Administration conspiring with bankers and real estate brokers at the expense of East New York homebuyers and taxpayers.[14]

In 1975 New York City fell into fiscal crisis. In the previous 10 years the city budget had doubled, and in 1974 expenses increased 16 percent, with revenues up only 2 percent.[15] Banks stopped lending the city money, and the city was forced to drastically restrict municipal services. Poor black neighborhoods, which were not politically powerful, were hit particularly hard. Children didn't get full days at school for lack of teachers, fire departments closed (at the height of an arson epidemic), the police force shrank (during a crime wave), libraries closed, potholes went unrepaired, street signs remained unfixed, and garbage was not collected for days or even weeks.[16] The blackout of 1977 and the resulting citywide looting and arsons symbolized an era of collapsing social order.[17]

East New Yorkers Jenn and I interviewed recalled the 1970s as a plunge into the abyss. Public space deteriorated. Drug dealers took over the parks, and rival gangs started to shoot at each other. Afraid of catching a bullet, tenants stopped taking their kids to the park. Girls were scared walking alone in the projects. People remembered seeing neighbors passed out in the hallways, people throwing spaghetti cans out of fifteenth-floor windows, and kids being killed. From the elevated train, one could see the vacant lots, the buildings falling into disrepair, the destitution in the streets. A police officer added: "A [police] car went in the projects, it was shot, that was a daily occurrence. I wouldn't spend more than ten seconds waiting for something."

Crime declined in the early 1980s but picked up again with the crack epidemic. It reached all-time highs between 1988 and 1993. "Statistics fail to convey the hopelessness of East New York," the *New York Times* wrote in 1989 in a profile entitled "East New York, Haunted by Crime, Fights for Its Life."[18] The precinct had the highest death toll in the city. In June of 1992 the *New York Times* titled a report on the neighborhood: "East New York, Under Siege; Life and Death in an Area Caught in Its Own Crossfire." The article opened:

> At 14 years old, Mario Jaime can recite the calibers and names of a dozen semiautomatic guns and assault weapons he has seen on the streets of his East New York

> neighborhood. His older brother was shot in the stomach by an intruder in the family's apartment a few months ago. A mural across the littered bullet-pocked street where he lives recalls Diamond, a friend shot more than 10 times in the corner bodega a year ago. Diamond was wearing a bulletproof vest. It did no good.[19]

"Crack is sold brazenly on the corners," the article went on. A few days before the reporter came, a stray bullet from the drug wars had hit a three-year-old toddler in the head. A year and a half later, in December of 1993, the *New York Times* completed its annual tally of homicides per precinct. With 125 homicides, East New York had beaten Harlem's record of 123 homicides in 1973, 20 years earlier. Describing the neighborhood as a "war zone," the reporter quoted a security guard: "Around here, it's the Wild West: Shoot first and ask questions later. Everybody is gun-happy. Buying guns is like buying candy around here."[20]

The local high school, Thomas Jefferson High School, became a "national symbol" of youth crime and urban despair when in 1992, on the morning Mayor David N. Dinkins was supposed to visit to address school reform, "two students, 17 and 16 years old, were shot and killed at point-blank range in the school's second-floor hallway in what the police said was a festering feud over a gold bracelet."[21] Violent street gangs were said to rule the land. East New York was also a hotspot for teen prostitution. In 1997, two *New York Times* articles detailed the indictment of a Mr. Stewart, who was pimping 11- to 14-year-old girls. "The police said Mr. Stewart had burned one of the girls with a cigarette for not bringing back enough money. He required them to earn $1,000 on weekday nights and $2,000 on the weekends, the police said .[22]

In the early 1990s, East New York made news for gruesome stories. In 1991 it was reported that "a newborn baby was rescued from a trash compactor in Brooklyn yesterday morning when two maintenance men heard the baby's cries just as they were about to start the crushing machine's motors, the police said." The mother was a 12-year-old who had not informed anyone of her pregnancy, nor did she admit to having had sex. "The boy was born in a six-story tenement on the corner of Stone Avenue, a depressed area of littered streets, empty lots and broken sidewalks."[23] The next day, the *New York Times* ran a longer article, including the following excerpt:

> At 12 years old, the New York City girl is already an orphan, a rape victim and a mother. Now, two days after her newborn son was rescued from the maw of a trash compactor, she has become something more—a symbol of the violence that stalks the young in some corners of this city. . . . At 4, a fire killed both her parents, and she passed into the care of an aunt, whom her neighbors in the Brownsville section of Brooklyn described as emotionally unstable. Drugs and alcohol invaded the home, the neighbors said. The girl was consigned to a class for slow learners and faithfully attended each day, perhaps her only triumph in a world where staying in school is a Herculean task. As if to punctuate the disorder of a life as troubled as it has been short, the girl's 21-year-old cousin and adoptive brother,

> Clarence Perry, was arrested yesterday as he threatened to fling himself off the roof of the housing- project building where they live. He told the police that he was the father of the baby. He was charged with rape. The girl was accused of putting the infant in a trash chute hours after she gave birth and letting the baby, a boy wrapped in a shopping bag, fall four stories into the compactor. Two maintenance men said they heard the baby's cries just as they were about to start the machine. . . . The girl has spent most of her life in the gritty streets of Brownsville . . . a place where crack is sold and where rival local gangs, the Co-ops and The Young Guns, frequently clash, often with automatic weapons. . . . He [a police sergeant] said the 12-year-old gave birth in the early morning in her bedroom in her fourth-floor apartment and held onto the baby until dawn. "She knew she had to go to school," he said. "It was getting to where something had to be done."[24]

The same day, in an unrelated incident in East New York, a 37-year-old woman had left her strangled newborn in a garbage bag.[25]

THE EAST NEW YORK RENAISSANCE

The story is familiar to urban scholars; greed, racism, and neglect happened everywhere.[26] But East New York didn't stay crime-ridden and devastated. It is still a poor neighborhood, but crime in East New York today is low compared to the early 1990s. Following the general pattern across the United States and New York City since 1993, crime has fallen (see fig. 4).

Granted, East New York still has higher than average crime rates. In 2006, 2007, and 2008 East New York received the *Village Voice*'s "Best place to get murdered, raped, or robbed in the city" award. I mention this dubious distinction because it speaks to a powerful current in discussions about the "ghetto." From birth we are exposed to an ocean of newspaper and TV reports, urban legends, movies, music videos, punditry, and even some social science about poor minority neighborhoods. As a consequence the "ghetto" is not just a place where poor black people live; it is a massive cultural signifier. The sum of these significations forms what I call "ghetto mythology." We are all familiar with ghetto mythology. It is the standard narrative that most people have about the "ghetto," based on movies and newspapers: poor black people, gang wars, drive-by shootings, drugs, and so forth. Myths are narratives that capture our imagination; they undergo constant reiterations with slight modification on the same themes,[27] from the "hood" movies of the 1990s to *The Wire* TV series. Faithful liberals know better than to reduce any neighborhood to a series of senseless murders and crack dens. A good deal of urban sociology aims at documenting the hidden social organization of poor neighborhoods or at evidencing the causal links between structural conditions (unemployment, deindustrialization, historical legacies, etc.) and undesirable behavior. Sociologists have argued forcefully against tendencies to study poor neighborhoods in terms of lacks and deficiencies and to highlight their exotic and unusual features.[28] Even so, the mythological ghetto casts a long shadow over our understanding of its present-day dy-

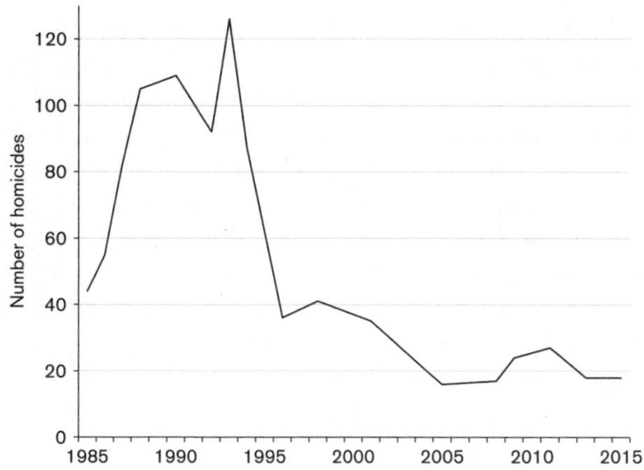

FIGURE 4. Number of homicides in the Seventy-Fifth Precinct, 1985–2015. Source: "Historical New York City Crime Data," NYPD, www1.nyc.gov/site/nypd/stats/crime-statistics/historical.page; various press articles.

namics: the ghetto mythology prevents us from seeing neighborhood change. And, thanks to falling crime, East New York did change.

The effects of crime on neighborhoods are well-known. Violent crime leads to white flight from, and white avoidance of, the neighborhood. This usually leads to declining public services, especially schools, which further detracts from the neighborhood's desirability. As criminologist John R. Hipp has shown, "neighborhoods with more crime tend to experience increasing levels of residential instability, more concentrated disadvantage, a diminishing retail environment, and more African-Americans ten years later."[29] But when crime drops, as it did in the 1990s, real estate prices improve. This has been especially true in New York City. There is now an emerging literature that backs up the intuitive idea that falling crime is a prime cause of gentrification and attracts wealthier and more educated people to the neighborhood. The detrimental effects of high crime on people's lives are well known; we also have recently learned that teenagers from poor neighborhoods who go to school during a crime drop are less likely to drop out and thus are much more likely to be more successful than their parents. Lower-crime communities also attract more bank investment (through mortgages).[30]

As the man quoted by Jonathan Rieder in this chapter's epigraph said, high crime mechanically depresses property values. For virtually everybody in the neighborhood, lower crime and neighborhood change were synonymous, interchangeable. The most obvious consequence of the crime drop in East New York was the real estate boom.

Jenn and I learned about the real estate boom in East New York while talking shop with fellow nonprofit employees from the Women's Prison Association (WPA), a natural partner for Family Justice. The WPA has managed real estate investments for more than 150 years. But in pre–subprime crisis East New York—this was back in 2006—something puzzled WPA operatives. They found it extremely difficult to buy apartments. Housing had become expensive. A house bought for $62,000 in 1987 was worth $350,000 in 2004.[31] Shops were improving in commercial streets. A shopping mall was built in 2000 and became a symbol of the East New York renaissance: it attracted a $192 million investment and powerful symbols of white middle class consumption, like a Bed, Bath and Beyond homeware store and ubiquitous American brands like Target and Staples. Supermarkets in East New York were scarce commodities, and they often carried the stigma of urban retail: the dominant chain was Food Dollar, a company that Manhattanites had never heard of. Banks were notoriously absent from poor minority neighborhoods. As a consequence, the mall and its upscale stores were uplifting the social status of East New York and its residents.

The residents themselves were also changing. Nepalese immigrants, Jewish Russians, West Indians, and Indians from Queens, as well as Latinos, were moving into East New York, driving real estate prices up. They had first looked for housing close to the border with Queens, far away from the projects, but little by little they were getting closer to the core. An East New York Catholic church had to add a sermon in Igbo to accommodate the newly arrived Nigerians.[32]

Among many East New Yorkers, change was obvious and welcome. The East Brooklyn world recognizes a transparent neighborhood hierarchy: Flatbush is better than East New York; Brownsville is worse. For a long time, East New Yorkers thought of themselves as the second-least attractive Brooklyn neighborhood. And now they were seeing Flatbush residents buying homes in their neighborhood. A lot of the people we talked to were anxious to be on the good side of real estate speculation. Jenn and I were told that as white people who obviously were neither cops nor teachers, we were probably seen as real estate brokers catching on to East New York real estate.

The crime drop explanation for the East New York renaissance seemed so obvious that people usually went straight to the reason they saw as most significant: homeownership.

THE HOMEOWNERSHIP NARRATIVE

Homeownership did not, of course, cause the crime drop, in East New York or elsewhere. But against the mythologized ghetto (of crack, gangs, and drive-by shootings), a new mythology emerged: the idea that the neighborhood was morally rejuvenated by homeownership. For instance, we asked a police officer what had changed during her tenure at the Seventy-Fifth Precinct in East New York. She immediately mentioned "homeownership." A politician said the same thing. In their view, shared by many in and outside of East New York, homeowners care more for their neighborhood, especially for their schools. Because homeowners' wealth increases as the neighborhood improves, they have a direct stake in lower crime. And in East New York the homeownership narrative was synonymous with the "Nehemiah homes." Bible-savvy readers will recognize the Old Testament prophet who rebuilt Jerusalem after its destruction by the Chaldeans. The name was not chosen by chance.

The story of the Nehemiah houses begins with the devastation of the late 1970s. Like many other poor minority neighborhoods, East New York's housing stock had experienced all the malfeasance described above. In 1978 church leaders across East Brooklyn decided to contact a community organizer. Community organizing is about mobilizing normal citizens into an organization with specific, realistic goals and achieving these goals through local activism. The organizer formed East Brooklyn Churches or EBC ("Churches" became "Congregations" as the coalition grew). One of the EBC's early successes was to force the city to replace street signs; 85 percent of East New York street signs had been missing, hindering the work of ambulances and the police.

In the early 1980s, EBC organizers decided that the solution to the problem of housing was building houses. Land was cheap. The organization discovered through a rogue developer that it was technically possible to produce low-cost housing and set about applying community organizing techniques to pressure the city into authorizing and supporting the construction of single-family homes. The plan was to increase homeownership to revitalize East New York. Homeowners cannot be evicted, the theory goes, and have a vested interest in improving the neighborhood. Pastor Johnny Ray Youngblood from St. Paul christened the program "Nehemiah."

The first Nehemiah house was built in 1984 in neighboring Brownsville and went for less than $40,000. In East New York the first Nehemiahs were built in 1987; half of the new residents moved from public housing.[33] To cut costs, organizers managed to get free land, tax cuts, and zero-interest loans from the city and the state, short-circuited local builders who were recommended by politicians, and resorted to many clever engineering tricks to build dirt-cheap homes. By 1997, 3,600 Nehemiahs had been built in East New York, crime was down, and the EBC started to get credit in the *New York Times:*

> The criminal justice ethnographer Richard Curtis lives in and studies Brownsville, where he witnessed the crackdown at close range. Mr. Curtis, who teaches at John Jay College of Criminal Justice, says churches, block associations and not-for-profit housing groups deserve more credit than they are given for reclaiming neighborhoods from the dealers. As abandoned buildings are redeveloped, families move in and crime-watch groups go into action. Dealers have fewer places to set up shop.[34]

New Nehemiahs did not go on the market but were awarded to qualified applicants through a lottery. In 1997, for example, applicants had to be first-time home buyers earning between $22,000 and $58,000, depending on family size. The down payment was $5,000, plus another $5,000 to $7,000 for closing costs.[35] Buyers could also customize their Nehemiah with extra security for about $2,000 extra (most people did).[36] The monthly installments were lower than private rentals in the same neighborhoods thanks to the city subsidy, which was repayable only if and when the house was sold at a profit. People soon realized that Nehemiahs were a fantastic deal.

An EBC organizer took me to a Nehemiah settlement. She had bought her house for $55,000 when East New York was "devastated." By 2007 the house was worth more than $300,000. She was keen to show me the chrome fences, the customized doors, the balconies that people had added. Nehemiah owners received identical houses, but over time they had invested in embellishments. The organizer was proud to show me these improvements, which indicated that people took care of their homes and of the architectural aesthetics of the street. According to her, Nehemiah owners had set the example in the neighborhood; once real estate started to go up, other homeowners began to invest in maintenance and beautification. In 2004 the *New York Times* again praised the EBC:

> Nehemiah and its parent organization, East Brooklyn Congregations, have been widely credited with restoring the economic and social stability of East New York and Brownsville, at a time when no one else would consider building there. Now private developers vie for small building sites once passed over by Nehemiah and put up market-rate houses without subsidies—and at a profit.[37]

There was a popular and media consensus that Nehemiah homes caused the crime drop in East New York. They probably didn't. But it created a narrative that put the neighborhood, its residents, and the crime drop in a positive light. Not everyone in East New York was happy with homeownership, though. One informant told me that these lotteries were "fixed" and "rigged" in favor of dues-paying St. Paul parishioners. The rising wealth and changing political attitudes of the propertied class didn't go unnoticed in the housing projects. Gentrification kicked many poor tenants out of New York City. This is the limitation of studying a neighborhood: the concerns of the people who have left are always silenced.

EAST NEW YORK THROUGH THE SUBPRIME CRISIS

I did most of the field research for this book in 2006. Soon after, the subprime crisis of 2007–8 occurred. Subprime mortgages are high-interest loans at adjustable rates made to people who are judged as most likely to default, because of low income, poor health, divorce, and so on. Subprime loans are expensive: a 30-year, $350,000 subprime mortgage typically costs $272,000 more in interest than a prime one.[38] Many studies have documented how subprime loans were concentrated in poor and minority neighborhoods.[39] Predatory lending was widespread at the peak of the bubble, when most people with the capacity to repay their loans had already been sold mortgages. Some of the predatory lending was outright fraud, exploiting the ignorance of first-time home buyers who were historically excluded from the mortgage market, and aimed at dispossessing people from their property (deed theft), sometimes by altering contracts, producing false income statements, and the like.[40] Most of the time, mortgage brokers only accepted mortgage applications they should have rejected. In poor black neighborhoods of New York City like Jamaica, Queens, 46 percent of the mortgages came from subprime lenders, against 3.6 percent in white Bay Ridge, Brooklyn, which had a similar median income.[41] As a result, default was more than three times as likely in New York minority neighborhoods as in white ones.[42]

Around 2005, home prices started to decline, interest rates increased, and many borrowers with adjustable rates were driven to ruin. The *New York Times* reported the case of a Ms. Thompson from East New York, who saw her monthly installments increase from $1,650 in 2004 to $3,000 in 2005.[43] Subprime borrowers defaulted massively, causing the collapse of the financial products with which they were securitized. About 40 percent of subprime borrowers with adjustable rates became unable to pay their installments for three months or more. Banks became insolvent, the ensuing credit crunch prevented homeowners from refinancing their loans, and many fell into foreclosure: the house seized by the bank and the money, already spent, lost. From 1990 to 2007 borrowers with subprime loans had an almost 20 percent chance of losing their home to foreclosure, seven times more than prime borrowers.[44] From September 2008 to September 2012 there were approximately four million completed foreclosures in the United States. The policy response to the foreclosure crisis was timid,[45] especially by comparison with government diligence about bailing out banks and insurance companies in 2008 and 2009. In particular, banks and federal agencies sold troubled loans at a discount to private equity and hedge fund firms, which in turn became "aggressive liquidators," "too quick to push homes into foreclosure."[46]

Foreclosures are always a financial catastrophe for home buyers. They also affect children, who may be moved to unfamiliar or less desirable schools as the family is forced to rent in cheaper neighborhoods.[47] Foreclosed buildings are not maintained, and vacant buildings degrade quickly, which brings home values down in the neighborhood and is associated with an increase in violent crime.[48] Foreclosures enable an industry of "scam artists and deed thieves," who claim they can fix the problem for a few thousand dollars but then disappear with desperate peoples' money.[49]

East New York fell squarely in the so-called foreclosures belt of New York City,[50] along with other poor minority neighborhoods. Yet, as of 2010, no Nehemiah owners had lost their home to foreclosures in Brownsville or East New York. This is remarkable, because minority owners in these poor neighborhoods were at the epicenter of the foreclosure crisis. Nehemiah organizers never tried to sell houses to insolvent families, never went for subprime mortgage financing schemes, and required applicants to attend ownership classes.[51] As devastating as the foreclosure crisis was in East New York, it did not affect crime rates, and the forces of gentrification continued at full speed.

Until the 2000s East New York was so removed from the collective consciousness of white New Yorkers that many did not even know the neighborhood existed. Crime and the fear of death at the hands of a random mugger made it *terra incognita*, where "here be dragons." With falling crime, things are changing. East New York is increasingly a functional component of the New York City real estate market. Indeed, even at the height of the subprime crisis, East New York already experienced among the highest rates of renter displacement because of increasing rents.[52]

In New York City, demand for housing is unlimited. This is of special concern for those at low incomes. Tenants are severely rent-burdened, and apartments are overcrowded. Public housing represents a small fraction of the total stock, about 6 to 8 percent. The only way most people at lower-middle incomes can pay rent in the city is through rent-stabilized apartments, which make up about 32 percent of the total residential stock (less than half of rental apartments). About 2.6 million people live in 990,000 rent-stabilized units, paying below market prices. But these units, which allow New York's service class to avoid having to commute from faraway New Jersey, are fast disappearing. Between 2007 and 2017, 172,000 rent-stabilized apartments have been "deregulated" thanks to market pressure and developer-friendly changes in regulations. Since 2011, massive amounts of capital have flowed into Brooklyn to buy out tenants, renovate buildings, and rent them to wealthier tenants at market rates.[53]

Now that East New York is safe enough for developers, it is a target for investment. To quote journalist Michael Greenberg:

> In April 2016, East New York in Central Brooklyn, one of the poorest districts in the city, became the first to be rezoned under de Blasio's plan. Two years earlier, investment groups, having learned of the impending change, began buying up older, rent-stabilized buildings and engaging in the familiar pattern of "unlocking" value through tenant harassment and eviction. Prices shot up. Short-term speculators flipped buildings for an average return of 125 percent, the highest appreciation in all of New York in 2016.
>
> The city has promised to spend $257 million on schools, parks, street repair, high-speed Internet service, and other improvements in a neighborhood whose residents have spent decades pleading for basic services. Subway stations will be renovated, buses will run more frequently, and police on foot patrol will give the streets a protected, reassuring air. As has happened during the early stages of gentrification in other Brooklyn neighborhoods, East New York will be more racially integrated—for a time.[54]

In sum, the change from the era of high crime is enormous. In 2015 more homes were flipped in East New York than in any other New York City neighborhood. These homes were resold within a year for thrice the price.[55] For poor communities of color such as those in East New York, the crime drop has had massive consequences.

CONCLUSION

From a distance, the "ghetto" is and always will be a place of crime and social problems. But, in the 2000s, falling crime has led to a new reality in East New York. As a result of the crime drop, real estate prices have increased, calling for a renewed attention to housing markets, tenancy, and eviction rates.[56] A new narrative has emerged, glorifying homeownership as moral rejuvenation. This narrative is, of course, incredibly self-serving for beneficiaries of real estate speculation and oblivious to the plight of the displaced.

The main point remains: the crime drop is an event of historic proportions. In East New York, as in many parts of the country, falling crime has transformed people's everyday quality of life. East New York exemplifies the implementation of a mix of social and penal policy that "works"—in the narrow sense that crime is contained. In the four remaining chapters of this book, I document the social and human cost of implementing this particular policy mix.

4

The Necessity of Harsh Policing

The only way to police a ghetto is to be oppressive.
—JAMES BALDWIN, "FIFTH AVENUE, UPTOWN"

Thus did the Tories of England long fancy that they were enthusiastic for the Kingdom, the Church and the beauties of the old English Constitution, until the day of danger wrung from them the admission that their enthusiasm was only for Ground Rent.
—KARL MARX, THE EIGHTEENTH BRUMAIRE OF LOUIS BONAPARTE

When it comes to police work in urban neighborhoods, the prevailing wisdom used to be that the police had abandoned them. Sudhir Venkatesh has described a housing project where police are absent and gangs are the main security providers, forcing other stakeholders to constantly make deals with their leaders.[1] A 2008 *Daily News* article about the Van Dyke Houses (a housing development on the border between Brownsville and East New York) illustrates this kind of neglect and underservicing:

> A Brooklyn woman was raped for a half-hour in a public housing stairwell bristling with security cameras, and the NYPD is investigating whether cops monitoring the live video somehow missed the attack. . . . Either they saw it and did nothing, which seems hard to believe, even for this unmotivated crew. Or they were busy looking at something else. Or they were asleep, which seems most likely," said a police source familiar with the lapse. The NYPD gives the job of monitoring Viper security cameras in public housing to cops on medical leave or, more frequently, to cops facing department disciplinary charges. Some 224 cameras cover the Van Dyke Houses in Brownsville. . . . Compounding the missed opportunity were two rookie cops on foot patrol in the complex. The duo was supposed to be making vertical sweeps of the housing project, but they lied about making the tours. The two cops recorded in their memobooks that they had made six to 10 sweeps, including the building in question around the time of the rape, but camera footage exposed their lie. Both are facing disciplinary action, sources said.[2]

In this account the police look bad because they are lazy and inept, especially so when the safety of poor black people is at stake.

But in recent years, and in the context of mass incarceration, a new perspective has emerged: poor black neighborhoods are no longer abandoned by the police. On the contrary, they are aggressively overpoliced.[3] This opposition between under- and overpolicing is probably simplistic but is best understood as an illustration of the changing patterns of punishment along the great adjustment of less eligibility I described in chapter 2. Punishment consists not only of incarceration but also of a police force that may be more or less courteous or repressive. Mass incarceration requires a consistent police infrastructure to identify and arrest offenders. American policing is now particularly punitive and has increased its legitimacy thanks to the crime drop. I argue that this harshness is a direct function of a society with poor prospects on low-income labor markets and restrictive social policy. In this context severe punishment is a structural necessity.

THE MAGIC OF THE CRIME DROP

In the 1970s the NYPD was in shambles. The riots of 1964 to 1968 had been precipitated by massive patterns of misconduct and brutality from white officers toward the newly arrived black residents. Corruption was pervasive. Detective Frank Serpico blew the whistle (resulting in an attempt on his life), and a major scandal ensued. The ensuing Knapp Commission report read as follows:

> We found corruption to be widespread. It took various forms depending upon the activity involved, appearing at its most sophisticated among plainclothesmen assigned to enforcing gambling laws. In the five plainclothes divisions where our investigations were concentrated we found a strikingly standardized pattern of corruption. Plainclothesmen, participating in what is known in police parlance as a pad, collected regular bi-weekly or monthly payments amounting to as much as $3,500 from each of the gambling establishments in the area under their jurisdiction, and divided the take in equal shares. The monthly share per man (called the nut) ranged from $300 and [$]400 in midtown Manhattan to $1,500 in Harlem. When supervisors were involved they received a share and a half. A newly assigned plainclothesman was not entitled to his share for about two months, while he was checked out for reliability, but the earnings lost by the delay were made up to him in the form of two months' severance pay when he left the division.[4]

In 1975 New York's fiscal crisis forced the city to fire 5,000 police officers and freeze hires until 1979. The department lost one-third of its workforce through attrition.[5] In the midst of a crime boom—serious crime was up 40 percent—police unions distributed the infamous flyer, "Welcome to Fear City." In 1980, hiring resumed, but new recruits were so needed that recruitment standards dropped. The NYPD was forced to hire officers with criminal records and little education. As a result, misconduct soared. Among many other scandals, one hit the Seventy-Fifth Precinct, which included East New York. Between 1986 and 1992 a group of officers worked for local drug dealers from the station house, informing them of police raids, disrupting competition, transporting drugs and money, and so on. Policemen also stole money, burglarized civilians, and the ringleader agreed to a kidnap-murder scheme (which did not go through).[6] This happened while homicides increased 60 percent in New York City and tripled throughout East New York. These scandals, as well as controversial shootings, led to the Mollen Commission, whose 1994 report concludes:

> Today's corruption is not the corruption of Knapp Commission days. Corruption then was largely a corruption of accommodation, of criminals and police officers giving and taking bribes, buying and selling protection. Corruption was, in its essence, consensual. Today's corruption is characterized by brutality, theft, abuse of authority and active police criminality.

A complete shift in perspective occurred in the early 1990s. This was the time of peak homicide, peak crack cocaine epidemics, and an increased presence of street homelessness and panhandlers. The subway, in particular, was *de facto* transformed into a giant homeless shelter. In 1990 William Bratton became Transit (Police) Chief and reclaimed the subway with a focus on minor offenses. Thanks to his successes at the expense of New York's most vulnerable, he became police commissioner in 1994, and, alongside Mayor Rudi Giuliani, implemented new police tactics. In the 1990s the NYPD repressed turnstile jumpers, drug addicts, panhandlers, and homeless people in affluent and touristic neighborhoods and systematically went after open-air drug markets in poorer neighborhoods. By the late 1990s, 10–15 percent of all arrests in New York City were marijuana-related, targeting mostly black and Latino users.[7]

Meanwhile something amazing happened: the crime drop.

The crime drop is a social fact of historic significance. It enables gentrification and transforms cities. It certainly transformed East New York. The crime drop happened exactly as Bratton and Giuliani were promoting their law-and-order agenda, and, Peter Manning argues, the NYPD managed to grab the credit.[8] For instance, a *New York Times* article unequivocally attributed the crime drop in East New York to good police work:

> A police crackdown on drug dealing in high-crime neighborhoods has driven down felony crimes from murder to car theft by wide margins in lower Manhattan, northern Brooklyn and the central Bronx. The most dramatic results were in the Brooklyn North command, where poor, crime-ridden neighborhoods like Brownsville and East New York once produced about a quarter of the city's shootings.[9]

Thanks to Bratton's tireless activism and public relations genius, and New York's iconic status, the idea that the NYPD was responsible for the crime drop in the city stuck. From every corner of the world, police officials and scholars went to visit the new Mecca of policing, and read the autobiography of its prophet (Bratton), soberly titled *Turnaround: How America's Top Cop Reversed the Crime Epidemic.* The New

York miracle was pushed on all fronts: in New York's tabloids, the press, and in academia.[10] Falling crime rates since the mid–1990s raised the profile of the agency considerably, in spite of the Abner Louima (sexually tortured in a police station, 1997) and Amadou Diallo (shot to death while unarmed, 1999) scandals. In New York the crime drop and the NYPD have become synonymous.

Policing did change in New York City, under and after Bratton. The most important innovation was CompStat, which uses crime data to make policing more rational and to achieve reductions in crime. CompStat involves making use of intelligence, crime statistics, and geographic patterns of criminality to better allocate police forces across space. (It is sometimes also called data-driven policing or hotspot policing.) It is also a management technique. Precinct commanders are constantly evaluated on the basis of crime statistics, and commanders who fail to deliver expected results are dismissed.[11] Between 1994 and 1995, three-fourths of all commanders were replaced. Police commanders are under pressure to deploy aggressive strategies to keep crime figures down. In today's NYPD, crime statistics—that is, proof that crime is down—are central to all operations, in the field, in the assessment of commanders, and in information provided to the public. Crime statistics have also become central instruments of self-promotion. Each precinct publishes a weekly update on crime statistics with the percent change from one, two, and five years before, as well as from 1993, the peak crime year in New York City. The latter comparison always shows massive drops in crime. In every police-community meeting, officers explain and interpret crime statistics.

There is consensus among criminologists that policing played its role, but it was not the only factor in New York City's crime drop. Crime drops (albeit less striking in scope) happened in other American cities.[12]

On the ground in East New York a lot of people Jenn and I met believed firmly in the NYPD's central role in the New York miracle. A prosecutor for Brooklyn's district attorney remembered the crime drop as "when Giuliani came in." Police officers had enormous respect for CompStat, which they identified with the software used to predict where crime is most likely to happen. "CompStat saved the city," an officer emphatically said. "If someone is robbing saying 'yo give me the money' or wears a yellow shirt, it's in CompStat." She insisted that CompStat had been designed by psychologists who knew about human nature. "We are creatures of habit," the officer said. "Ninety percent of arrested people in East New York live in East New York."

DEVELOPMENTS IN AMERICAN POLICING

The fact that police organizations in the United States have gotten most of the credit for the crime drop has immunized them against mainstream criticism. Yet as punishment in general—particularly in the form of mass incarceration—got harsher from the 1980s on, so did policing. I briefly review below some of the recent developments in American policing that have had the greatest impact on the lives of people like East New Yorkers.

Consider, for instance, the controversial practice, especially widespread in 2000s New York City, of stop-and-frisk. Stop-and-frisk is the practice of stopping people in the street to confirm their identity and make sure they don't carry a gun.[13] It is related to the War on Drugs, as many stops result in a drug arrest. Stop-and-frisk is used as much to get guns off the street as to disrupt open-air drug markets.

Stop-and-frisk is actually two legal actions. Police may *stop* people under suspicion of wrongdoing, and they may *frisk* stopped people under suspicion of weapon possession. About half of the people stopped are frisked. In practice, police officers stop and/or frisk whoever they want, typically young males of color. From 2002 to 2013 young black men accounted for 25.4 percent of stops in New York City, despite making up only 1.9 percent of the population. In contrast, young white men (2.2 percent of the population) accounted for 4.4 percent of stops. In the precinct of Greenwich Village (a rich white Manhattan neighborhood), blacks and Latinos represented 8 percent of the population but accounted for 78.5 percent of stops.

Between 2002 and 2013—the systematic practice was almost discontinued afterward—East New York experienced more than 265,000 stops, the highest number in New York City. Of the stops in East New York, 15.2 percent resulted in police use of force (usually without injury). This means that *a lot* of people in the neighborhood have been roughed up by the police. In 89 percent of the cases, stops yielded nothing—no weapon, no drugs, no arrest. (On average, the NYPD recovered one gun per 593 stops.)[14] There is no correlation between shootings and stop-and-frisks, and criminologists find the latter serve, at best, as a modest deterrent on crime.[15]

Stop-and-frisk has contributed to a style of relations between police and young black males characterized by intimidation and humiliation. This aggressive policing style is described in greater detail by Peter Moskos, a sociologist who has worked as a police officer in Baltimore.[16] One consequence of this policing style is that young men of color hate the police and teach children from a young age to be wary of the capricious and irrational violence wielded by police officers.[17] During the 2000s, stop-and-frisk defined police work for young black men in poor neighborhoods like East New York.

Because it has been used to disrupt drug dealing in the streets, stop-and-frisk is linked to the War on Drugs, which has been a priority in the United States since 1971.[18] The War on Drugs' contribution to mass incarceration has been overstated, but it is still a policy of significance.[19] By 2014, it was costing $51 billion per year and included military operations abroad and domestic law enforcement. The military effort, mostly in Afghanistan and Latin America, did not prevent retail drug prices from decreasing sharply. Between the 1980s and the 2000s, the price of crack fell by 54 percent, cocaine by 87 percent, and heroin by 93 percent. Even so, economists calculate that cocaine would be ten times cheaper if legally imported. No one disputes that drug epidemics bring misery. Urban black communities were devastated by heroin in the 1970s and crack in the 1980s. Opioids returned to rural white America in the 2010s. The question is how to handle this crisis, and the War on Drugs has been marred with issues. Although whites and blacks have roughly the same patterns of illicit drug use (according to the 2013 National Survey on Drug

Use and Health), blacks are 2.6 times more likely to be arrested for drug-related offenses. About 80 percent of all drug-related arrests are for possession only, not sale. Drugs that are more likely to be used by blacks are more severely punished; blacks get longer prison sentences; and police usually focus on open-air drug markets, where dealers and users are more likely to be black. People of color in general, and blacks in particular, are thus more likely to fall prey to American criminal justice. Because the War on Drugs is a federal priority, American police forces have financial incentives from the federal government to go after drug users and dealers. Police departments may lose funding if they fail to cooperate. The War on Drugs has also been a source of dollars to pursue the militarization of American police forces (assault rifles, armored vehicles and SWAT teams).

In addition, drug-related crimes are among the most lucrative under civil asset forfeiture laws: if you're convicted of a crime, the government may seize your assets to pay fines or provide for other forms of restitution. In the United States, civil asset forfeiture allows law enforcement agencies to seize property even if the owner is only a suspect. The most controversial aspect of the civil asset forfeiture program is that police departments can seize money, cars, and guns when they *think* that you may be involved in crime. This has led to countless abuses.[20] In theory, people whose goods have been seized can challenge the decision in court. In practice, most states enforce a *de jure* or *de facto* reversal of the burden of proof[21] —the complainants have to prove their innocence to get their money back. In addition, police officers routinely intimidate their victims into not going to court, for instance by threatening further investigations. The program is now a source of revenue for law enforcement agencies. From the 1980s to the 2000s, seizures in relation to the War on Drugs increased from $100 million to $2 billion. In New York State, local law enforcement (such as the NYPD) gets to keep 60 percent of what they seize, with loopholes that may be used to keep more.[22] For the NYPD this represents about $5 million per year[23] —admittedly a small fraction of its $4.8 billion annual budget.

A final concern with American policing is the number of people who are killed each year by the police.

One of the distinctive powers of police officers is their state-sanctioned right to take the life of citizens, given certain conditions. Therefore, a simple metric of police work is how many people they kill. We don't know how many people the police killed before the mid-2010s. When I first became interested in this issue, in the early 2000s, I read FBI statistics saying that "only" 400 people were shot by the police per year. Then, police killings of black men in the United States captured global attention. This started in 2013 with the acquittal of a neighborhood watch volunteer who had killed 17-year-old Trayvon Martin in Florida. In August of 2014 Michael Brown was killed by a police officer in Ferguson, Missouri. His death triggered protests and riots against the police, which prompted in turn a national discussion about racial profiling, police militarization, and routine misconduct. In 2015 the death of Freddie Gray in a police van triggered another wave of protest and riots in Baltimore. These riots were important events; the last significant wave of riots had happened 25 years ago, when the 1992 Los Angeles riots left 52 dead. Newspapers began to pay attention to police killings, especially when they concern children (12-year-old Tamir Rice, 2014) or when a smartphone has recorded a cold-blooded assassination (Walter Scott, 2015).

Public scrutiny led media organizations to count police killings themselves, and the numbers more than doubled. American officers kill more than 900 people a year —about 8 percent of all adult male victims of homicides are killed by the police.[24] To give perspective, over the past 40 years 35 people have received capital punishment annually. Between 1877 and 1950 the annual average number of recorded deaths in racist lynchings in the South was 56. British police forces kill on average fewer than one person a year (fig. 5). German police kill about eight people a year, the French police around 14. Granted, the United States is a bigger country. Nevertheless, per capita, American officers kill around 20 times more than their counterparts in France, another rich country with troubled inner cities. In figure 5, I have added Brazil for good measure, where police kill 2,200 people a year.[25]

One might object that the criminal situation is not comparable between the United States and continental Europe. The availability of guns and pervasiveness of gun homicides make for more dangerous policing in the United States, which might explain the discrepancy. Instead of the ratio of police killings per capita, therefore, consider the ratio of police killings per number of homicides (fig. 6).

Interestingly, American officers kill almost twice as many people as their Brazilian counterparts relative to the total number of homicides (fig. 7). In Brazil, police (or thugs sanctioned by the police) carrying out the killings of young males in the *favelas* are called "death squads" *(grupos de extermínio)* in progressive circles.[26] In truth, much police killing happens in California—188 deadly police shootings in 2015, against 19 in New York State.[27] Figure 7 compares police killings per one million people and shows the overrepresentation of blacks in the deadly use of force. Black men are 3.2 to 3.5 times as likely to be victims of police homicide as white men.[28] The problem of police shootings of black men is such that it affects black police officers themselves. In New York, in 1992, a black undercover police officer was mistakenly shot and wounded by fellow NYPD coworkers; another one was shot in 1994 and now lives in constant pain; and in 2009 an off-duty, armed black cop who was chasing a thief was shot dead by a white officer.[29]

With this context in mind I have counted 13 people killed by the police in East New York between 2001 and 2014.[30] Most of the victims were young, probably minority, and male. One of the deaths was officially recognized as illegitimate and made national news. In 2014 Akai Gurley, 28, was shot in an apparent accident. The police officer was walking in the dark in the Pink Houses stairs with his gun drawn; the gun went off, and the bullet ricocheted against the wall before striking Gurley in the chest as he went to visit his girlfriend. Gurley's death happened in the immediate aftermath of the Ferguson riots and the killing of Eric Garner. (In the process of being arrested for selling loosies [loose cigarettes], Garner was choked to death by police officers, who disregarded his repeating, "I can't breathe.")

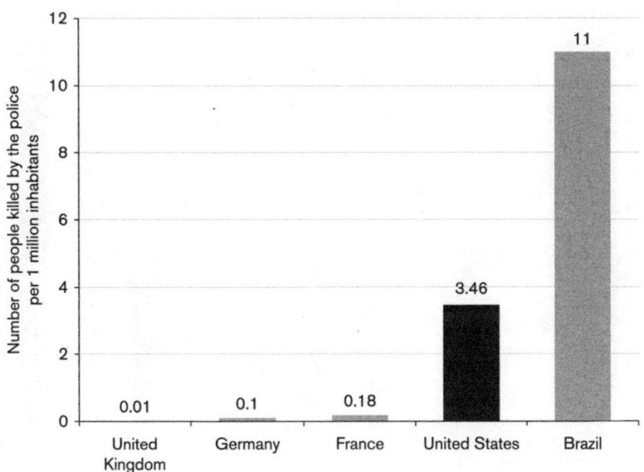

FIGURE 5. Number of people killed by the police per million inhabitants in selected countries. Source: see note 25 for references on police killings in selected countries.

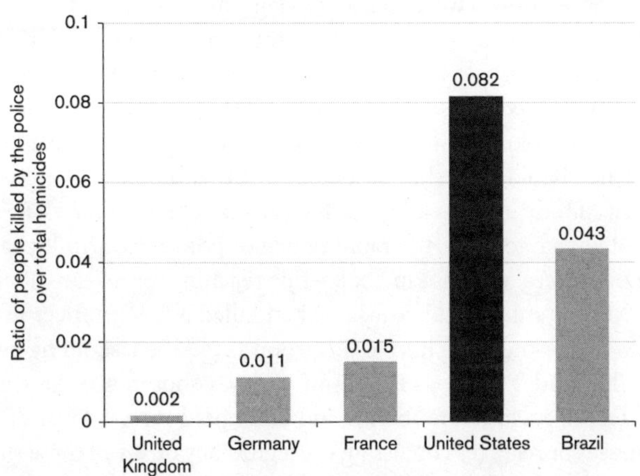

FIGURE 6. Ratio of people killed by the police over total homicides in selected countries. Source: see note 25 for references on police killings in selected countries; for homicide data see "Statistics and Data," United Nations Office on Drugs and Crime, https://dataunodc.un.org/crime/intentional-homicide-victims.

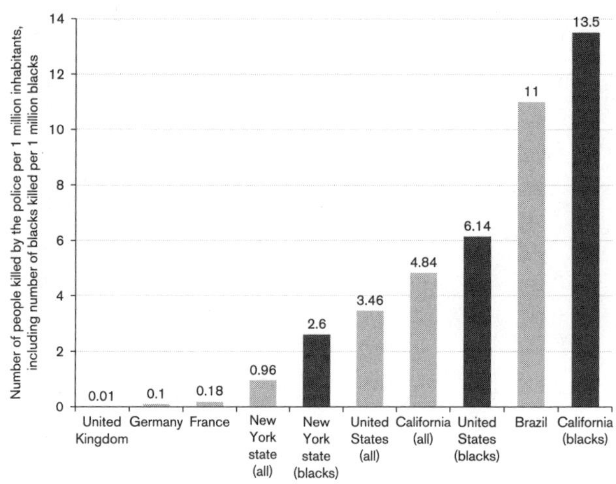

FIGURE 7. Number of people killed by police per million inhabitants, including number of blacks killed per million blacks, in selected US states and other countries. Source: *Washington Post* database of police killings, www.washingtonpost.com/graphics/national/police-shootings; see note 25 for references on police killings in selected countries.

The remaining shootings were considered legitimate by the NYPD. Shannon Vinson, 28, was shot in 2001 in his car while reaching for his gun. His girlfriend and her two kids were in the backseat. Vinson's gun had been used earlier to kill a man with whom he publicly feuded.[31] Renardo Powell, 25, was shot in 2003 after a gun battle along a stretch of five blocks while he was robbing a drug dealer.[32] Anthony Reid, 21, was shot after he chased, and shot at, people with whom he had argued in a bar.[33] Rashawn Sharif Moody, 18, was killed in 2004 while robbing a carwash. The employees were reportedly grateful for the rapid police response.[34] Darin Richardson, 23 or 29 according to sources, was shot in 2008 while reaching for his gun. Richardson was on the FBI's "Most Wanted" list because he had killed a police officer in Georgia. He had shot at him once, knocking him to the ground, and then, standing over him, shot the officer in the head.[35] Thomas Robinson, 50, was shot in 2013 during a robbery. His criminal record included robberies and attempted rape.[36] Press articles do not mention witnesses or relatives contesting the legitimacy of any of these shootings.

The deaths of Jamal Nixon, Darryl Green, and Kristen McKenzie were slightly more controversial, in that reporters immediately found people questioning the use of force. Kristen McKenzie was shot in 2007 in a nightclub when he was about to execute another officer. His sister, Andrea Pollidore, argued the cops "could have defused this situation." "They didn't have to kill him," said Pollidore, 33.[37] Jamal Nixon, 19, was killed on December 31, 2002. He was shooting in the air in an aimless and celebratory fashion. Police officers arrived on scene, and Nixon allegedly shot at them. Four years earlier, he already had been charged with shooting at a police officer.[38] The *New York Times* reported: "One of the friends, Lisa King, 30, questioned whether Mr. Nixon was only shooting in the air. 'They should know what's going on in the streets,' she said of the police." Darryl Green, 21, was shot outside a nightclub in 2005. It is unclear to this day exactly how the events unfolded. A witness said Green was surrendering, arms up, when he was shot. He did not have a criminal record.[39]

Three shootings clearly seem disputable or "lawful but awful." Jose Feliciano, a 44-year-old homeless man who frequently had seizures was killed in 2004. One day, he was swinging a fixture at a passer-by. A police officer from the neighboring precinct shot him. Many speculated that East New York police officers, who all knew Feliciano, would not have shot.[40] David Kostovski, 29, was killed as he brandished a broken wine bottle. He was mentally ill. A neighbor commented: "Did they have to kill him? . . . These cops got to stop this. They're shooting people like crazy."[41] Duane Browne, 26, was killed as he was rushing home to defend his half-brother against robbers. The officers mistook him for a robber and shot him because he had a gun. Police allegedly prevented paramedics from saving his life.[42]

The website *Fatal Encounters* lists two additional deaths.[43] Stacey Blount, a Gulf War veteran and mother of two, was struck by a van being pursued by the police. Her death generated some controversy: "State Sen. Eric Adams (D-Brooklyn), a former NYPD captain, said police must show restraint when following suspects on city streets. 'This is a textbook case why you do not speed through the streets of Brooklyn to apprehend a fleeing felon,' Adams said. 'Our city streets are not Hollywood.'"[44] Another incident involved a retired cop shooting his 18-year-old would-be robber, Manuel Ocampo.[45]

To the best of my knowledge, one police officer has been killed while working the beat in East New York since 2000. In 2011 Peter Figoski, 47, was shot in the face while responding to a burglary call. The killer, a 27-year-old man, was sentenced to 45 years to life.[46]

Compared to stop-and-frisk, police killings are rare events and are not as pressing an issue as in California or the South. It is striking how these recent developments only started to attract attention since the political activism, protests, and riots that occurred in both Ferguson and Baltimore in 2014 and 2015. In fact, until then, much attention went to community policing, the people-oriented, liberal, democratic policing that progressive police scholars hail as the model for police reform.

THE FEEBLENESS OF COMMUNITY POLICING

Community policing was a police reform born out of the crisis of the 1970s. Police-community relations were then at a low because of riots and corruption. Diligent scholars of various persuasions theorized that police misconduct and excessively bureaucratic tactics were alienating urban communities, causing riots, and generally threatening social order.[47] The goal of community policing was therefore to improve police legitimacy in urban neighborhoods through police-community meetings, pedestrian patrols, and the recruitment of minority officers.

Based on my research in East New York, I argue that community policing is peripheral to the NYPD's core strategy and that it is, in the end, a cynical public-relations device aimed at soothing some of the concerns that the public might have with harsher police tactics. This smokescreen theory of community policing is well-documented in police research.[48]

In East New York, community policing consisted mainly of police-community meetings. The most important of these were precinct meetings organized by the local police station (the Seventy-Third and Seventy-Fifth Precincts). On the police side the main participants were the precinct commander and police officers from the Community Affairs unit. Precinct meetings were open to the public and took place at the station or in a large room at a community center. When the attendants —sometimes more than 200 people, mostly senior citizens—took their seats or stood at the back of the room, a pastor would bless the gathering and say a prayer; participants would recite the pledge of allegiance, hand over heart, and occasionally sing *America the Beautiful.* Then guests would be invited to speak, such as representatives from local nonprofits promoting their programs or the district attorney's representative making an announcement. Then police officers would take over. Community affairs officers might give safety tips. The most anticipated moment was when the precinct commander would make his speech, to much applause. After a discussion of recent crime trends and community problems, he would respond to questions from the audience. At the end of the meeting the community council would organize a tombola. When the meeting was formally declared over, the participants would leave, except for the regular participants in local civic life, who would linger to chat with other influential people.

Such meetings are an opportunity for police and some segments of the population to discuss issues and concerns, and there is some value to communicative action. There might be a feel-good atmosphere, especially when the speaking officer is charismatic or good-looking. But meetings are supposed to bring police and the community together, and, of course, the "community" is not a homogeneous population. In East New York many senior citizens went to such meetings, where they mostly nodded, applauded, murmured, and ate cookies. The young males who were often stopped and frisked never attended. At best, community policing in East New York improved police legitimacy among the already convinced.

Meetings are also opportunities for law enforcement agencies to gather tips from the community or for community members to report criminals, that is, "to snitch." In almost all such meetings in East New York, there was a table where the NYPD had set out piles of tracts containing information about crime. The most common ones were about drugs and firearms. Some posters promised $1,000 rewards for information leading to the arrest of someone who illegally owns a gun or $500 to report on graffiti artists. Others described the features that one should be attentive to when describing a suspect, such as tattoos. Posters depicted threatening stylizations of criminals pointing a gun toward the viewer, with the tagline: "Remember: you don't have to leave your name." All these posters were in both English and Spanish.

In theory these calls for reporting crime are good policing, even if they are not necessarily in synch with the ideals of participatory democracy. The police in East New York, however, couldn't care less. One detective, in reference to a meeting we had both attended, was obviously disgruntled: "Two hours wasted. You go, you waste two hours, and that's it, only chatter." Years later, in an informal discussion I had with a police academy trainee, I asked which branch of the NYPD he'd like to join. He mentioned the pros and cons of different options, then concluded, with a smirk, "community affairs." When I asked why, he quipped, "Because you don't do shit! You just go to bullshit meetings, you do your twenty years and you get the pension" (NYPD officers receive low salaries but enjoy early retirement).

It is certainly a good thing that the police force organizes meetings with the population. But one cannot call community policing a "strategy" the way CompStat is a "strategy." CompStat and, until 2012, stop-and-frisk were central strategies for the NYPD; community policing was merely their after-sale service. This is exemplified at the national level by an oft-forgotten story about community-policing *money*. Between the 1994 crime bill and 2010 American police forces received $12 billion to implement community policing. Today, every self-respecting police department in the United States claims to engage in community policing. But early on, criminologists Peter B. Kraska and Victor E. Kappeler have suggested, police spent most of the money on militarizing their organizations.[49] They bought assault rifles, bullet-proof armor, night-vision goggles, and sometimes military vehicles. In particular, they invested in SWAT teams (combat units). In theory, SWAT teams were only supposed to intervene in the most dangerous situations, such as active shooters or terrorism. They quickly began to be used for mundane operations: small-time drug dealers, noisy parties, gambling rings. In spite of strict laws regulating police interventions in private homes, SWAT raids, particularly "no-knock raids," have become routine in many neighborhoods. Such raids are likely to go awry, with incidents of brutality, abuse, broken furniture, pets killed, and sometimes wrongful deaths. In 2003 the NYPD commissioner admitted that out of the 450 monthly home raids conducted by NYPD intervention teams, 10 percent went to the wrong door.[50]

In East New York, police-community meetings were mostly innocuous spectacles, free entertainment for senior citizens. Anyone can go to a rough neighborhood in New York and do a few ride-alongs with patrollers, attend precinct meetings, and get interviews with the Community Affairs unit. This is the communication facade that the NYPD has set to shield itself from meaningful civilian investigation. It works well. Everything that happens with the key units (drugs, street crime, strike teams, and so on) remains out of sight.

PROPOLICE HOMEOWNERS

In 1997, East New Yorkers asked Mayor Giuliani at a community meeting: Why are police officers routinely rude and abrasive toward young men who are not white? Why has East New York not received the same level of city services as more politically powerful neighborhoods?"[51] These two questions represent two opposite poles of frustration with the police.

Many, especially in public housing, were not enthused with the NYPD-saved-the-city story and precinct meetings. These people did not trust the police. The high school counselor spoke about undercover officers driving through the neighborhood, slowing down when they saw a young black man, stopping him, asking him to lift his jacket, turn, shake out his pants, and then they would go toward another prey. It's "walking while black!" she said, in reference to the "crime" of "driving while black," itself a pun on "driving under the influence," the usual cause for driver arrest. The slightest signals of insubordination, lack of docility, or ambiguous gestures by residents of poor neighborhoods may be perceived as threats by police, who have near-total discretionary power to stop-and-frisk, arrest, and detain civilians. As a consequence minority residents must be not only "streetwise" but also "copwise." They have to know how to behave to avoid a risky encounter with the police.[52]

"The police . . . they harass the kids all the time," a tenant association president told us. Her grandson had spent six months in jail for being nearby when a fight broke out. Another tenant association president, although formidably involved in the community, did not bother going to police-community precinct meetings. In Brownsville the community council president's own house had been raided at night by "crazy, out of control" cops. They yelled at her to go back into her bedroom and yelled at her nephew to show his ID. In fact, it was a wrong-door no-knock raid. When asked about the community's view about law enforcement, she immediately responded, "They hate the cops."

A recurrent complaint came about "rookie cops" who were "scared to death" and "out of control," who needed "sensitivity training, especially the rookies who get their guns and think they are big shots right away. It goes to their heads." For many residents, sending rookies into East New York was a slight: the criminal situation there required more experienced officers, which the NYPD preferred to keep to staff in whiter, more affluent neighborhoods. In addition to the litany of abuse, there was the idea that poor neighborhoods in general, and East New York in particular, were like a big playground for the police. The Seventy-Third Precinct (Brownsville) was apparently a "training precinct" for officers looking for promotions. According to someone else, the Seventy-Fifth Precinct was a "punishment precinct" for cops and a "promotion precinct" for inspectors. I do not know whether this is true. It is plausible that beat cops waiting for their early retirement would want to avoid working rough streets, while pyramid-climbers want to prove themselves in "the hood." It is equally plausible that making good friends in the Financial District cannot hurt a career.[53] The belief in the promotion and punishment precincts reinforced the idea that police officers were not after crime; they were not trying to protect and to serve but were merely chasing medals and promotions or being punished for stealing from precinct lockers or sleeping on the job.

Because actions speak louder than words, projectiles were thrown at East New York cops from windows and rooftops; residents called it "airmail." In 2004 a quiet 69-year-old war veteran called 911 to report a robbery and threw a bowling ball from the seventeenth floor onto the responding officers.[54] An officer who worked for the community-policing unit (called Community Affairs) of the Seventy-Fifth Precinct told us: "I'm very old-fashioned in my policing. I don't go in the projects. We are old-school. I avoid the projects." In 2003 an officer patrolling in East New York had been shot by a sniper while the officer was trying to arrest a man with a gun.[55]

But even in East New York, an epicenter of tensions, many residents held favorable views toward the NYPD and supported the tactics associated with the crime drop. This was especially the case among homeowners. Take St. Paul Baptist, the church that was a historical leader in the Nehemiah program and brought homeownership to thousands of East New Yorkers. Its pastor told me that part of his job entailed reporting crime to the police on behalf of congregants, making sure to protect identities and keep names out. To this effect, and to complain against rising crime, the pastor regularly met with the highest ranks of the police hierarchy. I also talked to an activist from the church. She knew everything about the legacies of slavery and institutional racism, police brutality, and the daily humiliations of being black in America. She knew the police were an important part of that, and she resented that the cops were not as responsive and amicable as she thought they were in white neighborhoods: "We homeowners we are with them [the police]," she said, "but they never say hi. If two cops say hi, it's like a party." But her main concern was not police abuse but rising crime. Her net worth was inversely correlated to crime rates, and the NYPD was supposed to keep the neighborhood improving. She told me that she loved Rudi Giuliani, the white, tough-on-crime conservative mayor of New York (1994–2001). And she disliked David Dinkins, Giuliani's black predecessor, "who only planted trees and did nothing for housing."

Another propolice group was affiliated with the Weed and Seed program. Weed and Seed is now a defunct federal initiative that funded local activists to improve police-community relations.[56] Whereas St. Paul congregants were progressives on economic issues and militant in racial discourse, the Weed and Seed affiliate was a religious conservative. He didn't like St. Paul, but he also was pro-NYPD. In the early 2000s his job had been to improve police-community relations. He knew this was not easy because cops, he said, "believe in repression, arresting, locking up people and throw[ing] away the key"—meaning they were skeptical about community policing. He saw it as his first mission, in the late 1990s, to let cops know they had "the community" on their side. Around the time of Amadou Diallo's murder (1999) he mounted a survey that showed that people, when behind closed doors, were in fact propolice. In recent years the Weed and Seed organizer had helped organize the "National Night Out against Crime" or the "Night without Crime."

Research shows consistently that minorities are less likely than whites to support the police, but many still do: "in a 2001 study conducted by the National Institute of Justice, 63 percent of Whites expressed a great deal of confidence in the police, as compared to 31 percent of African Americans."[57] East New York is not the only place where there has been class conflict within racial groups over "neighborhood revitalization."[58] Black homeowners in East New York knew about police brutality, had experienced racial profiling, and resented police killings as much as anyone else. But they fundamentally supported the NYPD's tactics, which they saw as bringing crime down, because low crime rates made their families safer and were the lifeblood of their financial health.

CONCLUSION

Policing is one of the first components in the long chain that makes the punishment apparatus. Prison is the end of this chain, and pervasive though it is in the era of mass incarceration, it is a rare event compared to the everyday operations of street policing.

In New York, as in many other cities in the United States, the police were able to capture the legitimacy boon granted by the crime drop, especially among homeowners, whom we know are the most politically active residents. This has given police officers across the five boroughs virtual immunity to criticism of the recent developments. Police have been able to be punitive and to enforce the most meaningless version of community policing without being confronted with large-scale riots. Only recently, the events in Ferguson and the increased visibility of police killings have started to shed light on the reality of policing in contemporary America.

My argument is that police behavior is to be understood in its structural context. There are no death squads in Scandinavian social democracies, just as there cannot be perfectly behaved, unarmed, nonviolent police officers in highly unequal societies. Police violence and misconduct are a function of the structure of less eligibility in a given country.[59] Where labor markets provide a decent life to all, and where welfare can be generous, street crime is minimal and police work can adhere to higher standards of courtesy, professionalism, and democracy. Where the lowest class of workers suffers less favorable living standards, and where welfare is meager, punishment will be harsh because it is the last resort of social order. In a society that is not pacified by the labor market, aggressive policing is a necessary evil: "the only way to police a ghetto is to be oppressive." Mass incarceration and harsh policing tactics are the price to be paid for a downward adjustment of less eligibility. Within this framework, racism hurts poor blacks twice over: by making racial minorities more likely to belong to the lowest class of workers, or to be structurally excluded from labor markets, and by aggravating the plight of minority clients of welfare and criminal justice institutions with additional humiliations, denial of service, abuse, and sometimes death.

I now turn to another dimension of punishment: what happens to prisoners once they have completed their sentence and are released.

5

Prisoner Reentry in Public Housing

In America, where wages are extremely high, the convicts easily find labour when they leave the prison; and this circumstance favours their good conduct when they have reentered society; in France, the situation of delivered convicts is infinitely less favourable; and even if they are resolved to lead an honest life, they are not unfrequently brought back to crime by a fatal necessity.

—GUSTAVE DE BEAUMONT AND ALEXIS DE TOCQUEVILLE, ON THE PENITENTIARY SYSTEM IN THE UNITED STATES

A released prisoner in the United States is frequently barred from voting, public housing, pensions, and disability benefits, and is lucky if he receives anything more than bus fare and, according to Jeff Smith, a routine farewell from a guard: "You'll be back, shitbird."

—ADAM HOCHSCHILD, OUR AWFUL PRISONS

Every year, hundreds of thousands of people are released from prison in the United States—about 650,000 in 2014. Former prisoners face dire job prospects because of discrimination and loss of skills. They have had no opportunity to save money while on the inside. They face increased health risks, are more likely to be homeless, and suffer the stigma of incarceration when they look for a job, many times facing these obstacles alone. They also are barred from voting. Their children are less likely to do well in school, which guarantees the persistence of misery over generations. More than half of released prisoners return to prison within three years.[1] These bleak facts define the experience of prisoner reentry in America.

In New York City in the early 2000s, about 300 people were released from prison or jail every day. Inmates released from Rikers Island (New York's main jail) were bused to Queens Plaza in the middle of the night. They were left there between 2 a.m. and 4 a.m. with a Metrocard and $10. Many had nowhere to go, ended up homeless, and quickly went back to jail.[2] Others returned to their families, which typically lived in poor, minority neighborhoods. Some had girlfriends or mothers in public housing.

The problem: in the United States it is forbidden for people with criminal records to live in public housing. Housing authorities are required to evict leaseholders for granting hospitality even to a husband or a son who comes back from prison or to anyone who has been convicted of a crime even in a distant past. In poor black neighborhoods like East New York, this law, called the One Strike ban, is yet another way to make reentry harder. This chapter is about the ban. I interpret policy efforts to make reentry more difficult as an ineluctable consequence of less eligibility.

The One Strike ban is popular and uncontroversial, but it creates problems for every government agency involved. In the story I am telling, three organizations—the New York Division of Parole, NYCHA, and Family Justice—play a central role. Parole is a law enforcement body that manages the provisional release of prisoners before the completion of their sentence (probation, administered by the New York City Department of Probation, also involves criminal supervision but as an alternative to incarceration). Since 2000, parole agencies across the United States have managed the supervision of about 800,000 parolees annually, compared to about 2.2 million inmates and 3.9 million probationers. NYCHA is the housing authority that manages public housing ("projects") in New York City. Family Justice is the nonprofit where I did my fieldwork, and it works with families of prisoners to reduce recidivism.

The two government agencies, Parole and NYCHA, found the ban on people with criminal records in public housing to be counterproductive and saw fit to partner with Family Justice to circumvent it. I explain how this law-evading partnership benefited both Parole and NYCHA.

"BETWEEN *RUCKER* AND A HARD PLACE"

Before the 1970s, public housing residents were not considered tenants but recipients of a government benefit.[3] Based on that understanding, housing authorities could evict or ban whomever they wished. Unwed mothers were barred from public housing until 1967.[4] Then, for a brief period in the 1970s, public housing residents became proper tenants. Court rulings at the time specifically forbade housing authorities to evict leaseholders based on the misdeeds of their relatives. This did not last.

In the context of the 1980s crack cocaine epidemic, housing authorities regained their discretionary power. In 1988 a Democratic Congress passed the Anti-Drug Abuse Act, which enabled public housing authorities to evict an entire family if one member, not necessarily the leaseholder, was producing or dealing drugs. That same year, Manhattan prosecutors launched the Narcotics Eviction Program. This aimed to evict drug dealers from their apartments in Manhattan private and public housing. Between 1988 and 2005 the program resulted in the eviction of 6,200 suspected drug dealers. In 1990 Congress passed the Affordable Housing Act, which required all public housing agencies to sign leases including provisions for the termination of tenancy if family members or guests engage in drug-related criminal activity.[5]

Things accelerated when President Bill Clinton said in his 1996 State of the Union address: "If you break the law, you no longer have a home in public housing, one strike and you're out. That should be the law everywhere in America." Clinton's phrase, "one strike," has since become synonymous with the ban on people with criminal records in public housing. In response, Congress passed the Housing Opportunity Program Extension Act of 1996, which recommended that public housing authorities do not provide housing to suspected drug users and evict leaseholders even if a guest commits a crime outside the tenant's building.

This was the law, but no one was sure of the extent to which it should be enforced. The answer came from Oakland, California, where the housing authority started eviction procedures against four tenants: two grandparents whose respective grandsons had smoked marijuana in the parking lot; a disabled 75-year-old whose caregiver was found to possess cocaine; and an aging woman named Pearlie Rucker, whose mentally disabled daughter had been arrested with a crack pipe a few blocks from the apartment. The Supreme Court unanimously ruled in 2002 that the ban was constitutional, and Pearlie Rucker was evicted.[6] *Rucker* became the name of the Supreme Court decision condoning no-fault evictions (also called "third-party-action evictions"). Since then, "numerous state courts have extended *Rucker* to sanction no-fault evictions for other criminal activity, including even nonviolent crimes such as forgery."[7]

After *Rucker*, Housing and Urban Development (HUD) Secretary Mel Martinez urged "compassion and common sense."[8] Instead, people got evicted from public housing for minor offenses. For instance, in smaller housing authorities, not returning a video rental has resulted in eviction. There is also the problem of how people get a criminal record in the first place. For example, some people, typically with mental disabilities, have become registered as sex offenders after taking a bad plea deal for urinating in public.[9]

In the post-*Rucker* world, housing authorities have to keep people with criminal records out of public housing. They pursue this goal by screening applicants, by evicting alleged or convicted criminals, and by evicting tenants who host them. In some housing authorities the number of evictions increased by 68 percent after 1996.[10] In Chicago the police department directly informs the Chicago Housing Authority of criminal arrests. Every month, the authority reviews 1,400 such reports, 7 percent of which are actionable for actual eviction. When the offender is not the leaseholder, the Chicago Housing Authority settles "approximately half" of these cases and requires that the offender leave public housing. About one-fourth of all One Strike evictions in Chicago in the late 1990s resulted from juvenile arrests until the police stopped transmitting information about children.[11] One Strike policies disproportionately affect racial minorities, as these demographics are more likely to commit crime, to be arrested, and to live in public housing.

In theory, tenants threatened by the ban could take their case to the courts and at least appeal adverse decisions. But public housing authorities do not have to meet the standard of proof used for criminal conviction when they determine whether a tenant (or a tenant's guest) has engaged in criminal activity. Tenants facing evictions typically lack the resources to effectively fight adverse decisions. In the case of the New York District Attorney policy to evict drug dealers, 55 percent of tenants vacate their house before the final court decision.[12]

The One Strike ban deprives an entire population of badly needed housing aid. Thus is mass incarceration applied to public housing. *Dura lex, sed lex*[13] —but Parole and NYCHA soon found the ban counterproductive.

PAROLE'S BACKSTORY

In the early 2000s, soon after the ban was put into place, Parole planned to open an office at the Van Dyke housing projects, one of the largest public housing complexes in New York City (1,600 housing units, 4,300 residents). It may seem odd for a law enforcement agency dealing with former prisoners to open an office in a place where its clients are legally forbidden, but Parole proceeded to do just that. They had found that many parolees lived in public housing, and they wanted to be close to their clients, to facilitate supervision. What is more logical and practical than a parole office where the parolees are?

Parole's plan caused a public outcry. The Van Dyke parole office was supposed to replace a public library and would be located in front of an elementary school. Residents didn't want a magnet for criminals and sex offenders so close to children. The Van Dyke Tenant Association president gathered a thousand signatures against the parole office, and the project was killed by grassroots NIMBY activism. Two years later, Parole found a solution. It was impossible for them to open an office in the projects, but it should be easier for a nonprofit.

The nonprofit in question was Family Justice. Working in the Lower East Side, it had seen the effect of the One Strike ban on clients. Carol Shapiro, the founder and CEO of Family Justice, secured a deal with Parole and NYCHA. Gentrification had made her Lower East Side operation less viable, and she was seeking to branch out into less-favored neighborhoods. Parole's New York City director guaranteed support and collaboration from local parole offices. NYCHA pledged office space to Family Justice within public housing. Carol Shapiro hired a project manager, Jenn, to open the Family Justice office in East New York in Brooklyn. In January of 2006, I joined the team to provide sociological expertise, and we started to reach out to stakeholders in East New York that February.

Family Justice's avowed goal was to provide support to the families of prisoners in public housing—where prisoners and former prisoners are not supposed to be, because of the ban. The goal was supported by Parole and NYCHA. Why would these respectable organizations seek to circumvent, and therefore undermine, federal law?

THE BAN, SEEN FROM PAROLE

Parole's logic is best understood in historical perspective. Postwar parole officers' job was to provide employment. Inmates came out of prison, the parole officer found them a job, and the parolee was on the way to becoming a productive member of society (or not). But, starting in the 1970s, unskilled jobs became a scarce commodity, and parole officers found themselves with a new function, that of "violating" (to send back to prison for violation) a large percentage of their unemployed parolees, who were forced back into crime. Between 1980 and 2001, parole returns to prison increased from 17 percent of prison admissions to 37 percent; today, more than half of parolees go back to prison before the end of their terms.[14] In Alice Goffman's account of life in the age of mass incarceration, young black men are constantly "on the run" and wanted by the police because they have violated the terms of their conditional release from prison.[15]

Parole officers, and Parole as an institution, present themselves in public as a punitive law enforcement agency. Jenn and I witnessed this firsthand at a parole orientation meeting. These weekly meetings were directed at the families of prisoners who were soon to be paroled. For two hours, mothers, wives, and girlfriends would sit and listen to parole officers going through the letter and the spirit of supervision. For these women these meetings were two hours of bad news, where officers projected minimal sympathy toward parolees and made sure that no one left thinking that they were bleeding hearts. At our meeting there were nine women in attendance. Some had already been visited by an officer at home, and the others would soon receive such visits under a policy called "community prep." Based on these prerelease visits, officers decide if the home is an acceptable environment for the parolee. They have much discretionary power in this regard and can, for instance, ask the family to get rid of a dog.

During the meeting, parole officers reiterated that parole was "incarceration in the community" and that they were "law enforcement." "Incarceration in the community" means there are strict rules restraining freedom. Parolees are on a 9 p.m. to 7 a.m. curfew and are supposed to sleep at their official address every night. "It is not possible to sleep at the girlfriend's," a parole officer said. Parolees are forbidden to use drugs or to drink alcohol. Parolees who are drug addicts before the release have to get into a rehab program; if they don't, they go back to jail. If they try to use a balloon of urine for a drug test (available for five dollars on the streets of Brooklyn), "it's automatically prison." They have to get an ID within two months following their release. If they fail to produce an ID, "they return to jail." At the meeting, families learned that some parolees, depending on crime, are not allowed to drive, to buy a car, or even to take driving lessons. "Don't sell cigarettes. Don't work off the books," another parole officer added, speaking to an imaginary parolee. "Any change in behavior, new sneakers, anything, we notice." Parolees also have to report their girlfriends. They cannot leave the five boroughs, let alone the state of New York.

The gist of the meeting was that parole was "no joke" and that parolees would not enjoy meaningful freedom before the actual term of the sentence. Another point was that parole officers had "discretion on most things, literally," as the Parole bureau chief explained. Parole officers have discretion on the frequency of the parole meetings and the severity of the supervision. Although arrests for serious offenses and drug-related concerns result in automatic violations, other concerns are at the discretion of the parole officer. This means that the parolee perpetually lives under the arbitrary threat of a whimsical violation. According to parole officers, the main violations are curfew, drugs, and arrest. Now all this looks like Parole just tries to find pretexts to violate parolees. Jenn and I certainly heard violation stories that fit with the punitive narrative. A probation (not parole) bureau chief proudly told us how one of her officers sent a mother of three to prison. She had been caught smoking pot in her house with her children present. The kids were sent to Children's Services and later to foster care. Another probation officer recommended theatrically that all violations result in jail time.

Parolees have good reason to take parole officers at their word, which makes supervision easier. Parole's unpopularity in Brownsville and East New York was obvious; as one (rather conservative) local politician told us, "Inmates are just jobs for them." A mother made this clear when she told Jenn about her son's parole officer. She explained, indignant, that the parole officer had intrusive questions, seemingly unrelated to supervision. He asked, for instance, whether the family had Section 8 housing subsidies, which she found humiliating and unnecessary. When she complained, he made it very clear that he was in charge and would lock up her son if necessary. "The way I see it," she said, "my son doesn't stand a chance. He'll make my son's life a living hell." From the point of view of their clients (parolees and their families), Parole's function is to send parolees back to prison—to "violate" them.

In reality, though, not all parolees are violated. More than 60 percent of first-time parolees do not return to prison.[16] Parole officers will not communicate this number to families, because parole is law enforcement, a business where the performance of toughness and rugged masculinity is paramount to avoid using violence. Many parole officers think that being unpleasant makes them more likely to be taken seriously. But Parole has defined so many reasons to violate parolees that they can send them back to prison practically at any moment for any reason. If Parole were just trying to send as many people as possible to prison, they could send virtually everyone. This is not happening (except for drug offenses, because of the War on Drugs) for the simple reason that it would defeat Parole's purpose as an organization.

Parole's broad function within American public policy is to save taxpayer money by organizing "incarceration in the community" rather than in prison.[17] Prison is expensive, costing up to $60,000 per prisoner per year in New York State. Parole is usually considered 10 to 20 times cheaper than prison; the average cost of parole per prisoner per year in the United States is $4,000 (I could not find the actual cost of parolees in New York). In addition to saving money, parole provides a legal and practical solution to overcrowded prisons and the resulting risk of prison riots. Parole has no purpose if it only sends people back to prison. When outside the public eye, parole officers readily admitted that they were not interested in returning parolees to prison. Their chief concern about working with Family Justice was about protecting their discretionary prerogatives, as opposed to enforcing mandatory violations. In a meeting at which Jenn presented on Family Justice, a parole officer insisted that he didn't want anyone telling him to "violate" a parolee. "I don't want to negotiate a re-arrest," he said. A Parole middle manager made it even clearer: "I try not to lock more people up." This all makes good sense, as parole is not especially conducive to crime: parolees "are rearrested, reconvicted, and reincarcerated less often than offenders who max out."[18]

Parole saves money, but there is a catch. Once a prisoner is paroled, he or she becomes the parole officer's problem. On one hand, the parolee cannot be "violated" on a whim, because it negates the purpose of the organization: to save taxpayer money. On the other hand, many parolees eventually end up back in prison anyway, and parole officers can only hope that the crime for which they are eventually incarcerated will occur after the parole period or, if not, for some minor offense that will not make it onto the news cycle. In their own admittance, a parole officer's deepest nightmare is to read in the *Daily News* that one of their parolees has just killed a little girl, because, as one said, "I become a co-defendant."[19]

Usually, parolees get violated for drug offenses and minor domestic violence incidents. This is all in the normal course of business for Parole. But to keep the risk of disaster under control, parole officers need to know where their parolees are. As Simon puts it, "Supervision has become just a temporary space between initial release from prison and inevitable return to prison. Their [parole officers'] task in such a system is to do the best they can to make sure they can find the parolee when the time comes to arrest him."[20] At the parole orientation meeting for families a parole officer said that the parolee's residence was "our number one pet peeve. We have to know where they are sleeping."

Parole officers have a typical caseload of 50 to 70 people, and they cannot afford to waste time looking for a parolee. They need a stable address, which public housing conveniently provides. But parolees are banned from public housing. As a matter of fact, there is an unofficial policy at Parole that it is not very urgent, or necessary, or even desirable to inform NYCHA of a parolee living illegally in public housing. Parole officers and brass will deny this to their last breath, as they should, but it is a plain and simple fact that Parole knows that some parolees live in public housing and are not informing NYCHA. Why would they? Living in public housing is forbidden, but this is not the type of offense that should send someone back to prison; if Mom is evicted, the parolee will be homeless, which maximizes the likelihood of bigger trouble; and nothing good will ever come from evicting Mom. Thus, Parole casually keeps lists of parolees in public housing.

All this is unknown to parolees, however, because parole officers cannot in good conscience advise their clients to jeopardize the family's lease on their home. Parolees therefore mistakenly believe that they should not inform their parole officer if they live in public housing. They cannot take the risk that Mom loses the apartment. This is a lose-lose situation.

In fact, the parole officers and supervisors we met did not like the ban. Their descriptions of One Strike showed how bizarre they found the policy. Parole officers routinely called it "the problem between NYCHA and Parole," as if it was a bureaucratic glitch and not federal law. Discussing the issue in an interview, a parole chief said: "I don't think living in public housing is a major issue." In his understanding, parolees couldn't live in a project *where they had committed the crime,* which is definitely not what the Supreme Court had ruled.

Police officers had similar concerns. When a robbery happens and the perpetrator is not known, police officers go through listings of neighborhood people who have recently been released from prison and who match descriptions and profiles. Parolees are the first ones they want to talk to. To do that, police officers need a stable address. If parolees lie about their whereabouts, it makes it more difficult for the police to clear or incriminate suspects. In fact, police officers are always trying to figure out who lives where, and who lives with whom, to make it easier to find persons of interest.[21]

All this led to a situation where Parole decided that the ban was counterproductive and detrimental to public safety—in short, absurd. But what about NYCHA?

THE BAN, SEEN FROM NYCHA

In theory, NYCHA has little to lose from the One Strike ban. There is such a long waiting line to get into public housing that denying access to people with criminal records just reduces the number of applications to process. People with criminal records have reduced earnings and higher propensity for crime: they are less desirable applicants than people without. The ban weeds out a subgroup (felons), which only has, from NYCHA's point of view, undesirable characteristics. The part where NYCHA has to evict people is thornier. NYCHA officials can use *Rucker*'s legal environment to maximize their discretionary power on whom to keep and whom to evict. In the case of admission to public housing (not evictions), NYCHA will not deny housing to someone who has been arrested for turnstile jumping in the subway. But if the application reveals a pattern of fare evasion, or another kind of disorderly conduct such as public drinking, NYCHA managers can decide that the applicant is ineligible for two years.[22] In 2013 NYCHA started 838 eviction procedures (legal proceedings, not actual evictions) on One Strike grounds.[23]

As long as NYCHA retains discretionary power on whether to evict or not, the ban seems like a resource in managing tenants. But there is a hitch.

Public housing authorities receive funding from HUD (US Department of Housing and Urban Development). To make sure that housing authorities are deserving of government money, HUD has devised a performance assessment system to evaluate housing authorities against a number of indicators: vacancies, rent collection, physical maintenance of buildings, and so forth. One of these indicators tracks how well the ban on people with criminal records is implemented:

> Under this performance evaluation system, a high-scoring PHA [public housing authority] is rewarded with less federal oversight and is eligible for more funding, but a low-scoring PHA is punished by being ineligible for additional funds and, ultimately, with a HUD takeover of its management.[24]

Thus, NYCHA's discretion is limited. They can keep good tenants, but at a cost: each noneviction weakens the score in HUD's performance assessment.

This is because, to a public housing authority, every tenant is a risk of unpaid rent.[25] Some tenants actually are reliable rent delinquents, experts at navigating courts and support systems, dedicated to their case, and known to landlords as "professional tenants."[26] The public housing authority will be happy to get rid of them, and the ban can be the pretext to enforce an eviction at low legal cost. Tenants who vandalize their apartments, who have a long contentious history with management, and whose children are local terrors are especially threatened by the ban.

But there are also "good" tenants—tenants who have never done anything wrong, who politely salute their neighbors, and who pay rent every month without making a fuss. Nothing would be more irrational than to evict one of these solid gold tenants, because no one knows how the replacement will behave. NYCHA managers have zero incentive to evict a good tenant who happens to have a son who comes back from prison. As a consequence, the ban is not only a resource for NYCHA managers: it is also a cause for headaches. They face a catch-22: if they evict, it may cost money, because they might get a worse replacement tenant. And if they don't evict, it may also cost money, because they might get less funding. So, what would you do in this position? The answer is: you will want to *not know* about people with criminal records.

The problem is that everyone knows about parolees in public housing, and it takes active and willful blindness for NYCHA managers to ignore it.

When I naively asked at the beginning of this research if parolees did live in public housing, Family Justice employees looked at me in disbelief: "Of course they do!" When I asked NYCHA Social Services employees, they reluctantly offered unconvincing denial. I then asked police officers, who also answered, "Of course they do," and when I told them that NYCHA employees denied it, they erupted in laughter, and mockingly asked, "Since when?!" A probation officer casually told Jenn that he had two or three probationers living at Van Dyke. When Jenn began to work on the project in early 2006, Parole records had 276 parolees in the housing projects of the Seventy-Third and Seventy-Fifth Precincts, according to an email communication. The number was likely higher, as parolees may take precautions to avoid jeopardizing the subsidized tenure of their loved ones, and it did not take into account all the people with criminal records who were not parolees. In July of 2006, Family Justice planned to serve more than 200 families of parolees in Unity and Van Dyke, according to internal documents.

NYCHA Social Services employees work at the front lines of implementation and are the most likely to discover unauthorized tenants. Informally, NYCHA social workers and housing assistants know a lot about tenants. My interviews suggest that some social workers even went the extra mile in helping tenants. For instance, they were not supposed to deliver legal advice, yet they advised tenants on how to get a show cause (a type of court order) when needed. By delivering inside advice to tenants, and by spending time with them, they got a lot of information (and gossip) about what was going on in apartments. NYCHA social workers certainly knew about unauthorized stays, but they used their inside knowledge of both tenants and the bureaucracy to do what they thought was right. As a matter of fact, a NYCHA management supervisor, who had worked all her life in public housing, could not remember a single time when a NYCHA social worker had reported a parolee who was illegally living in an apartment—not once. The supervisor apparently believed that Social Services was not required to report such matters, but social workers said they had to. Another supervisor expressed concerns that Family Justice would have to report illegal stays, as if that was a problem.

In other words, NYCHA social workers know about unauthorized tenants, but they don't report them. According to a Family Justice publication, if returning prisoners are discreet—if they spend as much time as possible out of public view, plan their exits and entrances according to staff schedule, or pretend that they are just passing by to help with a given chore—then social workers can pretend they don't know.[27] Their presence is an open secret, but they live in fear of detection. They are trapped, since they typically can't make private market rent.

Although the One Strike ban maximizes NYCHA's discretionary power and enables management to terminate the lease of troublesome residents, nothing indicates that in practice NYCHA ever tries to use this power. More likely, NYCHA employees collectively do their best to avoid finding people with criminal records, for economic and moral reasons. They are aware of the potential consequences. Having a lease terminated is a dramatic event for public housing tenants, because rent in the private market in New York City is unaffordable for many low-income families. Even in the poorest neighborhoods, rent for a two bedroom apartment exceeds $1,000, while public housing apartments can be rented for $300. NYCHA social workers certainly object to evicting tenants who only have committed the crime of hospitality. In addition, the One Strike ban limits social workers' ability to do their job. For instance, parolees cannot be referred to Victim Services because "Victim Services only helps people who are totally innocent," a NYCHA social worker said. In fact, there is a tacit understanding that the One Strike ban only applies to troublemakers.[28]

When NYCHA "discovers" someone living illegally in public housing, it may impose a "probation" sanction. When a family is under probation, NYCHA has the discretionary power to terminate the lease for any otherwise minor misbehavior, such as refusing the annual inspection or missing a rent payment. In the majority of cases NYCHA asks the leaseholder to ban the criminal family member (and will follow up on that). In effect, mothers have the choice between permanently barring their own son from visiting them or eviction. Then, if there is a problem, usually a combination of chronic nonpayment of rent and violation of the ban, NYCHA can pronounce permanent exclusion and arrange for eviction.

In fact, NYCHA only "discovers" unauthorized tenants (i.e., in a way that forces managers to register them in official records) when people make mistakes by self-reporting themselves. Sometimes, unauthorized residents are arrested by the police and, by mistake, report their family's address as their place of residence; the NYPD then has to notify NYCHA, which is forced into official registration. Other times, tenants may forget about the ban when they update the list of people living at home in an annual process called recertification. They may accidentally report an unauthorized tenant. This rarely happens because most tenants usually avoid adding adults to the list for fear of a rent increase. In other words, evictions are cruel; they make dubious economic sense, which results, in Jenn's words, in "an unspoken 'don't ask, don't tell' policy" within NYCHA.

In short, the law prevents people with criminal records from living in public housing, but it is inevitable that many of them will end up crashing at their mother's or girlfriend's apartment. The law is an inconvenience for Parole, whose officers would like parolees not to be forced to lie about where they live. Parole even tried to open an office in public housing to simplify the supervision of parolees living in public housing. The law also poses a problem for NYCHA. In theory the One Strike ban enables its managers to evict bad tenants, but in practice there are moral and economic reasons to not evict people.

Enter Family Justice.

In my analysis the main reason why NYCHA decided to collaborate with Family Justice is to maintain plausible deniability in providing social services to tenants. NYCHA management knows that poor people whose basic needs are met are less troublesome, behave better, and are more cooperative than poor people who are struggling. The ban prevents NYCHA from delivering services to struggling tenants. By supplying Family Justice with office space, NYCHA gets an on-site agency providing some measure of help (counseling, referrals) to this people with criminal records that NYCHA social workers can only help informally. Family Justice provides a veil of plausible deniability to NYCHA by being the contact point with tenants who are breaking the law. Because NYCHA does not have to know, these tenants do not make it into official records, and do not affect NYCHA's evaluation by HUD of the implementation of One Strike.

The real difficulty is in explaining what Parole gets from Family Justice.

MAKING FAMILIES PARTICIPATE IN PAROLE SUPERVISION

As we have seen, parole officers have to make sure that parolees are sent back to prison before they commit the horrible crime that will reflect badly on supervision. Parole officers need to be able to predict the trajectory of each parolee, but they don't have time to meet often enough for a proper assessment. How do they manage?

The solution is to rely on the people who know the parolee best: his or her own family.

Families may voluntarily provide information to parole officers. This is especially the case when a family wants to get rid of a relative for any given reason—romantic dispute, domestic violence, annoying friends, lack of financial support, and so forth. Here the family members just need to report a behavior that constitutes a violation of the parolee's terms, and the officer can proceed with incarceration—especially when all happens "in a manner which does not require the admission that the separation is desired."[29] This mechanism was widely described along the Parole hierarchy. A parole bureau chief told us that "the good PO [parole officer] is the PO that makes the family reports the wrongdoing of the parolee: 'Johnnie is doing good or bad.'" In a meeting where Jenn was presenting Family Justice to parole line officers, one of them said that a parole officer could gain a lot of information from the family, especially when the families wanted to get rid of the parolee.

Parole officers were not shy about presenting supervision to families at the orientation meeting: "If they [parolees] know you [family] gonna tell [about wrongdoing], they will stay [legit]. It's not snitching. It's preventing them from being arrested." For parole officers, it's best if parolees behave and stay at home: again, the point of parole is not to send people back to prison. A probation officer told Jenn that about 80 percent of the probationers' families were "supportive" and " stayed on top" of their loved ones on probation. I suspect that "staying on top" means exactly what I have just described. Studies of people under criminal supervision confirm this mechanism.[30]

Suppose, for instance, that Johnnie, the parolee, is arrested by the police. In theory the police should inform Parole, but this doesn't happen often in practice because cops have other things to do. Parole officers need to know about arrests because they are important information in assessing a case. Parolees, of course, have zero incentive to voluntarily report their own arrests since they might be violated. At the same time, an arrest is not a sufficient cause for violation. Parole officers therefore ask families to keep them informed about arrests.

The problem is when families do not want to cooperate. They may not want to see their loved ones going back to prison, or they feel strongly against cooperating with law enforcement, or they may be afraid of retaliation. Uncooperative families are a routine concern for parole officers, for which solutions abound. Police may just trash the apartment until families change their mind.[31] Subtler techniques exist.

One parole officer said at the family orientation meeting that she loved making home visits on Sundays because "that little two-year-old will tell it as well as a 40-year-old." She was suggesting to the audience that Parole would not hesitate to use devious means to achieve its goals. The most devious of all revolved around criminal liabilities. Unless a parolee is wanted by law enforcement, Parole officers need a warrant to search the house. But parolees and their family have to designate a private space that "belongs" to the parolee. Parole officers can search the parolee's bedroom or designated private space at their convenience, warrantless. Parole officers insisted that their searches were "thorough," because "we're law enforcement." By forcing the parolee to have a private space inside his family's apartment, Parole plays a dirty trick. Suppose a parolee wants to hide drugs. His private place, subject to warrantless searches, is risky. But if he hides drugs elsewhere in the apartment, then his family will be held responsible for not having cooperated with Parole and not having reported the drugs. "It's your home, be aware; if they do wrong, you get in trouble too," said a parole officer. Families have to watch really carefully over their parolee at home because they may become accomplices to his or her crimes. "Remember," the parole officer said, "if there are drugs in the house, and the parolee is not here, Mom can go to jail!"

And he added: "If you live in NYCHA you will lose your apartment." I believe this to be, humanitarian considerations aside, the key reason behind Parole's involvement with Family Justice.

To ensure compliance, Parole has to make reporting easy. As a parole bureau chief put it: "the problem is when families are afraid to say something." Families with parolees usually have a lot on their plate. These families are typically poor and cannot afford to lose the parolee's income. Even if the parolee is exploitative and abusive, reducing the emotional burden and economic cost of reporting, families face legal uncertainties: they cannot anticipate how the police, Child Services, or social workers will react to the incarceration of the parolee. They may have been themselves involved in crime and face retaliatory accusations with uncertain legal consequences. So, the ban on parolees in public housing brings another complication: cooperative families may lose their apartment over reporting a criminal.

In other words, the ban *disincentivizes* families living in public housing from performing their civic duty and informing on parolees. A law purportedly designed to improve safety in public housing and reward upstanding citizens actually prevents parole officers from doing their jobs and punishes tenants who cooperate with law enforcement. Such an institutional contradiction had to find its institutional solution. In East New York the solution—imperfect, incomplete, tentative—was Family Justice.

THE SERVICE THAT FAMILY JUSTICE RENDERED TO NYCHA AND PAROLE

In Parole jargon Family Justice is a *program,* a term they apply to a generic scheme, usually run by a do-gooding nonprofit, to which parolees can be referred. Individual parole officers usually hate when programs involve partnerships (more paperwork), but there aren't any more jobs to give parolees, and programs are all that's left.[32]

Family Justice planned to provide counseling to families of prisoners and parolees. Part of the job was done, informally, by NYCHA social workers, who were not supposed to know about the presence of parolees or to help. Family Justice was thus providing NYCHA with a layer of plausible deniability regarding helping the families of unauthorized guests. To Jenn this was a bureaucratic glitch, peripheral to her real mission. Jenn saw her work at Family Justice as a means to prevent kids from being drawn into the vicious circle of school failure, crime, prison, and untimely death. She was genuinely committed to helping people and connecting them with resources. In that sense, Family Justice was a social service agency.

Parole and probation officers fully concurred. They never missed an opportunity to boast they were "law enforcement" and not "social workers." I mentioned earlier how officers tended to emphatically display the masculine and punitive nature of their job, wearing bulletproof vests and carrying guns. In fact, some parole officers were reluctant to work with Family Justice because of an incident that had happened a few years ago. A former client who had absconded from Parole was trying to take refuge at a Family Justice satellite, and a parole officer had to use her gun. To make the long story short: parole officers did not fully trust Family Justice/La Bodega because, ultimately, parole was law enforcement (who shoot guns) and Family Justice social work (where criminals seek refuge).

The problem is, this opposition clearly carried meaning for many involved but was far from obvious on examining the partnership between Family Justice and Parole. For Parole, Family Justice was a channel for families to safely report on a parolee without endangering their lease. When Parole could not open an office to manage parolees in public housing—the project killed by tenant activism—it supported Family Justice to do it. In return, the nonprofit promised a close partnership, as the following excerpt from a letter from Family Justice to the parole regional director suggests:

> A family-focused approach to community supervision, if it relies on a genuine partnership with supervision agencies characterized by respect, collaboration and trust, can effectively increase compliance, promote public safety and prevent other generations from criminal justice involvement.[33]

This spirit of active collaboration was manifest in the Program Protocol for Probation, an internal Family Justice document from July of 2006. In the FAQ section, it sketches out an imaginary dialogue between a skeptical parole officer and Family Justice:

> Q: It sounds like family case managers just want to keep people out of jail but we have a job to do. We are law enforcement officers as much as we are caseworkers.
>
> A: This is not the case. Family Justice supports families to break cycles of criminal justice involvement. But we respect law enforcement and community supervision officers deeply, that's why we partner with you. We want to be useful to you and we want to be on your team. We understand that sometimes incarceration is necessary.

Family Justice promised to provide Parole information about parolees and indicated it was okay with surprise home visits. The protocol for partnering with Parole and Probation mentioned that Family Justice staff would get clients to sign a Consent to Release and Obtain Information form, provide branch chiefs with the client's real Van Dyke and Unity addresses, provide parole officers with Outreach and Referral Cards, and meet as often as requested by officers. It also promised to "always keep Probation Officers [and Parole Officers] apprised of the progress and setbacks their probationers are experiencing."[34] As a Family Justice employee said during a meeting with parole officers, "We don't want a menace to society to be at large either." In effect, Family Justice was offering intelligence to law enforcement.

The NYPD liked this kind of partnership. Police officers looking out for information are in the same position as parole officers: they know that families are afraid of losing their apartments, which is another incentive not to tell the truth. An inspector from the local police station was interested in the potential for intelligence. Maybe Family Justice could provide information about families who were below the police radar? "Your outreach is crucial," he said in a meeting with Family Justice and local police commanders.

As a consequence, and although Jenn and I thought of ourselves as the good guys, we were suspected of being agents for Parole. Remember that Parole had already tried to open an office at Van Dyke a few years ago. Several community leaders warned us that a lot of people would not trust Family Justice and would assume that our program would share incriminating information with NYCHA. One of them added candidly that it didn't help that we were white (he offered to help). Even probation employees believed it would be very tough to gain anyone's trust. The reality check came when we introduced Family Justice to the president of the Van Dyke Tenant Association—the woman who had single-handedly killed the first Parole project to open an office in lieu of the library. Her first question, hostile, was whether we worked for Parole. A month later, Jenn still thought that this woman saw her as a Parole agent.

Jenn and I fundamentally adhered to the idea that social and penal policies were ontologically different and that social policies were in essence benevolent and preferable to penal policies. Most people who work in the social service sector despise mass incarceration, repression, and violence and see social policy and social work as progressive, humanist work toward people who are fundamentally victims. Most law enforcement people also place a lot of meaning in this opposition: they value the masculine ethos of security policies, their effectiveness and authority, they perceive criminals as bad people who deserve punishment, and they deride social work as do-gooding, the work of bleeding hearts, counterproductive tolerance.

We see in the Parole/NYCHA/Family Justice story how difficult it is to empirically separate social and penal policy. This empirical blurring supports my conceptualization of welfare and punishment as part of a similar effort toward imposing social order. In fact, there is a long and contentious history between social workers and poor black neighborhoods. In the 1960s, Social Services used to stage surprise home inspections to check that women receiving welfare checks did not have a man in the house (making them ineligible).[35] Men had to sleep in cars or hide their belongings. As a soft-spoken physician, whose parents had gone through this, told us: "Social services were a curse."

CONCLUSION: PRISONER REENTRY AND LESS ELIGIBILITY

Does the One Strike ban work? Has it reduced crime in public housing? No one knows. Twenty years since its implementation, I cannot find any studies of the efficacy of the ban. Only Human Rights Watch cared to ask NYCHA officials.[36] The answer: "Crime is down in public housing, . . . but it looks similar to reductions in the city as a whole," the general manager said. Yet law enforcement officials, politicians, and NYCHA are under pressure to "do something" about high crime in poor neighborhoods. On March 1, 2006, one month after Jenn and I arrived in East New York, and even while NYCHA was providing Family Justice free space to assist the families of formerly incarcerated persons, New York City issued the Housing Trespass Program to "rid the projects of drug dealers." Under the Trespass Program those arrested for drug dealing on NYCHA premises were permanently banned from NYCHA property. If they ever set foot on public housing ground (including common areas), even as invited guests, the district attorney could prosecute them and have them locked up. In other words, while NYCHA and Parole were organizing a way around a legal ban to mitigate its perverse effects, another legal ban was being created.

On the surface, the takeaway from this chapter is that mass incarceration has gone so far and become so invasive that even law enforcement agencies are finding ways to circumvent its most counterproductive offshoots. Why not help former prisoners, the concerned reader will ask, even if only to prevent recidivism? It is good policy to train prisoners and to assist them after release. The Finns actually try to do just this, and they have social workers visit released prisoners to make sure they have a job.[37] Not so in the United States. Two-thirds of America's released prisoners return to prison within three years. The Second Chance Act of 2008 (a federal statute) "provides the princely sum of $20 monthly per new convict released, enough to buy them a sandwich each week."[38]

The actual reason why returning prisoners get nothing but even more vexing hurdles is penologist Hermann Mannheim's "principle of non-superiority," a variation on the principle of less eligibility: "the condition of the criminal when he paid the penalty for his crime should be at least not superior to that of the lowest classes of the non-criminal population."[39] Mannheim cited a trade-unionist who protested in 1933 against a perceived violation of the principle of nonsuperiority:

> My executive council feels very strongly that it is grossly unfair that honest lads and poor citizens should be deprived of the opportunity of training and employment, whilst it is proposed that persons who have committed offences against the law and community are assisted in this connection.[40]

In other words, it is a hard sell for societies to accept that criminals get handed out opportunities that are denied to honest, hardworking people. Again, nonsuperiority doesn't mean that released prisoners *should* be denied opportunities. It implies that released prisoners are unlikely to get anything that minimum-wage workers don't already have, as Beaumont and Tocqueville and Hochschild hinted at in the chapter epigraph. In theory we know what should be done: free education in prison, free training programs, free access to university after, free health care, and so on. Because all of this is already expensive for regular citizens, it is unthinkable that it is granted to criminals. Returning prisoners get nothing and are left to a life of crime (i.e., prison), informal economic activities (i.e., likely trouble with law enforcement), widespread employment discrimination, and, at best, dead-end jobs.[41] Less eligibility rules.

6

Nonprofits

Welfare on the Cheap

In civilized society he [man] stands all the times in need of the co-operation and assistance of great multitudes, while his whole life is scarce sufficient to gain the friendship of a few persons. . . . But man has almost constant occasion for the help of his brethren, and it is in vain for him to expect it from their benevolence only. He will be more likely to prevail if he can interest their self-love in his favour, and shew them it is for their own advantage to do for him what he requires of them. Whoever offers another a bargain of any kind, proposed to do this. Give me that which I want, and you shall have this which you want, is the meaning of every such offer. . . . It is not from the benevolence of the butcher, the brewer, or the baker, that we expect our dinner, but from their regard to their own interest. We address ourselves, not to their humanity but to their self-love, and never talk to them of our own necessities but of their advantage. Nobody but a beggar chuses to depend chiefly upon the benevolence of his fellow-citizens.

—ADAM SMITH, THE WEALTH OF NATIONS

Even an idiot can understand that someone who sleeps in a shelter at night will not be in the street with a blanket and a bottle of beer, that someone who has been given a meal will not go off and steal food, that someone who has been given shoes will not walk around barefoot, and that someone who has been given a clean t-shirt creates less of a mess than if he's wearing a t-shirt covered in blood.

—AN ITALIAN SOCIAL WORKER I INTERVIEWED IN 2004

Faust. *Who are you then?*
Mephistopheles. *Part of that power which would do evil eternally and eternally does good.*

—GOETHE, FAUST

In March of 2015 the Federation Employment and Guidance Service (FEGS) went bankrupt. FEGS was a "human services provider," a nonprofit that helped people get jobs, housing, or access to health care. It was a big provider, with a $250 million annual budget and 5,000 employees (including subsidiaries) serving 100,000 New Yorkers every year. The bankruptcy was major news. FEGS started out in 1934 as a small Jewish charity. It lived off government contracts, mostly from the city. With the organization stopping all activities, taxpayer money paid out in advance was being wasted. Employees were laid off or forced to accept lower salaries. Hundreds of unpaid creditors began to worry about their own survival. Clients who depended on services were left to themselves.

Prosecutors began to investigate. The general idea was that management was incompetent and greedy.[1] Among its financial sins, FEGS "invested money in offshore funds in the Cayman Islands, Greenland and Iceland, engaged in unusual auditing practices, increased executive salaries even as debts mounted, and may now owe the state tens of millions of dollars because of Medicaid overcharges."[2] FEGS invested $70 million in a back-office for-profit company that was unable to categorize revenues as "expected" or "realized."[3] The month before bankruptcy, a $19 million deficit was announced to funders, and the executive vice president got a $92,000 bonus.[4] The CEO who was in charge during the final years asked for $1.2 million in deferred compensation.[5]

The scandal reveals something about the new world of nonprofits delivering social services to the poor. In the United States, direct services now represent about 17 percent of federal welfare expenditure.[6] In 2010 the nonprofit sector represented 5.5 percent of GDP and employed about 10 percent of the domestic workforce. In this chapter I will discuss the rise and significance of nonprofits delivering welfare services and describe the operations of Family Justice, the nonprofit with which I did fieldwork in East New York. I put nonprofits in the context of the transformations of the welfare state and study them as political-economic entities. I will show that nonprofits are cogs in a system made dysfunctional by forces that are far beyond their reach. Nonprofitization is the symptom of an inferior welfare state.

THE RISE OF NONPROFITS IN SOCIAL WELFARE PROVISION

History will tell why FEGS went down. This section explains why it went up. The main reason derives from the transformation of the American welfare state. Federal spending in social welfare, measured as a share of GDP, was cut by 43 percent between 1980 and 2004, and welfare benefits became less likely to be in cash.[7] In 1979 a typical single-parent family (at high risk of poverty) got 25.4 percent of its post-tax income from cash welfare. In 2006 cash welfare accounted for only 13 percent of their income, with cash benefits amounts steadily decreasing (fig. 8).[8] From 1995 to 2012, the number of New Yorkers receiving cash assistance dropped from 1.2 million to 360,000.[9]

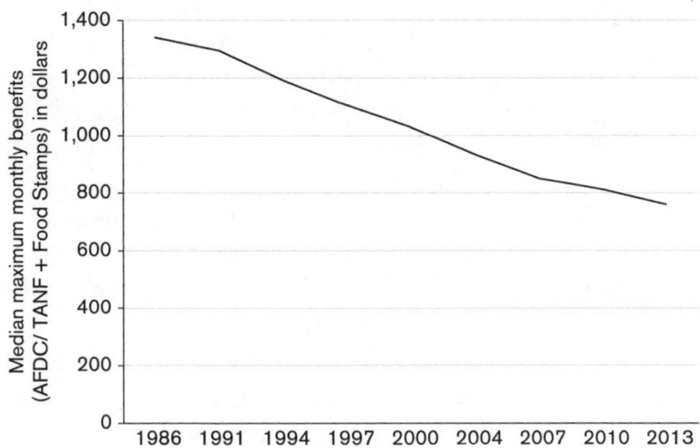

FIGURE 8. Median AFDC/TANF + Food Stamps maximum monthly benefits for a family of four in 2015 dollars, 50 states + District of Columbia. Source: David Brady, Professor in the School of Public Policy, University of California, Riverside (personal communication).

The poor now get many of their services in-kind, delivered by private nonprofit organizations that are funded mostly by local public authorities. There are two processes at play in the "nonprofitization" of welfare delivery: privatization and devolution.

Privatization concerns the providers and consumers of subsidized services.[10] This means that instead of funding public agencies, governments now increasingly fund nonprofits to deliver services. The main justification for privatization is to leverage the alleged benefits of competition. To achieve competition, public funders (governments) organize bidding processes and select the best proposals from applicants, who are usually nonprofits. Nonprofits do not pay corporate income tax, which gives them a competitive advantage over commercial organizations. They do pay employee taxes, but nonprofit workers do not enjoy the protections and benefits of public sector employees. Provided that requests for proposals are sufficiently competitive, the expected benefits of nonprofitization (compared to traditional public delivery) are as follows:

- cheaper services, and therefore greater public spending efficiency;
- more efficient organization, because of the allegedly superior management practices in the private sector and the stronger normative commitment of nonprofit personnel;
- greater ability of the funding body to reallocate spending according to need. Grants are contracts for a fixed duration. If a social problem becomes less important, or less politically sensitive, there is no inertia of public spending.[11]

Nonprofitization is just one way of privatizing services, and it is considered an inferior one by privatization theorists. Hard-core privatizers favor voucher systems in which the government subsidy goes to consumers (clients) instead of providers (nonprofits). With vouchers, people are able to buy the services they need on the marketplace. Vouchers are now used to subsidize access to private housing, replacing public housing managed by public agencies. Nonprofits are usually opposed to vouchers: they prefer the relative (albeit provisory) stability of grants, compared to waiting for customers like shopkeepers.[12]

The other process at play is devolution. This means that requests for proposals are organized by local, not federal, governments, who decide which nonprofit gets what.[13] The justification for devolution is that local authorities have a better grasp of local needs.

There is a consensus that public authorities (federal and local) are the main funders in the field of human services.[14] The following figure gives an idea of where the $6.1 billion in contracts for human services in New York City in 2015 came from. Compared to local governments, private philanthropy is a minor actor (fig. 9).

As a consequence of privatization and devolution, "the number of registered nonprofit human-service organizations increased by 33 percent and their total revenues (in constant dollars) increased by 73 percent" from 1995 to 2012.[15] In New York City alone, about 2,000 nonprofits were launched between 1990 and 2013,[16] and there are 200,000 employees working for nonprofits—a figure comparable to Wall Street rolls (albeit with vastly different salaries). These people work with 2.5 million New Yorkers.[17]

We are still a far cry from claiming that the welfare state is fully privatized. For instance, in New York City, food stamps amounted to $3.5 billion in 2012 (the number of recipients increased 85 percent from 2004 to 2012), and EITC (tax credit for the working poor) represented more than $2 billion in 2010.[18]

For nonprofits the consequences of welfare's nonprofitization are a desperate, constant, life-or-death concern for short-term money. What is, in the end, a nonprofit? It is an economic actor that tries "to cheat organizational death."[19]

Organizations try to stay alive, but most don't succeed. Companies usually die within their first year, and the average life span of (successful) companies listed in the S&P 500 is 15 years. Nonprofits are no exception. Most are financially stressed. They offer mediocre pay to their employees: "more than one-third of New York City's social service workers are eligible for safety net programs, compared to 24 percent of New Yorkers as a whole."[20] Nonprofit lobbies complain that governments are very stingy when it comes to calculating "indirect costs." For a nonprofit to deliver $100 worth of services, it needs an additional $18–20 for handling paperwork, grant writing, and so forth. Government agencies rarely grant more than 10 percent for indirect costs and sometimes zero. As a result, 60 percent of the bigger nonprofits have no more than three months of cash reserves.[21]

For most nonprofits, therefore, money is a pressing concern. Even the largest, most professionalized providers face organizational death, as the FEGS scandal showed. Nonprofit work cannot rest on goodwill alone. Past the youthful enthusiasm of their prime, nonprofits come "under yet more pressure to adopt a hierarchical organization with better-educated, better-paid, and better-trained staff mem-

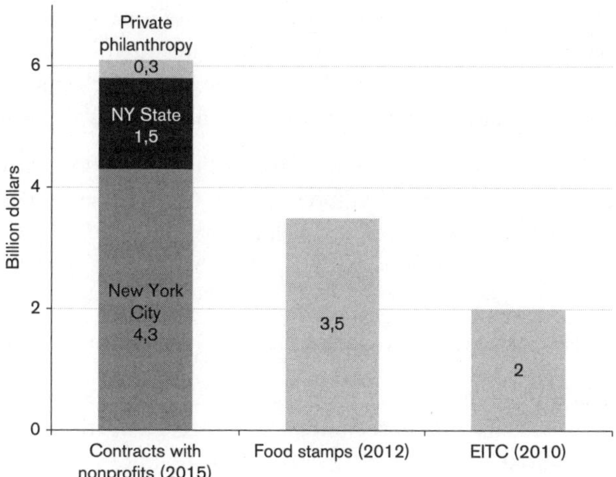

FIGURE 9. Order of magnitude for different types of aid to the poor in New York City in the early 2010s, in billions of dollars. Sources: Human Services Council Commission, New York nonprofits; and White, Creating collective capacity.

bers."[22] The main reason is that "nonprofits with higher bureaucratic orientation, stronger domain consensus with government, and longer government funding history" are more likely to get government contracts.[23] In other words, the organizations that get government money, and thus survive, are corporate structures with a professional workforce. They have to possess the financial know-how to accumulate assets so that they can survive rainy days.[24]

Professional, managerial nonprofits are better fit for survival than more grassroots organizations. Managerialism, also known to students of public administration under the name of New Public Management,[25] is the theory that organizations are best run by certified professionals using formal procedures and proven technologies such as performance indicators.[26] Sociologist Yeheskel Hasenfeld puts it best:

> Human services management . . . is awash with practice principles and models imported from business administration and New Public Management (NPM). These include, for example, entrepreneurship, branding and market niche positioning, revenue generating strategies, contracting out, logic models for program development and evaluation, and performance-based accountability systems. . . . The image of a successful organization is that of a well-oiled, highly productive and efficient machine. Managerial practices upholding this logic generate new forms of Taylorism. That is, work is structured to optimize productivity, increase the volume and speed by which clients are processed, reduce costs, and achieve prescriptive performance measures imposed on the workers by top managers.

> Client–worker relations become highly scripted by performance benchmarks and information processing algorithms. These are rationalized as "best practices" based on the latest research on effective interventions. The clients, in turn, become commodified: they are viewed as sources (or hindrances) of revenue.[27]

Managerialism, such as that exemplified by the FEGS scandal, is driven by privatization for two reasons: competition forces nonprofits to act as market actors, and nonprofits are monitored by funders through performance indicators. The implications of this double process of privatization and devolution raises several concerns.

GENERAL IMPLICATIONS OF NONPROFITIZATION

The expected benefits of privatization are the expected benefits of competition. The whole point of privatizing is to have multiple providers competing to deliver for optimal value.[28] Without competition privatization is pointless. Research shows that outside the biggest cities, competition is nonexistent.[29] In New York there are numerous nonprofits, but Carol Shapiro, for instance, didn't see other providers as competitors, more as "partners with common interests" who organized to raise awareness and get more funding from public authorities.

Instead, the main consequence of privatization is not competition but a classic principal/agent problem. There is the funding body (the principal) and the nonprofit provider (the agent). The funding body wants to save money, to know how money is spent, because it is accountable to taxpayers. Providers are in the messy business of managing humans (staff and clients). The particular resolution of this principal/agent situation in contemporary America is that government officials are constantly preparing requests for proposals, negotiating contracts, and, above all, monitoring nonprofits.[30] A recurrent grievance in the nonprofit sector is the multiplication of audits: nonprofits managing several grants get audited by different agencies at the same time, with up to 250 audits per year for big organizations. These frequently require the same information using different formats and generally create an insane amount of paperwork.[31] Writer Derek Jennings joined a nonprofit board and discovered how much bureaucracy was involved:

> I figured that serving on the board would be a good chance for me to become more knowledgeable about issues surrounding homelessness. . . . What I did not expect, however, was a two-year crash course on finances, balance sheets and cash vs. accrual accounting. . . . My limited understanding of the nonprofit sector was that it was where you went to "do good" and, essentially, escape the corporate world. . . . In today's economic landscape, the very survival of local charitable organizations is very much dependent upon how well they are able to function like a business. If it seems like a contradiction, it's because it is. If, say, rescuing abused animals is your passion, you want to be out there helping the sick puppies, not creating spreadsheets, doing paperwork or ensuring that you have all of your audit documentation in the proper format required to maintain your listing with

United Way or continue to receive state funding.[32]

To produce evaluations and to legitimize service models, a "considerable portion of the workers' time is devoted to mindless paperwork spelling out treatment goals, performance benchmarks, action plans and reported outcomes that have little bearing on their daily work." It follows that privatization does not improve the quality of care, nor does it cut costs.[33] But, as the bankruptcy of FEGS, the nonprofit with a $250 million budget, has shown, this doesn't mean that nonprofits are wealthy. Most are actually financially distressed,[34] especially when their purpose is not to speculate on housing. Struggling nonprofits therefore resort to selling services and charging fees,[35] which is one step toward becoming a full-fledged for-profit operation. This points to a growing competition between nonprofits and for-profit providers for the delivery of social services.[36] For instance, after the welfare reform, welfare offices (public administrations) across the United States have massively contracted a for-profit company called Maximus to find jobs for welfare recipients.[37]

Devolution brings two concerns. One is political decision making. Interest groups may influence politicians at the expense of needier, less influential constituencies. Because local politicians decide which nonprofits get money, some nonprofits—usually large, community-based and well-organized ones—have become intermediaries between voters and public officials. In short, politicians fund nonprofits to provide services, and nonprofits organize beneficiaries to keep politicians in office.[38]

Devolution's other concern is spatial justice—equal access for all Americans to quality welfare services. Which nonprofit gets the contract determines which of the poor will benefit, and direct services "vary greatly in their quality and effectiveness, depending on the skills and practices of the service providers."[39] There is a growing mismatch between where nonprofits are based and where poor people live. As a consequence, nonprofits face little to zero competition in many regions, especially rural areas. In a large urban area like Los Angeles County, there is no correlation between the poverty rate and government funding for nonprofits.[40]

There are also perverse effects for service providers desperately looking for dollars for survival. As social work professor Baorung Guo writes: "Theoretically, nonprofits presumably are not profit seekers because of lacking incentives to make profit. However, to adapt to the changing funding environment, many nonprofits have to 'act as profit seekers.' "[41] Under pressure from evaluators, nonprofits have zero incentive to claim failure. They need to constantly show success.[42] One consequence is the gaming of performance indicators to present acceptable data. Street-level practitioners have always played an important role in adapting policies to street-level realities by developing informal practices and generally using their discretion in the absence of direct oversight to their advantage. Now that they are evaluated through performance indicators, they use the same skills to produce the desired numbers.[43] Thus, performance indicators incentivize nonprofits to select the most desirable clients, those who are the most likely to comply and to show positive results.[44] As a consequence, "the clients who need the services the most may be least likely to receive them."[45] When numbers are not good, nonprofits may try redefining their goals in vague, buzzword-heavy terms.[46] The pressure to show results in a competitive environment has the same effects in other realms, including, of course, academia.

Another perverse effect of the hamster wheel of applying for grants is that nonprofits are incentivized to misrepresent the world to funders. They are under pressure to look innovative and reactive to new problems:

> If the new donor fashion is gender-based violence, the agents, sensibly enough, will say what needs to be said in order to get funding. And if the donors believe that beneficiaries are powerless, the brokers are particularly unlikely to tell the donors that their imagined beneficiaries already have agency and the ability to solve a particular problem. Rather, they are likely to portray their clients as in urgent need of assistance and enlightenment.[47]

Likewise, there is a contradiction between the two values of innovation and evidence-based devices. By definition, and as Carol Shapiro once pointed out to me, adopting evidence-based policies means not innovating; but funders, both governmental and philanthropic, love "innovation," clever new ideas. An infamous New York innovation was Opportunity NYC, launched in 2007. This conditional cash program gave poor people cash incentives for good behavior—"things like going to the dentist ($100) or holding down a full-time job ($150 per month). Children were rewarded for attending school regularly ($25 to $50 per month) or passing a high school Regents exam ($600)." It was brutally ended after three years in 2010 for lack of results. This was the perfect neoliberal program, relying on incentives and funded by philanthropists. It was a wasteful program: only one-third of the original $40 million allocated was spent on the poor ($14 million); the rest was for operating costs ($10.2 million) and evaluation ($9.6 million).[48]

In the enchanted world of civil society, nonprofits are independent of both state and corporate interests and can play a role in keeping a check on power, articulating grievances on behalf of the voiceless, and generally advocating on behalf of "society." In reality, nonprofits are "appendages" of the state "as they scramble for government dollars."[49] Today's nonprofits, because they specialize in specific issues and constituencies, are less likely to advocate for universal social rights.[50] Nonprofits dependent on government funding now see advocacy as a way of "solidifying funding relationships" and "brokering resources and promoting the organization rather than substantive policy change or client representation. . . . In order to be perceived as a legitimate partner to government, organizations reject confrontational methods and advocate as insiders."[51] In the professional, managerial nonprofit, power belongs to a "managerial elite" which has much in common with its government or corporate counterparts. These nonprofits are top-down hierarchical organizations where grassroots interests are less likely to have a voice. All this, combined with the managerial quest for best practices and evidence-based policies, results in depoliticization: the reduction of social problems to personal issues and the absence of challenge to structural inequality.[52] Writer Melissa Chadburn thus describes the emptiness of the nonprofit she worked for:

> What they said I was doing—what the foundations were paying us to do, what I thought I was doing—was working to prevent child abuse and neglect. . . . Then, on my first day, I was shown to my cubicle and handed a heap of papers that touted an ideology—a Theory of Change. On subsequent days, I sat at large round tables and looked on as a series of aggravating white liberals spouted the inherent value of this theory:
>
> *Relationship Based Organizing is a specific model that recognizes and harnesses the power, and inherent skills and talents of individuals to create and drive the changes they determine are necessary to improve the lives of their families, friends and neighbors.*[53]

Chadburn rightly concludes that her organization was into "poverty amelioration through behavioral change," as opposed to tax-driven redistribution or a self-respecting welfare state. Family Justice's model was similar: it involved convincing clients to be good citizens and did not involve actual transfer of income from the wealthy to the poor.

THE MANAGERIAL NONPROFIT: FAMILY JUSTICE

In my research, the nonprofit that embodied the professional, managerial approach was the one with which I did my fieldwork: Family Justice. Family Justice was part of a broader ecosystem where the constant need to secure funding makes nonprofits less likely to challenge structural inequality (not that it should). Before it was disbanded in 2009, Family Justice exemplified nonprofits that have flourished in the new ecosystem. (I will discuss another type of nonprofit in the next section.)

What was Family Justice? The ubiquitous, standardized capsule description on all its promotional material read: "Family Justice is a national nonprofit organization that draws on the unique strengths of families and neighborhoods to break cycles of involvement with the criminal justice system." Family Justice was an offshoot of a nonprofit founded in 1996, La Bodega de la familia (hereafter La Bodega), which sought to reduce drug use and was located in the Lower East Side (a Latino neighborhood in Manhattan), which, in the 1990s, was still poor and a giant drug supermarket. The alliance was named thus because it was founded in an abandoned convenience store where a shoot-out between robbers and police had left a robber dead and a cop paralyzed.

La Bodega was a successful program, which means it generated funding. In 2000 its energetic and persuasive founder, Carol Shapiro, created Family Justice, an umbrella organization to disseminate the lessons from the "Bodega model." In the early 2000s Family Justice offered training for various agencies across the United States, drawing on the La Bodega experience, which provided direct services ("family case management," more on this below) to Lower East Side residents. Because of gentrification, La Bodega was running out of clients and eventually closed in 2008. Back in

2005, the plan was to open a new La Bodega–type service provider in East New York, and that's where Jenn and I entered the story.

Family Justice's focus was on criminal justice. Carol Shapiro, the founder, had been an executive at New York's Department of Corrections and held a management position at Rikers Island. She understood early on that reentry was a major problem, and a funding opportunity, in the age of mass incarceration. Between 1991 and 2004 the percentage of prisoners participating in a reentry program increased from 17 percent to 31 percent.[54] At La Bodega most participants were poor, addicted to drugs, living in public housing, and had been referred there by Parole. In East New York, Family Justice was set to offer counseling to the families of prisoners. Aside from all the other hardships that come with having a relative in prison, there is a financial cost for families to keep in touch with prisoners. Families send money and pay for overcharged phone calls and for transportation to visit prisons located upstate; it costs them on average around $300 per month.[55]

Family Justice's slogan was "Families are part of the solution." *Family* was meant broadly; it included friends, neighbors, and virtually any concerned party. The idea was to consider returning prisoners in their social context and to draw on their own social networks to help them. The assumption behind this move was the strength-based approach. Too often, social workers and criminologists see people with criminal justice involvement as individuals with pathologies. Family Justice's distinctive edge was to see such people as embedded in rich social networks of friends and families whose power could be tapped for good. A Family Justice brochure read: "Even the most fragile of families have remarkable strength and resilience." Social workers at La Bodega practiced "family case management." They worked with clients to get them off drugs, providing counseling and referrals to other services, getting them appointments for job or training opportunities. They tried to involve the clients' families. Family Justice sought to tap not only interpersonal networks but also interinstitutional ones. Social workers maintained formal and informal partnerships with hospitals, rehab centers, and law enforcement agencies to make things easier for their clients: get a second chance with the parole officer, referrals to better medical treatment, and so forth. To that end, Family Justice social workers cultivated trust and goodwill with other agencies. Family Justice publications used a strength-based vocabulary. The organization was never to "teach" anyone but to *enhance existing practice.* A "problem" was a *challenge;* there were no "leaders"—a word that implies "followers"—only people who showed *leadership.*

Family Justice relied on science to prove its efficacy. Virtually every Family Justice document produced after 2002 cites a study conducted by the Vera Institute of Justice, which shows that after six months of family case management at La Bodega, drug use among clients had declined from 80 percent to 42 percent.[56] The study was based on two groups of returning prisoners: 50 La Bodega users and a comparison group of 56. In the comparison group drug use decreased from 61 percent to 48 percent during the same time frame.) Data analysis lent support to the strength-based approach:

> The reduction in drug use was not produced, as originally anticipated, by greater use of drug treatment among Bodega participants, but instead appears to be a direct result of pressure and support from Bodega case managers and family members themselves. (Executive summary)

The Vera study also shows that La Bodega clients had better access to health services and were less likely to be rearrested and convicted (9 percent against 16 percent for the comparison group).

There is, of course, enormous appeal to scientific evaluations for funding purposes. A large part of Family Justice's activity was geared toward presenting evidence of proximity to science. For instance, Family Justice promotional material referred to La Bodega as its "direct service learning center." This conveyed the idea that Family Justice, the primary organization, was a sort of think tank providing training and policy recommendations; and La Bodega, the subsidiary, was the laboratory for live experiments on best practices. Family Justice's long-term plan was to build an "inter-relational database" fed with data from La Bodega and the East New York satellite, managing dozens of indicators to prove the La Bodega model accurate.

Family Justice nurtured ties with prestigious universities. The award from the Kennedy School of Government at Harvard University that La Bodega got in 2003 was on every brochure. The chair of the board of trustees was a Columbia University sociology professor, Sudhir Venkatesh. Several academic studies were published using Family Justice data, including an article coauthored by Carol Shapiro.[57] Family Justice published policy briefs and quasi-academic articles. These publications used social scientific research designs and cited a wealth of academic references. One internal publication was a list of "research summaries" about the organization's core concepts (social capital, social networks, reentry, etc.), each time citing relevant scholars, such as Robert Putnam, Nan Lin, Michael Reisig, and Robert Sampson.

Alongside the respect for science was the pursuit of a professional/managerial orientation, manifest in the style of its brochures:

> The Bodega Model® is an award-winning, evidence-based methodology developed at Family Justice's direct-service arm, La Bodega de la Familia. The model draws on four disciplines: family systems practices, strength-based models, case management principles, and literature on partnership and collaboration—and is used to describe our approaches for both direct service application (where it has been evaluated) and government partnerships (where it received an award).

When Family Justice associates designed programs, they had to follow a specific method. They first had to articulate a "theory of change" (a "framework to understand how a program or policy will presumably achieve its goals"), with a "logic model," organized along inputs, activities, outputs, objectives and goals. Case managers drew "ecomaps" and "genograms" for their clients, and organized "diagonal workgroups" with representatives from other agencies.

Family Justice sought to emulate the result-oriented, professional/managerial ethos—the opposite of bloated, proverbially inefficient, public bureaucracies. Family Justice was committed to optimism and doing good. The nonprofit mystique of "doing good," of being "unencumbered and untainted by the politics of government or the greed of the market,"[58] is a well-identified theme in the literature. Nonprofits and NGOs more generally have been subjected to healthy criticism.[59] My point here is that doing good in the world of Family Justice meant a commitment to liberal values. These liberal values sometimes clashed with other stakeholders' values. The crass cynicism of some police officers or the unenlightened comments about gender issues from East New Yorkers accentuated the social and/or racial distance between typically white, elite university educated types and lower middle-class civil servants.

In fact, when it comes to delivering services in poor neighborhoods, *nonprofits* is a word that is applied to two different types of organizations. In a nutshell: one needs to distinguish Manhattan-based nonprofits (like FEGS or Family Justice) and their local, community-based counterparts, such as the local East New York nonprofits.

LOCAL NONPROFITS IN EAST NEW YORK

In general, local nonprofits are minimally bureaucratic, small operations with a limited life span.[60] Local nonprofits often lack a clear, public purpose. Manhattan-based nonprofits strive to be defined by a single issue or term (reentry, domestic violence, shelter, etc.) and a punchy slogan to maximize brand identification. In East New York, nonprofits delivered a range of services that made them difficult to categorize. Some of the confusion came from the fact that virtually all local nonprofit directors were simultaneously political activists. Another source of confusion was that housing-related nonprofits were often not-for-profit in name only, especially in the housing sector. Take, for instance, the Ocean Hill Brownsville Tenants Association (OHBTA). In 2007 OHBTA managed hundreds of housing units in Brownsville and East New York, including the 385-unit Noble Drew Ali Plaza building. In the early 2000s OHBTA started to evict tenants to replace them with more lucrative homeless people sent by, and paid for by, the city's Department of Homeless Services (to understand how landlords make more money with homeless people than with any other tenants, see chapter 7). OHBTA then neglected the buildings it owned, presumably to maximize profit, and in 2002 garnered a great deal of negative coverage in the media, even earning a spot on the *Village Voice*'s "Top ten worst landlords in NYC" list, for its predatory negligence.[61]

The local East New York nonprofits that Jenn and I met in 2006 lacked the infrastructure of professional grant writers and experts in city funding. In our eyes this only reinforced their authenticity, but in practice it means a great deal of economic vulnerability and dependence on political allegiances. Such nonprofits are often vehicles for political promotion, a stepping stone for young politicians as a means of generating income and building a favorable reputation among likely voters. To give a sense of these interrelations: the director of East New York Urban Youths Corps (a major affordable housing nonprofit) had spent his career as an aide for top local politicians. He had provided housing for, among many others, ManUp!, a nonprofit run by a former chief of staff for the local councilman and then assemblyman. For community-based East New York nonprofits, local elected officials were important sources of funding. This led to a number of corruption and mismanagement scandals over the years. Large nonprofits in poor neighborhoods may become full-fledged political actors that enter into a "triadic exchange" with politicians and clients: they mobilize their employees and clients to vote for local politicians who, thanks to devolution, make the decisions about which nonprofits get government contracts, recreating the political machines of yesteryear.[62]

While Manhattan-based organizations tended to downplay their religious origins (if they had any), in East New York many direct services to the poor were delivered by churches. The neighborhood's two megachurches—the progressive, Afrocentric St. Paul Community Baptist and the evangelical, prosperity-gospel Christian Community Center—were (and still are) major players with elaborate social programs such as managing schools or building affordable housing. Smaller churches also organized to capture grant money and deliver services. Many community leaders doubled down as pastors, imams, chaplains, or deacons. A community activist and nonprofit director told me flat out that he was here to "realize the kingdom of God" and that his nonprofit was "ministry first" and "business second." All meetings of three or more began with an introductory prayer, also known as inspiration, invocation, or spiritual introduction. The prayer regularly mixed spiritual themes and bureaucratic concerns ("God, help us with the decision making"). Public speeches often took the form of black church preaching: chiastic sentences ("we face darkness, but we see light"), call-and-response, Christian imagery, and spirited delivery resulting in collective approbation.[63]

The distinction between two types of nonprofits—the professional, managerial type and the local one—is important to bear in mind to avoid misconceptions about social policy in poor neighborhoods. Sociologists Patrick Sharkey and his colleagues have argued, for instance, that the rise of nonprofits had a causal effect on the crime drop.[64] They assume that nonprofits are a grassroots effort, the result of a "mobilization from within," as if all nonprofits that engage in urban- or crime-related work are local. This is not the case: a good deal of the work in poor neighborhoods is done by nonprofits like Family Justice, which are nothing local. What Sharkey and his colleagues show is the crime-reducing power not of nonprofits but of social policy: for instance, delivering services on substance abuse treatment has a strong effect on reducing crime.[65] Whether social-policy budgets are best spent on nonprofits or on other types of social service delivery (such as public administrations, vouchers, cash allowances, etc.) remains an empirical question.

IMPLICATIONS FOR SERVICES TO THE POOR

People who are unfamiliar with social policy often think the big problem is perverse effects: opportunists choosing welfare over work or capturing resources at the expense of others in greater need. In reality the problem is that social policies benefit only a fraction of the population entitled to them. For any program targeting a defined group, only a percentage even know about it. Of that percentage, only a fraction will actually apply. Only a handful of government programs are well-known to most (cash welfare, food stamps, Medicaid, etc.), and even for these the rate of non-takeup is significant—this is true even for universal, nonmeans-tested programs.[66] For example, the French have a minimal income program for the poor that is well-known to all, providing about $600 per month, plus $300 per child. The takeup rate is estimated at 50 percent.[67]

For local programs operated by anonymous nonprofits, it is a challenge, and a definite part of the operation, to inform people of the availability of a given program. Enter the dreaded referrals (a referral is when a social worker sends a client to a service provider).

Imagine that your son has a drug addiction problem, and you want to check him into rehab. If you're poor, you will need that service for free. Suppose an acquaintance tells you about a church, nonprofit, or government agency that helps people. After getting past a few gatekeepers (secretaries checking for eligibility, etc.), you meet a case manager. You tell your story, and the case manager tells you about this program that she can refer you to. If you're lucky, said program actually delivers services (for instance, rehab), and you've only been through two referrals (one informal, one formal).

Referrals are a normal component of social-service provision until they become an end in themselves, and the scarcity of actual services makes clients go through endless strings of meetings with social workers, each time reciting their life story—their failures and their humiliations. Referrals are easier than providing actual services. Interviewing two physicians at a health community center, Jenn soon realized that they did not treat anyone there; they were "just" doing referrals. Perhaps defensively, the doctors pointed out that they were not merely passing information to their clients: "we get them appointments," they said.

Even if referrals don't help, even if they only result in another referral or a dead end, they still perform two functions for social welfare organizations. The first one is to get rid of clients, who will take their complaints to someone else. The second one speaks to the age of performance indicators. A referral, even fruitless, is a measurable output. It belongs in a performance report, in the "achievements" category. Bureaucrats, whether nonprofit or government, are therefore interested in the possibility of making new referrals. For instance, when Jenn presented Family Justice to the NYCHA manager at Van Dyke, I was surprised that what suddenly sparked her interest was the word *referral.* The managers at Unity were also on the lookout, as Jenn recounts in her notes:

> Residents come to Management with all kinds of problems and expect Management to solve them. They don't know where to look to for help. She even remarked "it's too bad we aren't trained as social workers" because that is the position we are often forced into. She said that Management doesn't know where to

> refer aside from Safe Horizon at the PSA and NYCHA Social Services. (Jenn's notes, Feb. 21, 2006)

In sum, referrals are the by-product of a decentralized system where no one knows who does what, where organizations do not last, and where there is not one system of certification for reliable providers.

CONCLUSION: THE EVIL GENIUS OF NONPROFITS

Welfare scholars know what effective social policy looks like: massive transfers of money from the rich to the poor through punitive taxation. Instead, in the United States and specifically in East New York, social policy appears mostly in the guise of social services delivered by nonprofits. The scarcity of human services dollars, the way contracts are distributed, and the legal constraints on government spending have created this situation in which two types of nonprofits survive: the gritty, politically connected local ones (such as those we've seen in East New York) and the highly professional, managerial ones (such as Family Justice). The vast majority of these nonprofits do their best to meaningfully help the poor. But, as personally commendable as they are, there is only so much that nonprofits can do with their limited means. Empirical studies show that social services have less effect on redistribution than cash benefits.[68]

At this point in the discussion, someone usually raises the issue of the "hidden welfare state" to defend the honor of American social policy. The so-called hidden welfare state refers to tax deductions with social welfare objectives, such as home mortgage interest deduction, tax cuts for employer-subsidized health insurance plans, tax deductions for charitable contributions, and so forth. These are all for *working* people, typically middle-class, and the poor see almost none of it.[69] The added value of bringing up the hidden welfare state resides in its discussion of privatization. The usual analysis of tax deductions is that they are politically more feasible than granting direct benefits. There is more. Privatization allows for the creation of alternative policy-support coalitions.[70] According to privatization theorist Stuart Butler, the point of privatization is not so much to cut costs as to allow for the rise of interest groups supporting the newly created private entities.[71] The evil genius of funding nonprofits resides not in their lower costs but in the fact that their interest groups will spend a lot of energy fighting for more money for nonprofits, as opposed to more money for universal programs.

The growing importance of nonprofits is a symptom and a cause of the American welfare state's residual character.[72] In the final analysis the poor need a few hundred dollars more to make ends meet every month. Carol Shapiro, Jenn, and all the Family Justice staff were doing the best they could to help people in dire straits. But drawing on the "untapped resources of family and social networks" does not replace the money needed to make rent and pay for food and heating bills. Instead, a fraction of what is needed is spent on nonprofits, which are supposed to deliver direct services but which in reality catapult their clients into an endless loop of referrals, while administrators frantically check that performance indicators are met. This organization of relief is the symptom of a society where living conditions at the bottom of the labor market are so bad that welfare has to be reduced accordingly. Nonprofits struggling to survive and not paying their employees subsistence wages act out the theory of the upper limit: in a society where the living standards at the bottom of the labor market are so low, social policy will not be generous Scandinavian-style. The logic of less eligibility is inescapable.

But not all nonprofits are struggling. Some of those involved in managing homeless shelters have become multimillion-dollar empires. Why? And how does that relate to less eligibility? The answer is in the next chapter.

7

Reengineering Less Eligibility

The New York Homeless Shelter Industry

One question we face as a society—a broad question of justice and social policy—is whether we are willing to tolerate an economic system in which large numbers of people are homeless. Since the answer is evidently, "Yes," the question that remains is whether we are willing to allow those who are in this predicament to act as free agents, looking after their own needs, in public places—the only space available to them. It is a deeply frightening fact about the modern United States that those who have homes and jobs are willing to answer "Yes" to the first question and "No" to the second.

—JEREMY WALDRON, HOMELESSNESS AND THE ISSUE OF FREEDOM

Back in the 1950s, sociologists believed homelessness to be a problem of the past, resolved in an increasingly affluent society, where people would not "tolerate an economic system in which large numbers of people are homeless." Then a number of things happened. In the 1970s, unemployment peaked at 11 percent in New York. Between the early 1970s and the 1980s, real income from welfare decreased, making poor families more vulnerable. With urban renewal, flophouses disappeared from Manhattan. At the same time, the mentally ill were released from psychiatric hospitals as part of the deinstitutionalization movement. Between 1955 and 1987 the number of patients in mental hospitals dropped from 550,000 to 100,000 while the American population grew by nearly 50 percent. The decriminalization of public drunkenness and vagrancy made homeless people more visible. As a result, New Yorkers started to see a lot of homeless people in the streets.[1]

At that point, the story gets a New York twist. During the 1980s the city embraced a unique legal obligation to provide shelter to homeless people. A lawyer sued the city on behalf of a group of homeless men *(Callahan v. Carey)*, and in 1981 a New York judge, Richard W. Wallach, resuscitated a statute from the Great Depression to negotiate with Mayor Koch the "Callahan consent decree," establishing the first principles for a right-to-shelter for homeless men. Women were included in the consent decree in 1983 *(Eldredge v. Koch)* and families with children in 1986 *(McCain v. Koch).* Subsequent legal victories by homeless advocates established living standards with which the city had to comply. This legal obligation forced the Koch administration to hastily (and grudgingly) open temporary facilities with dire living conditions. By 1988, the shelter system—a sprawling network of intake centers, emergency housing, and longer-term shelters—was organized.[2]

New York City's shelter system is very expensive. In 2002 it was calculated that homeless people cost local governments more than $40,000 a year, whereas simply paying for their housing peaked around $24,000.[3] The latter program is called Housing First. As it happens, giving shelter to homeless people, no strings attached —no test, no forms, no mandatory detox or rehab, just a free apartment—is the most cost-effective way of dealing with the chronically homeless.[4] Housing First is designed for single men in the streets, not families. But it suggests, with little ambiguity, that we know the right policy answer to homelessness: make housing cheap and available to those in need.

This chapter analyzes New York City shelter policy, and it is not a "Housing First" feel-good story. New York has experienced a housing boom since the 1990s, which has exacerbated tensions in the housing market. New York judges have created a right-to-shelter that violates the principle of less eligibility. As a consequence, the city formally complies with its legal obligations and provides shelter, but the shelter policy's real objective is to reengineer less eligibility on the housing market. The program is designed to make sure that no one finds free shelter more desirable than what can be acquired by paying rent, and the city is spending a lot of money to deliberately make shelter unpleasant.

BASIC PRINCIPLES OF SHELTER POLICY

About 85 percent of homeless people are simply poor people who cannot make rent at some point in their lives. They are homeless in the sense that they are doubling up with relatives. Many work and have kids. They rarely end up on the street, and if they do, it is only for a few nights, usually after a quarrel with the relatives hosting them. The remaining 15 percent are chronically homeless. They consume more than half of shelter capacity, and they are the ones who cycle back and forth between shelters, jail, hospitals, and the streets.[5] New York City has to provide shelter for both populations, and this is the process that candidates for the shelter system have to go through.

Candidates need to reach out to an "intake center." Families have to go to the Bronx, to a facility called PATH, open 24 hours a day. Single male individuals apply to a separate intake center in Manhattan and single women in Brooklyn. Women who apply for shelter are screened (twice) for domestic violence.[6] Intake centers typically process people in a matter of hours and send them to an assessment shelter where Department of Homeless Services (DHS) employees determine whether applicants are truly in need. This may take up to ten days.[7] "Truly" homeless people are then sent into the shelter system.

Because availability is scarce, successful applicants usually have to spend weeks to months in transitional facilities such as hotels or private apartments (the so-called scatter- or cluster-site program) before more permanent places in housing or shelters are found.

Finally, if they don't find housing in the meantime, families (not single men) get access to the real shelters, known as "Tier II facilities," which usually are better quality than transitional housing. According to the New York City Department of Investigation, on any given night in 2015 there were about 2,000 families in hotels, 3,000 in private apartments, and 7,400 in Tier II facilities.[8]

To summarize the length of stays in New York City homeless facilities: intake centers (a few hours to a few nights) → assessment shelters (a few weeks) → transitional hotels or apartments (up to months) → Tier II facilities (possibly years).

In general, the typical family that makes it into the shelter system comprises a black single mother with two children. Between 2002 and 2012 the main reasons for entry, as coded by intake center administrators, were eviction (28 percent), overcrowding (23 percent), and domestic violence (23 percent). Over the course of the decade, eviction and domestic violence as a cause of entry rose at the expense of overcrowding. This statistic reflects tightening eligibility criteria and better screening for domestic violence.[9] In terms of geographic origin, East New York is one of the top three sending neighborhoods.

Most homeless shelters (both assessment and Tier II) are run by nonprofits. Contracting out to nonprofits of social policy is a way to both cut costs and make operations more flexible. The city doesn't own buildings managed by bureaucrats. Instead, it places requests for proposals, and nonprofits compete for contracts. It is up to nonprofits to secure buildings, manage staff, and provide food, security, and services according to city specifications. As of 2016 there were 240 shelters in New York City (up from 20 shelters in 1988).[10] Only nine of these shelters are directly managed by the city. All nine are punishment shelters, designed to get people out of the shelter system, and will be discussed in due course. The rest are run by a network of about 150 organizations, some of which operate multiple sites.[11] The transitional hotels and apartments are managed by private individuals or nonprofits. Shelter policy is thus almost entirely outsourced to private contractors.

Intake centers are run by the city's Department of Human Services. This is the crucial part of the business with which nonprofits can't be trusted since they live off contracts and their collective interest is to take as many people as possible into shelters. City bureaucrats make sure that people who get into the shelter system are in absolute, dire need. New York City's legal obligation to provide shelter to homeless people is expensive. From 1982 to 2015, DHS's budget increased from $50 million ($123 million in 2015 dollars)[12] to $953 million.

This brings us to money. It costs about $3,370 per month (as of 2015) to provide Tier II shelter to a typical family. This figure includes housing costs (rent or mortgage, maintenance), staff (including social workers and security guards), and food.[13] Tier II is the most expensive type of shelter.

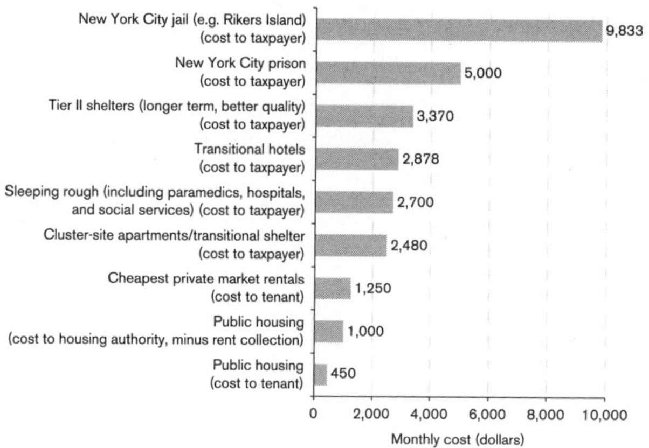

FIGURE 10. Estimates for monthly payer's costs for different situations for an individual (imprisonment, sleeping rough) or a family of three (shelter, public housing, and private rentals) in the early 2010s.

Services are a bit cheaper in transitional hotels ($2,880 per month) and apartments. A nasty cluster-site apartment for a homeless family in a rundown neighborhood costs $2,480 per month. If rented on the private market, the same unit will go for a maximum of $1,000 to $1,500. I myself rented rooms in Washington Heights and Bed-Stuy for $700 in the late 2000s.

To give a sense of the costs of different housing situations, figure 10 compares the cost to the payer of prison, shelter, public housing, private market housing, and sleeping rough (fig. 10).

In Tier II shelters, operating costs explain why sheltering homeless people is much more expensive than market-price housing. Operating costs are what nonprofits are paid for managing buildings and providing food, security, and counseling. (I have been unable to ascertain the proportion of the rental sum that accounts for services and security.)

This is where things get complicated. Many nonprofits struggle to make ends meet because they are not trying to make money: they have social justice ideals, which is why they can be trusted to spend money in the best interest of their clients.[14] But there is another type of shelter operator, who holds nonprofit status for the fiscal exemptions that enable revenue to be maximized. An illustrative example is that of a Brooklyn landlord who regularly appears in blogs and in the press because of various scandals related to his buildings. He operates a "cluster-site" apartment building at 60 Clarkson Avenue. Before 2014 the landlord used to contract a social service organization called CAMBA (Church Avenue Merchants and Business Association) to provide social services.[15] CAMBA's annual budget was $80 million in 2012.)[16] Since 2014, he is believed by tenants to have created his own nonprofit (called "We Always Care") to pocket the full amount of city funds dedicated to shelter residents. As of 2015, We Always Care was "in the middle of a two-year, $17.5-million city contract for operating its private shelters."[17]

Another documented instance of a *de facto* for-profit nonprofit has been described by anthropologist Martin Lamotte in the Bronx.[18] Lamotte documents the case of CASB (pseudonym), which manages two shelters, two senior centers, and owns 6,000 housing units. CASB contracts security and administration with for-profit CASB-owned-and-managed subsidiaries, an arrangement that maximizes revenue and optimizes the tax burden. These two examples show how profitable the homelessness market is.

These are the basic principles of New York City's homeless policy: there is a legal obligation for New York City to provide shelter to homeless people. The city contracts its shelter policy out to nonprofits. Many nonprofits managing shelters struggle on a contract-by-contract basis, but some become influential economic and political actors. Shelter policy costs a lot of money. These costs create a financial burden that every administration since Koch has tried to curb. For the city, there is a limited number of ways to cut costs: reduce the number of clients; shorten the stays; reduce the quality of stays.

The straightforward way to reduce the number of clients is to deny applicants their right-to-shelter. DHS sees to this at intake centers. The straightforward way to shorten the stays is for homeless people to find housing elsewhere. DHS sees to this, too: in 2009 the city started a scheme where nonprofits received a 10 percent bonus (compared with standard compensation) for the first six months of every sheltered family and then a 20 percent penalty after six months, to incentivize them to get residents out.[19] These two dimensions of cost cutting are ultimately subordinated to the third one: the reduction of the quality of stays.

Reducing the quality of stays means providing lower quality housing and services, in worse neighborhoods. This is because lower quality indirectly contributes to cutting costs: the less appealing the shelter system, the less likely homeless people will apply and the shorter their stays. That explains the false mystery of why conditions at some of NYC's shelters (especially hotels and cluster-sites) are so bad.

DICKENSIAN CONDITIONS: FALSE MYSTERY AND SMOKE & MIRRORS

Every few years, one of the key New York political players (mayor, comptroller, or governor) publishes a report documenting the nasty conditions in homeless shelters. New York politicians habitually commission and use these reports to attack rivals. The custom started with the Cuomo Commission in 1992, appointed by Mayor Dinkins (to criticize former mayor Koch) and chaired by Andrew Cuomo, who in turn used the report to gain prominence by turning his criticism toward the Dinkins administration. More recently, there has been the Department of Investigation report in 2015 (commissioned by Mayor de Blasio to attack former mayor Bloomberg) and a comptroller report in 2016 (a transparent attack on Mayor de Blasio).[20]

Reports typically indict the Dickensian conditions at some of the shelters' hundreds of health and safety violations: faulty fire alarms, peeling lead paint, mold, cockroaches, mice and rats, leaking plumbing, exposed wiring, broken heating systems, collapsed ceilings, and so forth.[21] This little game plays well with the press, which relishes horror stories. Moral outrage at bugs and mice is facile and harmless. At best, a handful of places are closed. Because of the need for shelter, structural equivalents open elsewhere, and the stage is set for the next report.

The obvious problem is to explain how and why the city manages to spend between $2,400 and $3,400 per family per month to provide squalid housing. This question is key to making sense of shelter policy. The technical answer—the *how* question—is that the city lets nonprofits maximize their profits at the expense of homeless people.

DHS contracts nonprofits to provide shelter. The contract specifies that providers have to keep up minimal standards of decency, because of legal obligations, and if only to avoid scandal. Amazingly, the most severe consequence for "nonperformance or negligent performance" is to lose the contract. Thus, the contracts with DHS do not specify "practically enforceable penalties." If a nonprofit puts a family in an apartment with peeling lead paint, collapsed ceiling, and swarming cockroaches, *and if the press finds out about it,* DHS cannot fine the nonprofit or make the nonprofit pay for alternative housing, let alone prosecute its directors. As the Department of Investigation puts it, "Without such terms, the City is depriving itself of a vital enforcement tool when a Contractor fails to satisfy its contract."[22]

In the private market, if an apartment is substandard, the renter may withhold rent, take the landlord to court, and demand repairs. Small landlords in poor neighborhoods spend a lot of time and money at the housing court; managing such costs is a crucial part of their business model.[23] But if the renter is DHS, landlords needn't care about all that. They will get paid, whatever the conditions. The only thing keeping them from mercilessly milking the situation is their good conscience. Shelter operators therefore have a massive incentive to maximize profit at the expense of quality, since they risk next to nothing, both in terms of severity and certainty of punishment.

It gets better: DHS does not always have a contract with providers. All the hotels, half of the cluster-site apartments, and even a few Tier II shelters hold no contracts with DHS. The absence of a contract typically happens when DHS needs emergency housing but doesn't have time to negotiate contracts, which means that these providers are paid more and are not required to provide services with minimum quality requirements.[24] As the 2015 Department of Investigation report states, "With no contract, DHS has lost a crucial point of leverage—it cannot enforce the provision of services through a breach of contract violation subject to basic contract law, giving DHS one less enforcement mechanism by which to hold providers accountable for poor conditions or services."[25]

In other words, shelters with contracts enjoy few inspections and no penalty for negligent performance, and shelters without contracts are not required to provide decent standards of living. DHS basically incentivizes shelter operators to *not* provide quality housing. Many shelter operators are decent people who do their best to provide a decent experience to their clients, but the implicit incentive is to save as much money as possible on maintenance and overall quality of housing since there is no reward for respecting contracts.

For nonprofits operating shelters, there are countless ways to save money. Shelter managers are sometimes stingy about security—a costly item with human resources headaches. Shelters for single men are said to be notoriously unsafe, so violent that many men prefer to sleep rough. Homeless women typically have fled situations of domestic violence and need protection from their abusers. Once in a while, scandals —the murder of a former teacher at a Harlem shelter[26] or of a mother and her two children at a Staten Island hotel[27] —shed light on the poor security conditions at shelter sites.

The simplest way to save money is to forgo building maintainance while collecting DHS money. Among the scandals covered by the press is that of the Brooklyn landlord mentioned earlier, who runs the 60 Clarkson Avenue cluster-site. The landlord bought 60 Clarkson at foreclosure in 1995 for $1.5 million.[28] This site attracted negative attention in the press between 2012 and 2015 because of shooting incidents. There were also reports of mice, cockroaches, burglars, and drug dealers. Since 2014, the landlord has received about $3,000 per month per unit, about 20 percent more than the city's average rate for cluster-site apartments. Adding insult to injury, 60 Clarkson has 83 apartments that used to be rent-stabilized at about $700 per month. In effect, therefore, the city has removed affordable housing from the market and given the landlord a per unit boon of $2,300 ($3,000 minus $700). To go from $700 (rent-stabilized) to $3,000 (the shelter industry), the landlord had to evict the original tenants. One can imagine that this was done thanks to legal action, psychological harassment, and buyouts.[29]

This is a somewhat exceptional case, one so egregious it captured even the *New York Times*' attention. Most of the time, nonprofits do not own the building they manage. When the building needs maintenance, the landlord and the nonprofit argue over who should pay. This allows for a delay in repairs and a convenient game of finger-pointing.

In addition, the biggest nonprofits have major political clout. In poor neighborhoods large nonprofits are able to influence local elections by mobilizing their employees and clients to make sure that elected officials keep funding them.[30] This makes for backroom political deals and corruption as contracts are awarded by elected officials. A few scandals have made it to the press. In 1998 the *New York Daily News* reported on East New York Urban Youths Corps, a shelter nonprofit whose managing director got fired for refusing to award a shady building contract to a man referred to as "the shadowy ruler of East New York politics."[31] East New York Urban Youth Corps now runs two shelters, one residence for senior citizens, and has remodeled more than 500 low-income rental units in East New York. They also provide space to influential local organizations. Likewise, in 2015 *Al Jazeera America* reported on a cluster-site that had been flagged several times as notoriously hazardous in official inquiries. This cluster-site was managed by Aguila Inc., a nonprofit that ran more than 200 cluster-site units in the Bronx. Because of misgivings about Aguila, in 2013 the comptroller had recommended that the city stop contracting with the nonprofit. A year later, the newly elected de Blasio administration awarded Aguila a $16 million contract.[32]

It is clear *how* these Dickensian conditions arise: nonprofits can cheat on their obligations without fear of penalty. Now let us consider the *why:* money is spent *in order to* make conditions unpleasant, if not with mold and rats then with humiliating rules.

ORGANIZING LESS ELIGIBILITY

In theory, homeless New Yorkers have a legally sanctioned right-to-shelter. When somebody needs a home, the city has to provide one. Given the astronomical cost of housing in New York, and the persistent poverty of many residents, the right-to-shelter seems too good to be true. It makes for a possible breakdown of less eligibility, especially since many shelters are decent, especially Tier II (longer term) sites. Of course, virtually everyone prefers paying rent to being homeless. But when it is difficult to generate an income, and when market prices force people into doubling up with relatives, people get squeezed, and some may rethink their hierarchy of preferences—especially when shelter is a guaranteed right. My argument is that New York City's shelter policy is designed to make sure that no one finds shelter more desirable than paying rent. The policy's logic is to reengineer less eligibility.

Less eligibility begins at intake centers, the first point of contact between homeless families and the shelter system. The mission of these centers is to prevent the homeless from making it into the shelter system and to route a maximum of applicants out. From 2003 to 2011 the proportion of applicants found eligible to enter the shelter system fell from 50 percent to 35 percent.[33] DHS employees try hard to find relatives whose homes applicants can sleep at or any other solution. A homelessness advocate explained the process to *Salon:*

> "You have to prove every place you and every member of your family slept in for the past two years. It's so they know every address they can investigate," says Kathryn Kliff, a staff attorney at Legal Aid Society in the Bronx. "Even if you're street homeless, you have to get documentation." Kliff counsels clients to get creative, like asking a bodega guy on the corner or "the guy that slept next to them" for official proof that they were, in fact, sleeping on the street.
>
> Even if a person you've formally lived with gives PATH a statement that you can't stay with them, that's not enough. "PATH always thinks that your close relatives will take you back," Kliff says, "and a lot of times they will, but a lot of times they won't, if there's some pretty bad family history of trauma or domestic violence, or lease restrictions."[34]

Intake centers are not just for screening out: they provide anti-eviction services, family mediation, and sometimes one-time rental assistance.[35] Employees of the shelter system are so diligent in finding creative solutions for homeless people to not be in shelter that they have been reported to advise families to sign a lease somewhere and not pay rent so they can qualify for federal assistance for people about to be evicted.[36] The *New Yorker* sarcastically commented:

> If you have no home in New York but own a cabin in Alaska, PATH may give you a plane ticket to Alaska. . . . Patiently and firmly and with endlessly bureaucratized persistence, it makes walking away and giving yourself up to fate seem the easier solution.[37]

Since 1996 (under Mayor Giuliani), the DHS has employed the services of professional fraud investigators who check every claim made by each applicant family. For an average of 20 to 30 daily applicants there is a staff of 155 fraud investigators who visit relatives and check records.[38] In spite (or because) of them, intake center social workers routinely make mistakes in determining applicants' eligibility, resulting in families unnecessarily sleeping rough (the city admits to a 10 percent error rate).

Single men also apply at intake centers, but their eligibility is automatically granted.[39] Conditions at single men's intake centers are notoriously harsh and deterrents in themselves. There, people sleep "in vast, warehouse-like shelters," in "barracks-style dormitories, lined up in cots with as many as 100 people."[40] The purpose is, of course, to save money but also to make people think twice before applying. According to homelessness advocates, many people prefer to sleep rough rather than to start the process at the intake center.[41] One homeless man, asked by the *Daily News* why he would prefer to spend the winter's months in the streets, responded that he was once woken up in a shelter by another man masturbating on his face.[42] These conditions are a historical constant: in the early 1980s, researchers Ellen Baxter and Kim Hopper were already documenting filthy conditions, overcrowding, endemic thefts and violence, abuse from predators, and staff members terrified of catching diseases.[43]

Less eligibility continues in the transitional shelters between the intake center and Tier II facilities. The principle is the same: make life purposefully uncomfortable to nudge people out, and punish uncooperative residents by transferring them to an even worse place. As I have already described, living conditions at hotels and cluster-site apartments are infamous. Moreover, their rules are designed to make the experience unpleasant. Some hotels don't allow food, forcing tenants to eat out for each meal; others don't allow birthday parties. In some places, "residents must sign in daily to prove continued residency, and if they go more than 48 hours without signing in, they have to move out and report back to a temporary shelter in the Bronx."[44] Residents may not complain, organize, or do anything other than comply because they could be sent to even worse facilities. In Brooklyn, for instance, 75 Catherine Street is notoriously worse than the already nasty 60 Clarkson.[45]

Finally, less eligibility extends to the management of users in Tier II shelters, where conditions are usually better. Tier II shelters are designed to make life uncomfortable but without the mice, bugs, and mold. The point is to prevent clients from forming a sense of home: most people get emotionally attached to the place they live, and the more they are attached, the more they will try to stay. Landlords know they have to pollute the privacy and destroy the sense of home of the tenants they want to get rid of with intrusive visits, harassment, insults, and so forth.[46] In Tier II shelters, managers also prevent the formation of a sense of home thanks to hostile rules. Residents cannot bring personal furniture, nor can they own microwaves, toasters, or hairdryers. They have to observe curfews, sign in and out at all times, and cannot receive family or friends, even for birthdays or Christmas.[47] The logic of the rules is to communicate to residents that paying rent for their own apartment is the only means to nurturing a meaningful private life.

In addition to rules making shelter life uncomfortable and unattractive, noncompliant or uncooperative residents are threatened with being transferred to less desirable shelters, sometimes referred to as "next-step shelters," a program started in 2007. Says the *New York Times:* "such shelters offer more intensive case management, but among families, they are known for stricter rules and more crowded conditions."[48] Next-step shelters are run by the city itself and place a strong emphasis on getting families out. Case managers escort residents to job interviews and apartment viewings; there is no living room for families to watch TV.[49] Stricter rules involve

> having to meet with caseworkers seven days a week and attend daily life-enhancing workshops, both of which are required even of those with jobs. Residents must also leave the premises no later than 9 a.m. every day and return no later than 8 p.m. And even though passes are given to those who have jobs or school schedules that go past 8 p.m., residents must call their caseworkers each afternoon to renew them.[50]

Next-step shelters impose all sorts of humiliations on residents, like making them go through airport-like security at the entrance, confiscating cell phones with cameras, providing spoiled food and shared bathroom facilities for thirty people, and making residents ask each time for a single-serving supply of toilet paper.[51]

Behind these Dickensian conditions there is, once again, the principle of less eligibility, applied to the housing market: to make sure that no one finds shelter more desirable than paying rent. Applicants are deterred from entering the system at intake centers; they have to endure appalling conditions during the transitional, cluster-site phase; and in long-term Tier II shelters, clients are prevented from feeling at home in pernicious ways, to make private rentals more appealing. These pernicious ways are expensive and taxpayer-funded. The city *pays* to make shelter life unpleasant.

THE DINKINS MOMENT

The careful reader will have noticed that I have been vague about the degree to which the shelter policy is intentional. I have written of the policy's "logic," but what of the policy makers' intentions?

It so happens that Mayor Bloomberg's administration (2002–13) openly embraced the logic of less eligibility. In 2013 Bloomberg himself made the point that New York City's legal obligation to provide shelter was excessive: "You can arrive in your private jet at Kennedy Airport, take a private limousine and go straight to the shelter system and walk in the door and we've got to give you shelter."[52] In 2012, asked about the record number of homeless people in shelters (in the aftermath of the Great Recession), Bloomberg responded that shelters were "so much more pleasurable. We have made our shelter system so much better that, unfortunately, when people are in it, or, fortunately, depending on what your objective is, it is a much more pleasurable experience than they ever had before." To appease the ensuing scandal, he conceded that a shelter is "not the Plaza Hotel."[53] Bloomberg's top administrators championed a conception of potential and actual homeless people as reckless free riders, calculating the minimum effort for the best comfort, and decried the "perverse incentives" within the shelter system. Because no humiliation was too small, shelter residents received monthly invoices from DHS telling them how much they have cost the city.[54] One might think that Bloomberg's policy was informed by a pessimistic conception of human nature peopled with pathological exploiters of loopholes. Given different policy makers, one might assume that the policy could be more humane, more generous.

It cannot. Policy makers' intentions are irrelevant. Less eligibility imposes itself, for its logic is inescapable.

As I mentioned earlier, in the 1980s Mayor Koch was forced to open shelters. Koch's shelter system—at that time managed by the city, not by nonprofits—was notoriously unpleasant, but it welcomed every applicant without determining eligibility, in strict application of the law. In 1990 David Dinkins became the first African American mayor of New York and pledged to reform shelters. He appointed the Cuomo Commission to investigate the shelter system in the Koch years. Dinkins wanted to help the poorest and saw affordable housing as a solution to homelessness. He decided to facilitate homeless families' access to public housing, that is, to get permanent and subsidized housing to homeless applicants. Soon, the number of applicants shot up by 17.2 percent.[55] In public housing, residents organized demonstrations to protest the priority given to the sheltered homeless over the residents' own relatives. (NYCHA apartments have many unofficial residents who are on waiting lists for public housing.) NYCHA residents were joined by their administrators, who objected to being sent insolvent tenants, precipitating the financial crisis of public housing.[56] Dinkins's generous policy seemed to have created a perverse incentive to become homeless, an incentive that some families pursued, organizing their own homelessness to get into NYCHA.[57] By 1993, the Dinkins administration had established eligibility criteria for families as a means of rejecting suspected free riders.[58]

Dinkins's good intentions have been widely interpreted as a vindication of the "perversity thesis" (social policy creates the needy it is supposed to assist). The issue is, of course, extraordinarily contentious. No one "wants" their children to be homeless, to go from hotel to shelter, and so forth. Yet the only argument to claim that

Dinkins' policy of placement into subsidized housing did *not* incentivize applications to the shelter system appeared in a single unpublished paper by two Columbia University economists. They argued that the policy's perverse incentive was offset by its effectiveness in reducing homelessness.[59] What the authors prove is not the lack of incentive but the effectiveness of permanent housing solutions.

The perversity thesis made conservative publications happy. Yale law professor Robert C. Ellickson pointed out that the three cities that adopted a right-to-shelter (New York, Westchester, and New Haven) all experienced a surge in homelessness. At the end of the 1980s the per capita incidence of homelessness was five times higher in New York City than in other big cities; six times higher in New Haven than in the neighboring towns of Hartford and Bridgeport; and eight times higher in Westchester than in adjacent Nassau County.[60] According to Ellickson, lower rates of homelessness in more restrictive cities demonstrate that the right-to-shelter incentivizes homelessness.

Because neighborhoods strongly objected to opening new shelters, the Dinkins administration had to rely on large, inhumane barrack shelters and "welfare hotels," a situation that deterred many homeless people from seeking shelter. People sleeping rough became more visible, and New Yorkers complained more about street camps. Dinkins quickly resorted to evictions of street camps with bulldozers and the NYPD, further gaining the contempt of homelessness advocates.[61] The attempt at a progressive homelessness policy was a failure. Playing on the visibility of street homelessness, Rudy Giuliani was elected mayor on a law-and-order platform with an emphasis on "cleaning up" the streets and removing "squeegee men." Under Giuliani the NYPD enforced a particularly aggressive policing of the street homeless, criminalizing car washing, loitering, camping, and publicly feeding the homeless.[62]

The hard lessons of the Dinkins experiment have informed homelessness policy ever since: the best policy intentions are ruthlessly punished by the principle of less eligibility. Social policy can only be as generous as structural conditions allow.

CONCLUSION

Homelessness is not a sad-but-inevitable consequence of advanced societies. There are, for instance, very few homeless people in Scandinavia or the Netherlands.[63] In societies where poverty is contained and housing made affordable, services for people going through a rough patch can contain homelessness.[64] In New York City today, everything converges to precipitate a homelessness crisis: a low-income proletariat, insane real estate prices, and a right-to-shelter municipal policy.

The usual formulations of the principle of less eligibility focus on the determining role of the labor market. We see here how it can be extended to the housing market. People who don't own property have to pay rent to a landlord, the same way people who don't have capital have to work to make a living. To work and to pay rent are both vital necessities that give employers/landlords enormous power over workers/renters to determine wages/rent, which is why progressive governments implement minimum wage/rent control.[65] A functioning low-wage labor market needs a steady supply of people willing to work and thus rests on the principle of less eligibility for the organization of welfare and punishment. A functioning low-income housing market requires that poor people are incentivized to pay market-price rent.

Because homelessness creates so many problems, it is obviously best for everybody that the poor have a home, and this is why social-democratic countries regulate low-income housing. In Amsterdam (The Netherlands), for instance, 52 percent of the housing supply is public housing. In Germany an elaborate system of rent control keeps housing costs lower than in other, much poorer, European countries. As rent-stabilized homes in New York City are fast disappearing, and with scarce public housing, many will not be able to make rent and will get evicted or will no longer be welcome at the relatives' habitations where they were doubling up. Some of these people—about 8,000 to 10,000 families every year, including victims of domestic violence—will end up in the shelter system.

The particularity of New York City is that policy makers have to make do with the legal obligation to provide shelter for the city's homeless and, in theory, decent shelter. This is a breach in less eligibility: if rent is high, income unlikely, and shelter available, there will be candidates for the shelter system. The trick is to make shelter life not so unpleasant that it violates the law (and common decency) but unpleasant enough that no one would want to stay in the system of their own will.

The logic of homelessness policy is to deter people from staying in the shelter system by degrading their experience and signify to families that their best interest is to pay rent in private market housing. Within the shelter system, at all stages of the process, there is a cynically transparent hierarchy in the quality of different places, which functions as a carrot-and-stick system designed to keep homeless people in line. The "services" that come with shelter, paid for by New York taxpayers, are really means to make shelter life unpleasant. Vexing rules and the pollution of privacy are carefully organized to punish those who overstay and to reward those who comply—but not to the point of making shelter more appealing than rent. A homeless family costs taxpayers about $3,000 per month; at least half of that money is for disciplining clients. Tax money is spent on making poor people's life miserable. New York City's shelter policy exemplifies the reengineering of less eligibility on the housing market.

We can thus reconstitute the continuum in desirability of the different housing situations. Higher-income people make a trade-off between homeownership and market rentals (depending on regulations, likelihood of moving, etc.); in the United States, massive subsidies toward homeownership guarantee its most desirable status. To put things in context: homeowner tax breaks cost about $144 billion (in 2008), three-fourths of which went to homeowners earning more than $100,000 a year. Federal contributions to low-income recipients amounted to $46 billion; Section 8 housing vouchers (in 2012) cost less than $19 billion.

Low-income people try to get into subsidized housing, but because it is scarce, they have to pay market-price rent, which is the only option for privacy, dignity, and a sense of home. If they are evicted, they end up in shelters. One way or another, shelters have to be less desirable than paying rent, and in New York City, because of legal constraints, this takes an active process.

Evicted people may also end up in the streets. Because no one likes to see homeless people in the streets, sleeping rough also has to be made unpleasant, with aggressive policing and the criminalization of street homelessness. Periodically, the city organizes clearances of makeshift homeless encampments.[66] For the most recalcitrant there is always prison. Of those in the single-men shelter system in the 1990s, 23 percent had been incarcerated within the past two years. [67] Almost 12 percent of New York State former prisoners in the 1990s went to shelter within two years of their release, and recent homelessness was 7.5 to 11.3 times as likely among jail inmates as in the general population.[68] Homelessness experts Stephen Metraux and Dennis P. Culhane conclude that shelter and prison form an "'institutional circuit' that acts as a surrogate for stable housing."[69] In effect, and more generally, jails have become the last-recourse safety net, especially for people with mental disabilities.[70] The institutional circuit underlines the continuity in social and penal policy on which the theory of less eligibility rests.

Conclusion

All efforts to reform the punishment of criminals are inevitably limited by the situation of the lowest socially significant proletarian class which society wants to deter from criminal acts. All reform efforts, however humanitarian and well meaning, which go beyond this restriction, are condemned to utopianism.

— GEORG RUSCHE, LABOR MARKET AND PENAL SANCTION

I did most of my research for this book in a poor black neighborhood, at the acme of subprime lending. I spent six months discussing real estate speculation with homeowners and activists, and I didn't see what was to come, never registered that it wouldn't end well. I learned about the subprime crisis when it appeared in the news, and I pieced together the puzzle later. I have learned my lesson: without a theory we are blind and deaf.

In this book I have laid out a theory of social order: the living standards of the lowest class of workers determine the maximum generosity of the welfare state, and punishment is to make a life of crime less attractive than a life of collecting welfare benefits, if they exist. Within these bounds societies are free to implement whatever mix of welfare and punishment they please, but they must have the administrative capacity to set incentives right for potential criminals, or they will face endemic crime. I have not offered a systematic test of the theory, which remains to be done, but I have used the theory to interpret American postwar history and to suggest its relevance: declining living standards for low-income workers have lowered the upper limit for welfare and punishment, resulting in a shift toward more restrictive poor relief and harsher punishment. I have used East New York as a strategic case to analyze the local consequences of this adjustment as manifestations of the principle of less eligibility. Police aggressiveness, for instance, is a structural necessity in a society where the labor market fails to integrate large numbers of young men. People who are released from prison are unlikely to find policies that would improve their chances at successful reintegration when law-abiding people are already denied these policies. Social services to the poor will not match the demand. The logic of less eligibility will even be found on the housing market.

In itself, the theory of the upper limit is conceptually agnostic as to the mix of welfare and punishment that should be implemented. It says nothing about where the upper limit should be. It only explains the coherence of a given mix of social and penal policy. Conservatives can point to the American example to argue that redistribution is neither a necessary nor sufficient component of social order. The success of the great adjustment after the 1970s and the overall economic dynamism of the United States speaks for the low-wage, punitive model. Conservatives fully embrace, in practice, the principle of less eligibility. They typically seek to lower minimum wages, remove labor protections, weaken unions, challenge redistributive policies, and aggravate inequalities. Their hostility to welfare and support for punishment is perfectly coherent.

The underlying conception of social order for the conservative position is Hobbesian. Social order is when people are not killing each other. Assuming a given society, it means the absence of civil war and political stability.[1] Hobbesians regard political stability and security, defined as low crime, as the paramount concern of the state. Hobbesians purport to describe social order as it is: a constant, iron-fisted effort to crush enemies and to incapacitate criminals.

In contrast, the *doux-commerce* thesis, proposed by Enlightenment thinkers such as Montesquieu, Condorcet, and Thomas Paine, holds that economic relations provide for social order.[2] In their view "universal opulence" makes for a "well governed society" (Adam Smith in the *Wealth of Nations*). This idea is intuitive and central to social-democratic political thought.[3] When everyone is busy living a middle-class lifestyle (high wages, housing security in a low-crime neighborhood, participation in consumerism, health care, decent education for the kids), the *doux-commerce* thesis holds, there is little space for social problems to creep in. For instance, postwar Scandinavian welfare capitalism has been relatively successful in achieving high living standards for all, low crime, and political stability.

To Hobbesians it is unclear that shared prosperity is possible or even desirable. In that sense they see *doux-commerce* theorists as normative political philosophers who think of social order as it should be, not as it is. *Doux-commerce* theorists retort: it is a near-universal truth that people who are structurally excluded from, or only precariously attached to, labor markets are most likely to make for begging, vagrancy, epidemics, disorder, and crime. Therefore, social order is only achieved when complex arrangements limit inequality and organize generous redistribution.

I happen to side with the *doux-commerce* crowd. As I have suggested by exploring patterns of penal and social policy in East New York and New York City at large, the cost of making low wages attractive is significant. Taxpayer money and human lives are wasted for the sole purpose of making criminal justice harsh and access to social benefits restrictive. The American solution to social order (meager welfare, harsh punishment) creates a life of hardship for a vast proletariat of working poor and a life of humiliation for welfare recipients. It also creates a permanent criminal class that requires a monster of a criminal justice system, which cycles people back and forth in and out of prison, destroying families and precipitating more hardship.

The theory of the upper limit suggests that by raising the living standards for the lowest class of workers, societies may escape the costs of imposing low-wage work. I therefore recommend that societies move toward aggressively redistributive efforts to implement the highest possible living standards at minimum wages so as to dispense with social problems originating in the concentration of both wealth and poverty. To make welfare more generous and punishment more humane, to get rid of mass incarceration and police killings, we need to raise the minimum wage, ruthlessly crush the informal economy, and integrate as many people as possible into labor markets. The rest, as Rusche wrote in 1933, is "utopianism." Single-focus reformers (for instance death penalty abolitionists) are wasting their time as long as they are not actively participating in movements fighting for more livable wages and higher living standards for all. The key to reforming welfare and punishment lies in the economic standing of the working class. Having an economic focus does not mean one is blind to racial inequalities. In societies where economic inequalities are deeply racialized, raising the upper limit will obviously benefit people of color first and does not contradict additional affirmative efforts to disentangle the stereotypes of racial minorities as "underclass."[4]

More specifically, the theory of the upper limit calls attention to the situation of low-income men. Because men commit most of the crime in most societies, the particular structure of choice to which they are confined determines the mix of welfare and punishment. Where the upper limit is high, men's potential for crime is mostly absorbed by the labor market and social policies, which removes the need for harsh punishment and, critically, enables a higher quality of life for everybody. Where low-wage work pays little, (young) men are more likely to be involved in crime, especially where punishment apparatuses are not developed enough to set incentives right. Furthermore, men without a steady income are much less likely to be married.[5] For all its evils, family stability has well-identified positive outcomes on financial health and helps keep male children out of delinquency. The policy implication is that in highly unequal societies, it would make sense to favor men in low-income labor markets—perhaps another reason to raise the upper limit.

Many can agree that the poor should be better off, but what about inequalities in wealth within a society? There are good reasons to seek the reduction of inequalities, beyond welfare and punishment concerns. Highly unequal societies are less livable—more criminal, more unstable, less healthy—than social democracies.[6] Because there is little evidence that inequality is conducive to growth,[7] relative equality does not seem to come at the cost of an economic penalty. Philosophers debate whether inequalities are more or less tolerable in the pursuit of making the worst-off better off. At one end is the Marxist position that inequality should be abolished; at the other end is the "sufficiency view" (as long as the poor are taken care of, the concern for inequalities is irrelevant); and in the middle is the Rawlsian position for maximizing the well-being of the worst-off.[8] From an empirical point of view, the debate is resolved. The only existing societies that have significantly addressed relative poverty are the ones that have aggressively reduced inequalities.[9]

The problems of (relatively) equal societies lie elsewhere. Societies have a tendency to grow unequal over time because growth is, in the long run, lower than capital returns.[10] As long as capital returns exceed growth rates, wealth inequalities are indefinitely aggravated. Over the past two centuries, only the postwar decades have experienced higher growth rates than capital returns. To some extent, then, social democracy in Western Europe is a historical accident because inequality is built into the historical dynamic of capitalism. As we return to a regime of sluggish economic growth, we see Western societies become more and more based on inherited wealth. This empowers the social groups and special interests that seek to maximize capital returns and promises us a long night of lower taxes, lower wages, lower welfare benefits, and harsher punishment.

Optimists will argue that inequality is not inexorable and that resolute public policy can make a difference.[11] This is tautologically true in the sense that states are the only actors in potential capacity to reduce inequalities. I thus tend to side with more realistic thinkers, like Thomas Piketty, Branko Milanovic, and Walter Scheidel, who show that only catastrophes—epidemics, wars, and genocides—are able to significantly reduce inequalities.[12] In the normal run of things, the grip of economic elites on policy making and the lack of growth simply ensure an inequality-generating status quo.

Provided that catastrophes happen (and climate change will see to it), there remains the problem of the political will for a welfare state. As Western societies are increasingly polarized along ethnic lines, and as we know ethnic factionalism to be the enemy of redistribution policies, existing welfare states are imperiled and future welfare states less likely.[13] The current trend among progressives to embrace open borders is, on this regard, concerning. The mobility of capital and labor is probably the surest way to lower the upper limit in Western societies.

In fact, as this scenario unfolds before our eyes, we understand why the theory of less eligibility has long been dismissed as unserious and dystopian. Most of our social-scientific concepts are born out of the era of postwar prosperity, when high growth and low capital returns made for more equal societies and, crucially, reasonable optimism. It made sense, at the time, to think of punishment as a residual intervention, to think of abolishing prisons, to think of crime as a mild form of deviance that deserved greater tolerance. It made sense to think of welfare as a symptom of human progress or the bedrock of citizenship. Most of the conceptual tools that social scientists routinely use belong to a world that no longer exists, a world made optimistic by historically aberrant postwar growth. It is perhaps time to update our conceptions about society and politics accordingly.

The theory of less eligibility, with all its limitations, is a small step in the direction of acknowledging the world as it is.

NOTES

INTRODUCTION

1. I discuss these numbers in chapter 4.

2. Too many prisons make bad people worse. There is a better way, *The Economist,* May 27, 2017, www.economist.com/news/international/21722654-world-can-learn-how-norway-treats-its-offenders-too-many-prisons-make-bad-people.

3. In old English, *eligible* means desirable, attractive, appealing, hence the idea that welfare has to be "less eligible" (attractive) than work.

4. Scheper-Hughes, *Death without weeping.*

5. See Gottschalk, *The prison and the gallows;* Gottschalk, *Caught;* Pfaff, *Locked In;* see also Jacobs & Jackson, On the politics of imprisonments.

6. Alexander, *The new Jim Crow;* see also Murakawa, *The first civil right;* Hinton, *From the War on Poverty;* and Tonry, Explanations of American punishment policies.

7. Garland, *The culture of control;* Wacquant, *Punishing the poor.*

8. Baumer & Wolff, Evaluating contemporary crime drop(s); Tonry, Why crime rates are falling.

9. Sharkey, *Uneasy Peace,* 112.

10. Zimring, *The city that became safe.*

11. See, e.g., Wehner & Levin, Crime, drugs, welfare. Wehner and Levin were policy advisers to President George W. Bush. Writing just before the financial crisis of 2008, they argue that since 1993 the United States has experienced an amazing turnaround, citing the crime drop, receding welfare rolls, and declining social problems of all sorts.

12. See, e.g., Villarreal, Fear and spectacular drug violence, for a study of Monterrey (Mexico) during a spike in violence by drug cartels from 2009 to 2012.

13. Sharkey, *Uneasy Peace.*

14. This argument is best made in Villarreal, Fear and spectacular drug violence, 137.

15. In fairness, in my experience everyone is a constructivist when it comes to assessing facts they don't like.

16. Wilson, *The truly disadvantaged,* 140.

17. Wilson, 4, 6–10.

18. Wildeman, Parental imprisonment.

19. See, e.g., Soss, Fording, & Schram, *Disciplining the poor;* Miller, Devolving the carceral state; and Duvoux, *Les oubliés du rêve américain.*

20. As sociologist Nicole Marwell argued, what happens in poor neighborhoods is the result of decisions of real estate companies and boards, administrations, firms, nonprofits, and so forth. Unlike aggregated statistics, organizations act and are observable. See Marwell, *Bargaining for Brooklyn;* drawing on Perrow, A society of organizations.

21. Leon Neyfakh, The ethics of ethnography, *Slate,* June 18, 2015, http://www.slate.com/articles/news_and_politics/crime/2015/06/alice_goffman_s_on_the_run_is_the_sociologist_to_blame_for_the_inconsistencies.html; Lubet, *Interrogating Ethnography.*

1. THE UPPER LIMIT

Epigraph: American jurist Richard A. Posner is a leading intellectual of the "law and economics" field in legal theory, closely associated with the Chicago School of economics.

1. Beckett & Western, Governing social marginality welfare; Cavadino & Dignan, Penal policy and political economy; Lacey, *The prisoners' dilemma.*

2. Pratt, Scandinavian exceptionalism; Pratt & Eriksson, *Contrasts in punishment.* For another example of cultural explanation see Whitman, *Harsh justice.*

3. Lacey & Soskice, Why are the truly disadvantaged American, 2; see also Lacey, Soskice, & Hope, Understanding the determinants.

4. Savelsberg, Knowledge, domination, and criminal punishment.

5. Wacquant, *Punishing the poor.*

6. I borrow the term *upper limit* from Sieh, Less eligibility.

7. See Rusche & Kirchheimer, *Punishment and social structure;* Geremek, *Litość i szubienica,* French translation: *La potence ou la pitié;* Garland, *Punishment and welfare;* Procacci, *Gouverner la misère;* Van Leeuwen, Logic of charity; Castel, *Les métamorphoses;* among many others. As Richard A. Posner writes, "criminal law is designed primarily for the nonaffluent" (An economic theory of the criminal law, 1204–5).

8. Castel, *Les métamorphoses,* chap. 1.

9. Geremek, *Litość i szubienica,* French translation, 77.

10. Castel, *Les métamorphoses.*

11. Geremek, *Litość i szubienica.*

12. Van Parijs & Vanderborght, *Basic income,* 55–56.

13. tenBroek, California's dual system, 273–74; Stanziani, The traveling panopticon.

14. tenBroek, California's dual system, 259.

15. Ravallion, *The idea of antipoverty policy,* 12.

16. Ravallion, 12.

17. Boyer, *An economic history.*

18. Van Leeuwen, Logic of charity, 606.

19. Solar, Poor relief.

20. Stanziani, The traveling panopticon, 731.

21. Clark & Page, Welfare reform, 1834.

22. In 1795 the justices of Speenhamland (southern England) decided to extend the (Old) Poor Law and make it more generous. In the *Great Transformation,* Hungarian economic historian Karl Polanyi analyzed the Speenhamland system as a *de facto* universal poor allowance (Polanyi, *The great transformation,* chap. 7; see also Block & Somers, In the shadow of Speenhamland). In 1796 Prime Minister William Pitt sought but failed to extend Speenhamland to the entire kingdom (Van Parijs & Vanderborght, *Basic income,* 57). Whether Speenhamland was nationally implemented or not, the only thing that really matters for my argument is that relief spending kept growing and that Victorian elites decided to act on it, hence the New Poor Law of 1834.

23. *Poor Law Commissioners' Report of 1834,* pt. 2, sec. 1.

24. Ravallion, *The idea of antipoverty policy,* 22.

25. Clark & Page, Welfare reform, 1834.

26. Feinstein, Pessimism perpetuated.

27. Stanziani, The traveling panopticon, 740.

28. Van Parijs & Vanderborght, *Basic income,* 266n22; Stanziani, The traveling panopticon, 736. Memorable slogans were engraved on the entrances of workhouses across Europe: in Hamburg, *labore nutrior, laborer plector* (with work I am fed, with work I am punished); in Dessau, *Miseris et Malis* (For the poor and the wicked ones); in Amsterdam's Spinhuis, "Be without fear! I am not vengeful of evil, but I force towards good. My hand is heavy, but my heart is full of love." See Geremek, *Litość i szubienica,* French translation, 274.

29. Carré, *La prison des pauvres.*

30. Ravallion, *The idea of antipoverty policy.*

31. Roberts, How cruel, 106.

32. Lindert & Williamson, English workers' living standards; Crafts, English workers' living standards; Feinstein, Pessimism perpetuated; Clark, The condition.

33. Hobsbawm, The British standard of living; Floud, Wachter, & Gregory, *Height, Health and History;* Nicholas & Steckel, Heights and living standards; Huck, Infant mortality and living standards.

34. De Swaan, *In care of the state;* Ravallion, *The idea of antipoverty policy.*

35. Van Parijs & Vanderborght, *Basic income,* 65–66.

36. Kohler-Hausmann, Guns and butter, 92.

37. Korpi & Palme, The paradox of redistribution; Lee & Koo, The welfare states and poverty; Kenworthy, *Progress for the Poor;* Brady, *Rich democracies, poor people;* Brady & Bostic, Paradoxes of social policy.

38. Titmuss, *Problems of social policy.*

39. Heclo, *Modern social politics;* Garland, *Punishment and welfare;* Garland, The welfare state.

40. Korpi, *The democratic class struggle;* Esping-Andersen, *The three worlds.*

41. Meltzer & Richard, A rational theory; for an argument that we should disregard this theory for lack of basic evidence, see Brady, Blome, & Kleider, How politics and institutions shape.

42. Alesina & Glaeser, *Fighting poverty;* Finseraas, Immigration and preferences for redistribution; Gilens, *Why Americans hate welfare;* Eger, Even in Sweden. Friederike Römer actually finds that European welfare states remain relatively generous toward migrants; see Römer, Generous to all.

43. Piven & Cloward, *Regulating the poor.*

44. Jessop, Towards a Schumpeterian workfare state? 263.

45. Soss, Fording, & Schram, *Disciplining the poor,* 197.

46. Besley & Coate, Workfare versus welfare.

47. Typically, Murray, *Losing ground.*

48. Stanziani, Serfs, slaves, or wage earners?; Stanziani, The traveling panopticon.

49. Korpi & Palme, The paradox of redistribution; Brady & Bostic, Paradoxes of social policy.

50. Ravallion, *The idea of antipoverty policy,* 64.

51. Cited in Garland, *Punishment and welfare,* 47.

52. Besley and Coate, Workfare versus welfare.

53. Ravallion, *The idea of antipoverty policy.*

54. Marx, Salanauskaite, & Verbist, For the poor, 22.

55. Cantillon, The paradox.

56. Jessop, Towards a Schumpeterian workfare state?

57. Piketty, *Le capital au 21e siècle.*

58. For instance, Donzelot, *La police des familles;* Cohen, *Visions of social control;* and Garland, *Punishment and welfare;* see also Soss, Fording, & Schram, *Disciplining the poor;* and, for recent statements, Soss & Weaver, Learning from Ferguson.

59. For instance, Piven & Cloward, *Regulating the poor;* O'Connor, *The fiscal crisis;* and Offe, *Contradictions of the welfare state.*

60. For instance, Wacquant, *Punishing the poor;* and Hinton, From the war.

61. See Garland, *Punishment and modern society,* for a review.

62. Nagin, Deterrence.

63. Canela-Cacho, Blumstein, & Cohen, Relationship between the offending frequency.

64. Liedka, Piehl, & Useem, The crime-control effect. See also Roeder, Eisen, & Bowling, *What caused the crime decline?*

65. Nagin, Deterrence. Research suggests that the experience of punishments tends to increase offending (because of the stigma of criminal records on labor markets, lost skills, and new criminal skills and contacts acquired in prison). Scholars therefore focus more on general deterrence.

66. Helland & Tabarrok, Does three strikes deter?

67. Becker, Crime and punishment.

68. Lappi-Seppälä, Trust, welfare, and political culture; for a contrarian view see Enns as cited in Lacey, Soskice, & Hope, Understanding the determinants, 199.

69. Ehrlich, Crime, punishment and the market.

70. Chiricos, Rates of crime and unemployment; Freeman, The economics of crime.

71. Grogger, Market wages and youth crime; Gould, Weinberg, & Mustard, Crime rates and local labor; Entorf & Spengler, Socio-economic and demographic factors; Machin & Meghir, Crime and economic incentives; Fougère, Kramarz, & Pouget, Youth unemployment; Grönqvist, Youth unemployment and crime; all cited in Draca & Machin, Crime and economic incentives.

72. Cited in Draca and Machin, Crime and economic incentives.

73. Ehrlich, Crime, 64.

74. Nagin, Deterrence, 100.

75. Piven, A response to Wacquant.

76. Garland, Penality and the penal state.

77. Rusche & Kirchheimer, *Punishment and social structure.* Insights from *Punishment and social structure,* and the concept of less eligibility, are also used by Alessandro De Giorgi. While his work is most useful in making sense of the political economy of punishment, De Giorgi has little interest in welfare, and his project concerns more the contemporary contours of capitalism and the criminalization of migrants—a numerically small population. See De Giorgi, *Rethinking the political economy*; De Giorgi, Toward a political economy; and De Giorgi, Immigration control.

78. Even welfare can be made wasteful. To operate a workhouse was 63 percent costlier than to just distribute money to people (Clark & Page, Welfare reform, 1834). Workhouses needed guards, prison-like security, etc. From an accountant's perspective they were wasteful. Yet the principle of less eligibility *demanded* that poor relief (i.e., the workhouse) be made wasteful in order to make relief less attractive than low-wage work.

79. Rusche, Prison revolts, 42.

80. As cited by De Giorgi, Punishment and political economy, 47.

81. Castel, *Les métamorphoses,* 146.

82. Nagin, Deterrence.

83. See Draca & Machin, Crime and economic incentives.

84. Danziger, Haveman, & Plotnick, How income transfer programs; Moffitt, Incentive effects; and, more recently, Hoynes & Schanzenbach, Work incentives.

85. For the US, for instance, see Hannon & DeFronzo, The truly disadvantaged; for Brazil see Chioda, De Mello, & Soares, Spillovers; for cross-national studies see Messner & Rosenfeld, Political restraint; and Savage, Bennett, & Danner, Economic assistance and crime.

86. Beckett & Western, Governing social marginality; Downes & Hansen, Welfare and punishment; Lappi-Seppälä, Trust, welfare, and political culture; Lappi-Seppälä, Explaining imprisonment in Europe.

87. Respectively, Soss, Fording, & Schram, *Disciplining the poor,* 139; Garland, *Punishment and welfare;* and Garland, *Punishment and modern society.* Other authors seem to hesitate. In *Poor Discipline*—a book that rests on a less eligibility argument (with parole becoming more punitive as work disappears)—Jonathan Simon inexplicably abandons the idea in the final pages, as if he were dealing with a defective doctrine. Hermann Mannheim's *Dilemmas of Penal Reform* opens its conclusion with an enigmatic formulation about "the alleged or real demands of the principle of less eligibility" (212).

88. Pratt, Scandinavian exceptionalism; Lappi-Seppälä & Tonry, Crime, criminal justice, and criminology. Lappi-Seppälä explains the social-penal mix in Scandinavian countries with a political-institutional argument drawing on Arend Lijphart's typology of democracies. Some scholars from Nordic countries criticize the idea that Nordic penal policies are milder; see, e.g., Ugelvik & Dullum, *Penal exceptionalism;* Smith, A critical look; and Barker, Nordic exceptionalism revisited, on the grounds that Nordic penal policies could be even more progressive.

89. Ekunwe & Jones, Finnish criminal policy.

90. Ward, Inmate rights and prison reform.

91. Lappi-Seppälä & Tonry, Crime, criminal justice, and criminology; Adam Hochschild, Our awful prisons: How they can be changed, *New York Review of Books,* May 26, 2016, www.nybooks.com/articles/2016/05/26/our-awful-prisons-how-they-can-be-changed/.

92. Tonry, *Sentencing fragments,* 26.

93. Sieh, Less eligibility, 171–72.

94. Ward, Inmate rights, 241.

95. De Giorgi, Immigration control; Melossi, Punishment and migration.

96. Blaug, The myth, 177.

97. Garland, *Punishment and welfare.*

98. Mannheim, *The dilemma of penal reform;* Rusche & Kirchheimer, *Punishment and social structure.*

99. According to Sieh, Less eligibility, 159.

100. See, e.g., Block & Somers, In the shadow; Somers & Block, From poverty to perversity; and Kenworthy, Do social-welfare policies reduce poverty?

101. Van Oorschot, Non-take-up of social security benefits; Warin, Le non-recours au RSA.

102. Van Leeuwen, Logic of charity, 598.

103. Geremek, *Litość i szubienica,* French translation, 254–55.

104. Van Leeuwen, Logic of charity, 558.

105. Garland, *Punishment and welfare.*

106. Savelsberg, Knowledge; see also Lacey, Soskice, & Hope, Understanding the determinants.

107. The common criticism of this type of theory is that it is determinist (it is, within the bounds that I have delimited) and economically reductionist (it is not, as I have suggested regarding the determination of the upper limit). See De Giorgi, Punishment and political economy, for a compendium of critiques to Rusche's original argument; more recently, Lacey, Soskice, & Hope, Understanding the determinants, 203–4. See esp. Healy, Fuck nuance, on the impossibility of any theory to account for every nuance of social life.

108. Wacquant, *Punishing the poor.* Wacquant doesn't use the concept of less eligibility—only once, in *Punishing the poor,* does he employ it to make a side point on prison conditions (184). Wacquant has greater ambitions than making a "less eligibility" argument. First, he perceives materialist (or instrumental) approaches as reductionist and articulates the political economy of punishment with a symbolic, Durkheimian perspective. Under neoliberalism, he argues, the middle classes become economically anxious. The new punitiveness helps soothe the declining middle classes' anxiety and reaffirms their moral worth. Second, Wacquant proposes a theory of the neoliberal state. In his view welfare belongs to the "left hand" of the state (i.e., it is potentially benevolent, along with education, health policy, etc.), while punishment belongs to its "right hand" (police, prisons, border control, etc.), and the key to understanding change is to study conflicts within the "bureaucratic field"—see Wacquant, *Les prisons de la misère;* Wacquant, Deadly symbiosis; and Wacquant, *Punishing the poor*). I have learned a lot from Wacquant, starting with the insight that welfare and punishment have to be thought in relation to each other. Nonetheless, I stress what I perceive to be limitations in Wacquant's framework. First, he promotes a state-centered theory in which economic processes are secondary; see Dawson, The hollow shell. In *Punishing the poor* the neoliberal state has all the agency: it transforms the economy, operates the shift from welfare to workfare, and organizes mass incarceration. Most of the book's theoretical effort goes toward defining the neoliberal state, eventually relabeled the "centaur state"; for other criticism along these lines see Nelken, Denouncing the penal state; Lacey, Punishment, (neo)liberalism and social democracy; and Clarno, Beyond the state. A focus on the state's economic omnipotence is unrealistic, as I have suggested in my discussion of what determines the upper limit. Second, Wacquant tends to see neoliberalism, workfare, and law-and-order politics as pernicious ideologies that spread across continents. That is, he does not see the evolution of social and penal policy as structurally determined by the transformation of labor markets. His analysis of lenient penal policies in Scandinavian countries is that they "have best resisted the drift toward the punitive containment of urban marginality" (Wacquant, *Punishing the poor,* 303), as if leniency and punitiveness were caused by shifting ideas. This is because, I think, he refuses to admit that sensibilities may be grounded in empirical realities. Wacquant seems to hold a constructivist understanding of punishment as unrelated to crime rates. In addition, it is always

unclear, in Wacquant's work, whether or not poverty causes crime (a point noted in Piven, A response to Wacquant, 114–15).

109. Ravallion, *The idea of antipoverty policy,* 2.

110. Cited in Ravallion, *The idea of antipoverty policy,* 79.

111. Castel, *Les métamorphoses.*

112. Marx, *Capital.*

113. Stanziani, Serfs, slaves, or wage earners; Stanziani, The traveling panopticon.

114. Geremek, *Litość i szubienica,* French translation, 296–97.

115. Ravallion, *The idea of antipoverty policy.*

2. THE GREAT ADJUSTMENT

Epigraphs: Steven Rattner, Volcker asserts U.S. must trim living standard, *New York Times,* Oct. 18, 1979, www.nytimes.com/1979/10/18/archives/volcker-asserts-us-must-trim-living-standard-warns-of-inflation.html.

Henry Rollins, Henry Rollins: America's real safety net is drugs, alcohol, cheap food and free porn, *LA Weekly,* July 6, 2017, www.laweekly.com/music/henry-rollins-americas-real-safety-net-is-drugs-alcohol-cheap-food-and-free-porn-8392156.

1. Sanders, *Roots of reform;* Prasad, *The land of too much.*

2. Skocpol, *Protecting soldiers and mothers.*

3. Belgium followed in 1974, Ireland in 1975, France in 1988, Mexico in 1997, Chile in 2002, Brazil in 2003. Timeline by Van Parijs & Vanderborght, *Basic income,* 67–69. Of course, France's 1988 minimal income is far more generous than the United States' 1935 ADC.

4. Garland, *The culture of control.*

5. Van Parijs & Vanderborght (*Basic income,* 90) analyze the Family Assistance Plan as a household-based negative income tax.

6. Quadagno, Welfare capitalism. Poor southern white workers' living standards were much better than blacks', but they were also pulled down by the competition on the low-income labor market.

7. Donna Murch, Paying for punishment, *Boston Review,* August 1, 2016. https://bostonreview.net/us/donna-murch-paying-punishment.

8. Lieberman, *Shifting the color line;* Katznelson, *When affirmative action was white.*

9. Piven & Cloward, *Regulating the poor,* chap. 7; Kelley, *Hammer and hoe.*

10. Grossman, *Land of hope;* Gregory, *The southern diaspora.*

11. Hinton, *From the war on poverty,* 28.

12. Hinton, 66.

13. Hinton, 50–51.

14. Wilson & Aponte, Urban poverty, 238.

15. Piven & Cloward, *Regulating the poor,* chap. 6.

16. Piven & Cloward, chap. 9.

17. Piven & Cloward, 331–34.

18. National Research Council, *The dynamics of disability.*

19. Reich had argued that the benefits-as-gratuity theory led to invasions of privacy (the infamous midnight raids) and to the imposition of arbitrary moral standards. See Reich, Midnight welfare searches; and Reich, The new property.

20. Hinton, *From the war on poverty,* 277.

21. Sampson, Raudenbush, & Earls, Neighborhoods and violent crime.

22. Wilson, *The truly disadvantaged.* See also Waldinger, *Still the promised city?*; and Waldinger & Lichter, *How the other half works.*

23. Wilson & Aponte, Urban poverty, 240.

24. Edin & Lein, *Making ends meet.*

25. Kleiman, *When brute force fails.*

26. Kleiman, chap. 1.

27. Baumer & Wolff, Evaluating contemporary crime drop(s), 9. Among the causes for rising (violent) crime rates, scholars mention lower levels of social control, the decline of the traditional family, the rise of heroin addiction, declining political legitimacy in the context of the turbulent 1960s, and the decline in punitiveness; see Wilson, *Thinking about crime*; LaFree, Declining violent crime rates; and Garland, *The culture of control.* It is not my intent to adjudicate, as we are dealing with extremely complex phenomena. What is certain is that the demographic shock hypothesis, often presented as the most obvious (e.g., in Weaver, Frontlash), is the least convincing. This hypothesis holds that the sudden expansion of the population caused by the baby boom in the 1940s created a bigger cohort of young males in the 1960s, therefore more crime. This is likely false for a number of reasons. First, the increasing number of young males does not match the increase in homicides. In Detroit, between 1960 and 1971, homicides grew fivefold over the increase of young males (Wilson, *Thinking about crime*). Second, we know variations of crime rates to be linear phenomena, so "tipping point" effects are out of the discussion; see McDowall & Loftin, Are US crime rate trends; McDowall & Loftin, Do US city crime rates. Third, the crime drop in the 1990s happened in the context of a growing young male population; see Blumstein & Rosenfeld, Explaining recent trends.

28. Gans, The ghetto rebellions; Oberschall, The Los Angeles riot.

29. Flamm, *Law and order,* 88.

30. Flamm, 146.

31. Downes, Social and political characteristics, 509.

32. Flamm, Law and order; Edsall & Edsall, *Chain reaction;* Weaver, Frontlash, coined the term *frontlash* to suggest that the reaction was more against civil rights than against crime.

33. Rieder, *Canarsie.*

34. Citations from Rieder, *Canarsie,* 103 and 108.

35. Abramowitz & Teixeira, The decline.

36. Detailed historical accounts of how crime became politicized in the 1960s include Flamm, *Law and order;* and Weaver, Frontlash. Weaver (Frontlash, 263–64)

and Beckett *(Making crime pay)* have argued that politicians promoted law and order framings of the troubles in the 1960s *before* public opinion shifted toward law and order. This interpretation is rejected by political scientist Peter K. Enns (as reviewed in Lacey, Soskice, & Hope, Understanding the determinants, 199): "A recent careful econometric study of US data by the political scientist P. K. Enns (2014, 2016) shows that violent crime rates, at least in the United States, are indeed closely correlated not only with the development of penal policy as measured by the rate of change in the imprisonment rate but also with public levels of punitiveness (again carefully measured), which seems likely to be a key driver of politicians' electoral concern with developing effective penal policies."

37. Heathcote, Perri, & Violante, Unequal we stand.

38. Heathcote, Perri, & Violante, 27.

39. Heathcote, Perri, & Violante, 15.

40. See, e.g., Piketty, Saez, & Zucman, Distributional national accounts.

41. Hirsch, *Social limits to growth;* Sen, Poor, relatively speaking.

42. Heathcote, Perri, & Violante, Unequal we stand, 16.

43. Kenworthy & Marx, *In-work poverty,* 12.

44. Autor, Manning, & Smith, The contribution.

45. Charette et al., *Projecting trends.*

46. Jones & Schmitt, Update on low-wage workers.

47. Kalleberg, Reskin, & Hudson, Bad jobs in America; Kalleberg, *Good jobs, bad jobs;* Hollister, Employment stability in the US; Katz & Krueger, The rise and nature.

48. Cited in Western et al., Economic insecurity, 352.

49. Gottschalk & Moffitt, The rising instability.

50. Western et al., Economic insecurity (citing Sandoval, Rank, & Hirschl, The increasing risk of poverty).

51. Hollister, Employment stability, 307–8.

52. Autor, Katz, & Kearney, The polarization of the US; Autor, Katz, & Kearney, Trends in US wage inequality.

53. Western & Rosenfeld, Unions, norms, and the rise; see also Brady, *Rich democracies, poor people.*

54. Davis, After the corporation.

55. Surowiecki, The pay.

56. Lee & Koo, The welfare states and poverty, 712.

57. Heathcote, Perri, & Violante, Unequal we stand, 30.

58. Dwyer, The care economy?

59. Western et al., Economic insecurity.

60. Bosworth, Burtless, & Zhang, Later retirement, 87.

61. Hinton, *From the war on poverty,* 94.

62. Hinton, 241.

63. Kohler-Hausmann, *Getting Tough;* see also Garland, *The culture of control.*

64. Tonry, Explanations of American punishment policies; Campbell & Schoenfeld, The transformation.

65. Tonry, *Sentencing fragments.*

66. Wacquant, Deadly symbiosis.

67. Soss, Fording, & Schram, *Disciplining the poor,* 108.

68. Cited in Wacquant, *Punishing the poor,* 69.

69. Travis & Lawrence, *Beyond the prison gates,* 8.

70. Kohler-Hausmann, Guns and butter, 96–97.

71. Moynihan, *The politics of a guaranteed income.*

72. Soss, Fording, & Schram, *Disciplining the poor,* 39.

73. Greenstein, Losing faith in "Losing Ground" (cited in Wilson, *The truly disadvantaged,* 94). See also Rossi, *Down and out in America,* on declining real income from welfare in the 1970s as a cause for homelessness.

74. Gustafson, The criminalization of poverty, 652.

75. Gustafson, 652.

76. Gustafson, 659.

77. Hinton, *From the war on poverty,* 315.

78. Gustafson, The criminalization of poverty, 666.

79. Gustafson, 662-3.

80. Gustafson, 681.

81. Gustafson, 683.

82. Gustafson, 4 (citing Hasenfeld, Ghose, & Larson, The logic of sanctioning).

83. Lein et al., Social policy, 743.

84. Danziger, The decline of cash welfare, 525.

85. Soss, Fording, & Schram, *Disciplining the poor,* 98–99, 101.

86. Beckett & Western, Governing social marginality, 45.

87. Shoesmith, Crime, teenage abortion, and unwantedness.

88. Lauritsen, Rezey, & Heimer, When choice of data matters.

89. Ousey & Kubrin, Immigration and crime.

90. Farrell, Tilley, & Tseloni, Why the crime drop?; Tonry, Why crime rates are falling.

91. Aebi & Linde, Is there a crime drop.

92. Blumstein, The crime drop in America; Baumer & Wolff, Evaluating contemporary crime drop(s).

93. Blumstein, The crime drop in America; Baumer & Wolff, Evaluating contemporary crime drop(s).

94. Roeder, Eisen, & Bowling, *What caused the crime decline?* This report (sponsored by the Brennan Center for Justice) is often cited to refute the crime-reducing effect of mass incarceration. What it does show is that increases in incarceration after 2000 stopped yielding crime reductions.

95. Pierce & Schott, The surprisingly swift decline.

96. Feler & Senses, Trade shocks.

97. Autor, Dorn, & Hanson, When work disappears.

98. Case & Deaton, Rising morbidity and mortality.

99. Case & Deaton, Mortality and morbidity.

100. Autor, Dorn, & Hanson, When work disappears; Pierce & Schott, Trade liberalization and mortality; Case & Deaton, Mortality and morbidity.

101. Deiana, *The bitter side.*

102. Oliver, White rural imprisonment rates.

103. Josh Keller & Adam Pearce, A small Indiana county sends more people to prison than San Francisco and Durham, N.C., combined. Why? *New York Times,* Sept. 3, 2016, https://www.nytimes.com/2016/09/02/upshot/new-geography-of-prisons.html. The reader may be surprised by these dropping admissions numbers. For incarceration rates to stabilize, as they have in the 2010s, admissions need to drop, because of the nature of prison sentences, which extend over time. The recent drop in prison admissions does not mean that American punishment is less severe. In 2017, the American rate of incarceration was around 650 prisoners per 100,000 inhabitants, down 12 percent from 2008. Given rates of homicides, I have calculated that if American incarceration followed the OECD average, the United States would imprison 388 persons per 100,000 inhabitants. I suggest taking "prison downsizing" seriously if the actual incarceration rate falls more significantly. Furthermore, severity is not the same as capacity. Holding capacity constant, the crime drop will reduce the prison population. Lower incarceration rates will not mean that severity is reduced: criminals will still be subjected to a punitive criminal justice system; only there will be fewer criminals, because the rewards of crime, factoring the probability of punishment, are so meager.

104. Pamela Oliver, Education, Poverty, and Rural vs. Urban Incarceration Rates, *Race, Politics, Justice* (blog), July 14, 2017, http://www.ssc.wisc.edu/soc/racepoliticsjustice/2017/07/14/education-poverty-and-rural-vs-urban-incarceration-rates/.

105. Keller & Pearce, A small Indiana county.

106. Josh Katz, Drug deaths in America are rising faster than ever. *New York Times,* June 5, 2017, www.nytimes.com/interactive/2017/06/05/upshot/opioid-epidemic-drug-overdose-deaths-are-rising-faster-than-ever.html.

107. The incarceration rate for American whites is still four times as high as France's or Germany's total rate of incarceration and comparable to the rate of incarceration of Western European minorities (about 440 per 100,000). See Gottschalk, *Caught;* and De Giorgi, Immigration control, 155 (2007 figures).

108. Eberstadt, *Men without work.*

109. Groves, Welfare reform.

110. Western & Beckett, How unregulated is the US; Groves, Welfare reform.

111. Kenworthy & Marx, *In-work poverty,* 7.

112. Marx, Marchal, & Nolan, Mind the gap, 9.

113. Milkman, González, & Ikeler, Wage and hour violations; see also Cooper & Kroeger, Employers steal billions.

114. U.S. Bureau of Labor Statistics, National compensation survey; see also Mishel et al., *The state of working America.*

115. Stacy Cowley, Many low-income workers say "No" to health insurance, *New York Times,* Oct. 19, 2015, www.nytimes.com/2015/10/20/business/many-low

-income-workers-say-no-to-health-insurance.html.

116. Allegretto et al., *Fast food, poverty wages.*

117. Sykes et al., Dignity and dreams, 246.

118. Kenworthy & Marx, *In-work poverty,* 3.

119. Moffitt & Pauley, *Trends in the distribution.*

120. Halpern-Meekin et al., *It's not like I'm poor.*

121. Kenworthy & Marx, *In-work poverty.*

122. Kasy, Who wins, who loses?; see also Rothstein, Is the EITC as good.

123. Tach & Edin, The social safety net.

124. Lee & Koo, The welfare states and poverty, 718.

125. Brady, Finnigan, & Hübgen, Rethinking the risks of poverty.

126. Edin & Shaefer, *$2.00 a Day.*

127. Harris, *A pound of flesh.*

128. Donna Murch, Paying for punishment, *Boston Review,* August 1, 2016, https://bostonreview.net/us/donna-murch-paying-punishment.

3. THE CRIME DROP AND THE EAST NEW YORK RENAISSANCE

1. Thabit, *How East New York became a ghetto,* 7.

2. For detailed accounts of blockbusting in Brownsville and East New York see Pritchett, *Brownsville, Brooklyn;* and Thabit, *How East New York became a ghetto.*

3. Thabit, *How East New York became a ghetto,* 31.

4. Pritchett, *Brownsville, Brooklyn;* Rieder, *Canarsie.*

5. Flamm, *Law and order,* 5.

6. Thabit, *How East New York became a ghetto,* 15–16.

7. Thabit, 39.

8. Thabit, 9.

9. Rieder, *Canarsie,* 25.

10. Von Hoffman, *House by house,* 22.

11. Hinton, *From the War on Poverty,* 300.

12. Thabit, *How East New York became a ghetto,* 119.

13. Thabit, 169.

14. Thabit, 179.

15. Phillips-Fein, *Fear City,* chap. 3.

16. Thabit, *How East New York became a ghetto,* 70–81.

17. See Mahler, *Ladies and gentlemen,* for a sobering journalistic account.

18. Felicia R. Lee, East New York, haunted by crime, fights for its life, *New York Times,* Jan. 5, 1989, www.nytimes.com/1989/01/05/nyregion/east-new-york-haunted-by-crime-fights-for-its-life.html.

19. Donatella Lorch, East New York, under siege; life and death in an area caught in its own crossfire, *New York Times,* June 5, 1992, www.nytimes.com/1992/06/05/nyregion/east-new-york-under-siege-life-and-death-in-an-area-caught-in-its-own-crossfire.html.

20. George James, East New York homicide breaks a deadly record, *New York Times,* Dec. 20, 1993, www.nytimes.com/1993/12/20/nyregion/east-new-york-homicide-breaks-a-deadly-record.html.

21. Somini Sengupta, Wrestling with "Jeff," *New York Times,* June 1, 1997, www.nytimes.com/1997/06/01/nyregion/wrestling-with-jeff.html.

22. Kit R. Roane, Man accused of forcing four girls to be prostitutes, *New York Times,* August 13, 1997, www.nytimes.com/1997/08/13/nyregion/man-accused-of-forcing-four-girls-to-be-prostitutes.html.

23. James C. McKinley Jr., Baby saved from compactor, where mother, 12, says she put him, *New York Times,* March 28, 1991, www.nytimes.com/1991/03/28/nyregion/baby-saved-from-compactor-where-mother–12-says-she-put-him.html.

24. Chris Hedges, A child-mother in the jaws of New York, *New York Times,* March 29, 1991, www.nytimes.com/1991/03/29/nyregion/a-child-mother-in-the-jaws-of-new-york.html.

25. McKinley, Baby saved from compactor.

26. See Hirsch, *Making the second ghetto,* on Chicago; and Sugrue, *Origins of the urban crisis,* on Detroit.

27. See Levi-Strauss, The structural study of myth.

28. See, e.g., Wacquant, Three pernicious premises in the study of the American ghetto; and Small, De-exoticizing ghetto poverty.

29. Hipp, A dynamic view of neighborhoods, 205.

30. Liska & Bellair, Violent-crime rates and racial composition; Pope & Pope, Crime and property values; Schwartz, Susin, & Voicu, Has falling crime driven New York City's real estate boom? 101; Ellen, Horn, & Reed, Has Falling Crime Invited Gentrification?; Harding, Collateral consequences of violence in disadvantaged neighborhoods; Sampson, *Great American city;* Sharkey & Torrats-Espinosa, The Effect of Violent Crime; Vélez & Richardson, The political economy.

31. Dennis Hevesi, The boom spreads: This house is valued at $350,000, *New York Times,* August 7, 2005, www.nytimes.com/2005/08/07/realestate/the-boom-spreads-this-house-is-valued-at-350000.html.

32. John Soltes, Harsh words amid the hallelujahs, *New York Times,* July 22, 2007, www.nytimes.com/2007/07/22/nyregion/thecity/22nige.html.

33. Von Hoffman, *House by house,* 69.

34. Effective drug crime tactics, *New York Times,* Sept. 2, 1996, www.nytimes.com/1996/09/02/opinion/effective-drug-crime-tactics.html.

35. Rachelle Garbarine, 645 modular houses going up in Brooklyn, *New York Times,* July 4, 1997, www.nytimes.com/1997/07/04/nyregion/645-modular-houses-going-up-in-brooklyn.html.

36. Alan S. Oser, A housing program's next generation, *New York Times,* Dec. 21, 1997, www.nytimes.com/1997/12/21/realestate/a-housing-program-s-next-generation.html.

37. Josh Barbanel, Steady focus, evolving vision, *New York Times,* May 16, 2004, www.nytimes.com/2004/05/16/realestate/steady-focus-evolving-vision.html.

38. Michael Powell & Janet Roberts, Minorities affected most as New York foreclosures rise, *New York Times,* May 15, 2009, www.nytimes.com/2009/05/16/nyregion/16foreclose.html.

39. Rugh & Massey, Racial segregation and the American foreclosure crisis.

40. Sylvain Cypel, Ces petits propriétaires américains, premières victimes des "subprimes," *Le Monde,* Sept. 20, 2007.

41. Been, Ellen, & Madar, The high cost of segregation.

42. Powell & Roberts, Minorities affected most.

43. Derrick Henry & Janet Roberts, Long Island foreclosures rise, with no end in sight. *New York Times,* May 13, 2009, www.nytimes.com/2009/05/17/nyregion/long-island/17mortli.html.

44. Gerardi, Shapiro, & Willen, Subprime outcomes.

45. Immergluck, Too little, too late.

46. Matthew Goldstein, As banks retreat, private equity rushes to buy troubled home mortgages, *New York Times,* Sept. 28, 2015, www.nytimes.com/2015/09/29/business/dealbook/as-banks-retreat-private-equity-rushes-to-buy-troubled-home-mortgages.html?ref = topics.

47. Powell & Roberts, Minorities affected most.

48. Schuetz, Been, & Ellen, Neighborhood effects; Ellen, Lacoe, & Sharygin, Do foreclosures cause crime?

49. Michael Powell & Janet Roberts, Minorities affected most as New York foreclosures rise, *New York Times,* May 15, 2009, www.nytimes.com/2009/05/16/nyregion/16foreclose.html.

50. Michael Powell, That comeback trail for the economy? Here, it's littered with foreclosures, *New York Times,* Feb. 7, 2012, http://query.nytimes.com/gst/fullpage.html?res = 9E06E3D71E3AF934A35751C0A9649D8B63.

51. Michael Powell, Old-fashioned bulwark in a tide of foreclosures, *New York Times,* March 5, 2010, www.nytimes.com/2010/03/07/nyregion/07foreclose.html.

52. Wyly et al., Displacing New York.

53. On all this, and what follows, I borrow from Greenberg, Tenants under siege.

54. Greenberg, Tenants under siege.

55. Center for NYC Neighborhoods, *The Impact of Property Flipping.*

56. Thery, *Larry's clique;* Desmond, *Evicted.*

4. THE NECESSITY OF HARSH POLICING

1. Venkatesh, *American project;* Venkatesh, *Off the books;* see also Anderson, *Code of the street;* and Jacobs & Wright, *Street justice.*

2. Alison Gendar, Despite security cameras, cops miss Brooklyn public housing rape, *Daily News,* March 14, 2008, www.nydailynews.com/new-york/brooklyn/security-cameras-cops-brooklyn-public-housing-rape-article–1.285563.

3. See, e.g., Wacquant, *Punishing the poor;* Rios, *Punished;* and Goffman, *On the run.*

4. Cited in White, The New York City Police Department, 76.

5. White, 77–78.

6. This scandal is the subject of the documentary *The Seven Five* (dir. Tiller Russell, 2014).

7. White, The New York City Police Department, 83.

8. See Manning, Theorizing policing. Although Manning argues that the crime drop was a statistical artifact manipulated by the media to make Bratton look good, the data now show beyond reasonable doubt the reality of falling crime rates.

9. Effective drug crime tactics. *New York Times,* Sept. 2, 1996, www.nytimes.com/1996/09/02/opinion/effective-drug-crime-tactics.html.

10. See, e.g., Zimring, *The city that became safe;* Kelling & Bratton, Declining crime rates; Bratton & Malinowski, Police performance management; and, for a detailed analysis of the Bratton mythmaking, Manning, Theorizing policing.

11. See Willis, Mastrofski, & Weisburd, Making sense of COMPSTAT.

12. Blumstein, The crime drop in America, 24; Baumer & Wolff, Evaluating contemporary crime drop(s). For a spirited debate on the centrality of the NYPD in New York's crime drop, see Zimring, *The city that became safe*, and Eterno & Silverman, *The crime numbers game.*

13. NYCLU, *Stop-and-frisk,* 2.

14. NYCLU, 1.

15. Rosenfeld & Fornango, The impact of police stops; Weisburd, Telep, & Lawton, Could innovations in policing; Messner & Baumer, Stop, question, and assess; Weisburd et al., Do stop.

16. See Moskos, *Cop in the hood.*

17. Harding, *Living the drama.*

18. These paragraphs about the War on Drugs are based on German Lopez's Vox.com "cards": www.vox.com/cards/war-on-drugs-marijuana-cocaine-heroin-meth.

19. For arguments against the centrality of the War on Drugs in the making of mass incarceration, see Gottschalk, *Caught;* and Pfaff, *Locked In.*

20. See, e.g., Michael Sallah, Robert O'Harrow Jr., Steven Rich, and Gabe Silverman, Stop and seize, *Washington Post,* Sept. 6, 2014, www.washingtonpost.com/sf/investigative/2014/09/06/stop-and-seize.

21. Dara Lind, How police can take your stuff, sell it, and pay for armored cars with the money, Vox.com, March 28, 2016,www.vox.com/2014/10/14/6969335/civil-asset-forfeiture-what-is-how-work-equitable-sharing-police-seizure.

22. Williams et al., *Policing for profit.*

23. Max Rivlin-Nadler, How the NYPD's use of civil forfeiture robs innocent New Yorkers, Gothamist.com, Jan. 14, 2014, gothamist.com/2014/01/14/nypd_civil_forfeiture.php.

24. Edwards, Esposito, & Lee, Risk of police-involved death.

25. Police organizations do not usually communicate on police killings. I draw the American figures from the *Washington Post* database, www.washingtonpost.com/graphics/national/police-shootings; the German and British figures from Don't shoot, *The Economist*, Dec. 11, 2014, www.economist.com/news/united-states/21636044-americas-police-kill-too-many-people-some-forces-are-showing

-how-smarter-less; the French from discussions with activists against police violence; and the Brazilian from the Brazilian Forum on Public Safety, as reported in Brazil police kill six people a day – NGO, *BBC*, Nov. 12, 2014, bbc.com/news/world-latin-america-30015465. Recent efforts to uncover the reality of police killings in Brazil suggest higher numbers (5,000 in 2017); see Mortos por policiais no Brasil, *G1*, May 23, 2018, especiais.g1.globo.com/monitor-da-violencia/2018/mortos-por-policiais-no-brasil.

26. Human Rights Watch, *Lethal Force.*

27. Source: *Washington Post* database, retrieved at https://www.washingtonpost.com/graphics/national/police-shootings.

28. Edwards et al., Risk of police-involved death.

29. Michael Powell, On diverse force, blacks still face special peril, *New York Times,* May 30, 2009, www.nytimes.com/2009/05/31/nyregion/31friendly.html.

30. Thanks to fatalencounters.org; and vox.com, http://anandkatakam.cartodb.com/viz/e13166bc–854f–11e4-abdb–0e018d66dc29/public_map.

31. John Marzulli, Officers kill slaying suspect, *New York Daily News,* Oct. 10, 2001, www.nydailynews.com/archives/news/officers-kill-slaying-suspect-article–1.927504.

32. Michele McPhee, Shot cop's heroic tale: Sergeant took three slugs but refused to die, *New York Daily News,* Oct. 31, 2003, www.nydailynews.com/archives/news/shot-heroic-tale-sergeant-slugs-refused-die-article–1.516159.

33. Kevin Flynn, 2 dead after firing at officers, police say, *New York Times,* Jan. 2, 2003, www.nytimes.com/2003/01/02/nyregion/2-dead-after-firing-at-officers-police-say.html.

34. David W. Chen, Carwash robbery suspect is killed by police, *New York Times,* August 31, 2004, www.nytimes.com/2004/08/31/nyregion/carwash-robbery-suspect-is-killed-by-police.html.

35. Sarah Garland, Brooklyn police shooting victim was on FBI Most Wanted List, *New York Sun,* Jan. 3, 2008, www.nysun.com/new-york/brooklyn-police-shooting-victim-was-on-fbi-most/68857.

36. Danielle Tcholakian and Laura Shin, Suspect named in Brooklyn police-involved shooting, *Metro,* June 19, 2013, http://www.metro.us/local/updated-suspect-named-in-brooklyn-police-involved-shooting/tmWmfs—-5fHyboQAlsKBY.

37. Veronika Belenkaya, Mike Jaccarino, Alison Gendar, & Robert F. Moore, Clubgoer killed pointing gun at detective's head, cops say, *New York Daily News,* March 11, 2007, www.nydailynews.com/news/crime/shoot-saves-officer-article–1.216366.

38. Flynn, 2 dead.

39. Kareem Fahim, One is dead and one hurt in a shootout in Brooklyn, *New York Times,* Oct. 23, 2005, www.nytimes.com/2005/10/23/nyregion/23shot.html?_r=0.

40. Michael Wilson, Man swinging light fixture killed by police in Brooklyn, *New York Times,* Nov. 23, 2004, www.nytimes.com/2004/11/23/nyregion/23shot

.html?pagewanted=print&position=&_r=0.

41. Robert D. McFadden & Al Baker, Police kill a man armed with a broken bottle, *New York Times,* Nov. 19, 2007, www.nytimes.com/2007/11/19/nyregion/19shoot.html.

42. Matthew Lysiak, Rocco Parascandola, & Corky Siemaszko, A Brooklyn police officer responding to a robbery shoots and kills an armed man allegedly rushing to defend his home from intruders, *New York Daily News,* Jan. 13, 2012, www.nydailynews.com/new-york/cops-kill-armed-brooklyn-man-girlfriend-victim-investigating-break-in-home-article-1.1005646.

43. For these and many other fatal encounters between police and the citizenry, visit the Fatal Encounters database: http://www.fatalencounters.org.

44. Alison Gendar & Nicole Bode, NYPD probe eyes cop car chase in fatal Brooklyn hit-run, *New York Daily News,* Dec. 31, 2008, www.nydailynews.com/new-york/brooklyn/nypd-probe-eyes-car-chase-fatal-brooklyn-hit-run-article-1.355655.

45. Barry Paddock & Thomas Tracy, Teen shot and killed after he tries to rob ex-cop on Brooklyn street: police, *New York Daily News,* May 28, 2014, www.nydailynews.com/new-york/nyc-crime/teen-shot-killed-rob-driver-brooklyn-street-sources-article-1.1806542.

46. Jamie Schram, NYPD officer dead after being shot in the face during B'klyn burglary call, *New York Post,* Dec. 12, 2011, http://nypost.com/2011/12/12/nypd-officer-dead-after-being-shot-in-the-face-during-bklyn-burglary-call.

47. Goldstein, Improving policing; Trojanowicz, *An evaluation;* Wilson, & Kelling, Broken windows.

48. See, e.g., Manning, Community policing as a drama; and Mastrofski, Community policing.

49. Kraska, & Kappeler, Militarizing American police.

50. Balko, *Rise of the warrior cop.*

51. David Firestone, Off is Turf, Giuliani gets a real earful, *New York Times,* March 26, 1997, www.nytimes.com/1997/03/26/nyregion/off-his-turf-giuliani-gets-a-real-earful.html.

52. Stuart, Becoming "copwise."

53. Pam Martens, Financial giants put New York City cops on their payroll, *Counterpunch,* Oct. 10, 2011, www.counterpunch.org/2011/10/10/financial-giants-put-new-york-city-cops-on-their-payroll.

54. Michael Brick, Bowling ball from 17th floor almost hits 3 Brooklyn officers. *New York Times,* March 24, 2004, www.nytimes.com/2004/03/24/nyregion/bowling-ball-from-17th-floor-almost-hits-3-brooklyn-officers.html.

55. Patrick Healy, Rooftop sniper wounds officer in Brooklyn, *New York Times,* July 3, 2003, www.nytimes.com/2003/07/03/nyregion/rooftop-sniper-wounds-officer-in-brooklyn.html.

56. See Herbert, *Citizens, cops, and power.*

57. Tyler, Policing in black and white, 323.

58. See, e.g., Pattillo, Negotiating blackness; and Hyra, Racial uplift?

59. There is of course tremendous intranational variation in policing patterns. See Jobard, Proposition on the theory of policing.

5. PRISONER REENTRY IN PUBLIC HOUSING

1. Pager, The mark of a criminal record; Western, The impact of incarceration; Mallik-Kane & Visher, *Health and prisoner reentry,* 82; Metraux & Culhane, Homeless shelter use and reincarceration; Edin & Kefalas, *Promises I can keep*; Uggen & Manza, Democratic contraction? Foster & Hagan, The mass incarceration of parents; Morsy & Rothstein, *Mass incarceration and children's outcomes*; and Visher & Travis, Transitions from prison to community. Some inmates do work in prison, for wages vastly lower than what is paid outside. But prison work remains quantitatively small (about 80,000 working prisoners in c. 2000, according to Thompson, Why mass incarceration matters).

2. Metraux & Culhane, Homeless shelter use and reincarceration.

3. I borrow my title for this section from Michael Zmora's 2009 article; see Zmora, Between Rucker and a hard place.

4. Zmora, 1967.

5. Zmora, 1969; Levy, Collateral consequences; Mock, Punishing the innocent.

6. Department of Housing and Urban Development v. Rucker, 535 U.S. 125, 128 (2002).

7. Zmora, Between Rucker and a hard place, 1962.

8. Zmora, 1973–74.

9. Human Rights Watch, *No second chance.*

10. Renzetti, "One Strike and You're Out," 693.

11. Rodney, Am I my mother's keeper? 754–55.

12. Rodney, 754; Mock, Punishing the innocent, 1495; Levy, Collateral consequences, 554.

13. "The law is harsh, but it is the law."

14. Buckle, & Zajac, But some of them don't, 240.

15. Goffman, On the run.

16. Travis, *Beyond the prison gates*, 18 (data from the 1990s for the United States). Only 20 percent of "re-releasees" (prisoners who have already been on parole and thus have more stable criminal involvements) avoid returning to prison.

17. Simon, *Poor discipline,* 113, 229.

18. Schlager & Robbins, Does parole work? 234.

19. See also Simon, *Poor discipline,* 99, 111.

20. Simon, 201.

21. Goffman, When the police knock, 216.

22. Human Rights Watch, *No second chance,* 48.

23. Rachelle Blidner, Public housing safety policy can hit whole family, Associated Press, Sept. 14, 2014, http://bigstory.ap.org/article/public-housing-safety-policy-can-hit-whole-family.

24. Renzetti, "One strike and you're out," 697.

25. Bloom, Learning from New York.
26. Thery, *Larry's clique.*
27. Hebert, *The invisible tenant.*
28. Hebert, 8 .
29. Simon, *Poor discipline,* 194–95.
30. Goffman, On the run, 348–51.
31. See Goffman, When the police knock, 216.
32. Simon, *Poor discipline.*
33. Family Justice to Parole Regional Director, Feb. 1, 2006.
34. *Partnering with Family Justice in Brownsville/East New York: Program Protocol for Probation*, undated Family Justice document.
35. Reich, Midnight welfare searches.
36. See Human Rights Watch, *No second chance,* 36.
37. Ekunwe & Jones, Finnish criminal policy.
38. Wacquant, Prisoner reentry as myth, 614.
39. Mannheim, *The dilemma of penal reform,* 57.
40. Mannheim, 76.
41. Sykes & Geller, Mass incarceration; Pager, Western, & Sugie, Sequencing disadvantage; Western, The impact of incarceration.

6. NONPROFITS

1. Rachel L. Swarns, With little warning, agency aiding New York's most vulnerable crumbles, *New York Times,* Feb. 8, 2015, www.nytimes.com/2015/02/09/nyregion/with-little-warning-agency-aiding-new-york-citys-most-vulnerable-crumbles.html?_r = 0.
2. Laura Nahmias, Dan Goldberg, and Nidhi Prakash, The wrecking of a blue-chip New York nonprofit, *Politico,* March 13, 2015, www.politico.com/states/new-york/albany/story/2015/03/the-wrecking-of-a-blue-chip-new-york-nonprofit–087679.
3. Ruth McCambridge, The FEGS autopsy: Bad nonprofit business in a tough operating environment, *Nonprofit Quarterly,* Feb. 26, 2016, https://nonprofitquarterly.org/2016/02/26/the-fegs-autopsy-a-case-of-bad-nonprofit-business-in-a-tough-operating-environment.
4. Josh Nathan-Kazis, FEGS execs got fat payouts as bankruptcy loomed amid rampant mismanagement, *Forward,* Sept. 30, 2015, http://forward.com/news/national/321474/fegs-execs-got-payouts-while-staffers-struggled-and-services-suffered.
5. Rachel L. Swarns, Nonprofit's chief during its fall seeks $1.2 million payday, and outrage ensues, *New York Times,* May 3, 2015, www.nytimes.com/2015/05/04/nyregion/as-former-fegs-chief-executive-waits-for-payday-so-do-her-ex-employees.html.
6. Marwell & Gullickson, Inequality in the spatial allocation, 320.
7. Hasenfeld & Garrow, Nonprofit human-service organizations, 303.

8. Danziger, The decline of cash welfare, 525.

9. White, Creating collective capacity, 6.

10. Savas, Competition and choice.

11. Fisher, Doing good?; Austin, The changing relationship; Garrow, Receipt of government revenue.

12. Savas, Competition and choice, 90.

13. Marwell & Gullickson, Inequality in the spatial allocation, 324.

14. Garrow, Receipt of government revenue, 445.

15. Hasenfeld & Garrow, Nonprofit human-service organizations, 308. This was theorized in Lipsky & Smith, *Nonprofits for hire.*

16. Calculated from Sharkey, Torrats-Espinosa, & Takyar, Community and the crime decline.

17. Human Services Council Commission, New York nonprofits, 1.

18. White, Creating collective capacity, 8–9.

19. Watkins, Swidler & Hannan, Outsourcing social transformation, 293; see also Weisbrod, *The voluntary nonprofit sector;* Weisbrod, *The nonprofit economy;* Hansmann, The role of nonprofit enterprise; Salamon, Of market failure; and Marwell & McInerney, The nonprofit/for-profit continuum.

20. Human Services Council Commission, New York nonprofits, 14.

21. Human Services Council Commission, 3.

22. Watkins et al., Outsourcing social transformation, 293.

23. Lu, Which nonprofit gets more, 297.

24. Calabrese, The accumulation of nonprofit profits.

25. Hood, A public management; see also Faucher-King & Le Galès, *The New Labour experiment,* for the exemplary case of the British public service under New Labour governments.

26. Parker, *Against management.*

27. Hasenfeld, What exactly is human services management? 2.

28. Savas, Competition and choice.

29. Girth et al., Public service delivery.

30. Hasenfeld & Garrow, Nonprofit human-service organizations, 306.

31. Human Services Council Commission, New York nonprofits, 9.

32. Derek Jennings, Necessary evil: The business of nonprofits, *Indy Week,* Sept. 13, 2006, www.indyweek.com/indyweek/necessary-evil-the-business-of-nonprofits/Content?oid = 1199012.

33. Hasenfeld, What exactly is human services management? 3; Hasenfeld & Garrow, Nonprofit human-service organizations, 305.

34. Human Services Council Commission, New York nonprofits.

35. Guo, Charity for profit?; Child, Whither the turn?

36. Savas, Competition and choice; Marwell & McInerney, The nonprofit/for-profit continuum.

37. Soss, Fording, & Schram, *Disciplining the poor.*

38. Marwell, Privatizing the welfare state; Marwell, *Bargaining for Brooklyn.*

39. Marwell, Privatizing the welfare state, 266–67.

40. Allard, *Out of reach;* Girth et al., Outsourcing public service delivery; Garrow, Receipt of government revenue.

41. Guo, Charity for profit, 124.

42. Watkins et al., Outsourcing social transformation, 295.

43. Brodkin, Bureaucracy redux; Brodkin, Policy work.

44. Soss et al., *Disciplining the poor.*

45. Hasenfeld, What exactly is human services management? 3.

46. Watkins et al., Outsourcing social transformation, 296–97.

47. Watkins et al., 295 .

48. Julie Bosman, City will stop paying the poor for good behavior, *New York Times,* March 30, 2010, www.nytimes.com/2010/03/31/nyregion/31cash.html. Opportunity NYC was not, strictly speaking, an innovation. It was based on the Mexican Progresa/Oportunitades/Prospera conditional cash transfer programs.

49. Savas, Competition and choice, 90.

50. Marwell, *Bargaining for Brooklyn,* 234, Hasenfeld & Garrow, Nonprofit human-service organizations, 297.

51. Mosley, Keeping the lights on, 841.

52. Hasenfeld, What exactly is human services management? 2–3; Hasenfeld & Garrow, Nonprofit human-service organizations, 309; see also Ferguson, *The anti-politics machine.*

53. Melissa Chadburn, Resilience is futile: How well-meaning nonprofits perpetuate poverty, *Jezebel,* July 14, 2015, http://jezebel.com/resilience-is-futile-how-well-meaning-nonprofits-perpe–1716461384.

54. Phelps, Rehabilitation in the punitive era.

55. Grinstead et al., The financial cost.

56. Sullivan et al., *Families as a resource.*

57. See Shapiro & Schwartz, Coming home.

58. Fisher, Doing good? 442.

59. See, e.g., Ferguson, *The anti-politics machine;* Duffield, *Global governance;* and Krause, *The good project.*

60. Garrow, Racial and ethnic composition, 161.

61. Nick Judd, Saving home: Former Met buys notorious complex, *City Limits,* Jan. 8, 2007, http://citylimits.org/2007/01/08/saving-home-former-metbuys-notorious-complex; Charlene A. Joseph and Kendall J. Matthews, Abdur Rahman Farrakhan, *Village Voice,* June 27, 2006, www.villagevoice.com/news/abdur-rahman-farrakhan–6418641.

62. Marwell, Privatizing the welfare state; Marwell, *Bargaining for Brooklyn.*

63. For an account of the influence of church culture in black public life see Pattillo-McCoy, Church culture .

64. Sharkey, Torrats-Espinosa, & Takyar, Community and the crime decline.

65. Wen, Hockenberry, & Cummings, The effect of Medicaid expansion, also find that substance abuse treatment policies reduce crime.

66. Currie, The take-up of social benefits.

67. See Warin, Le non-recours au RSA.

68. Marical et al., Publicly-provided services; Esping-Andersen & Myles, Economic inequality and the welfare state.

69. Howard, *The hidden welfare state;* Hacker, Privatizing risk; Mettler, *The submerged state.*

70. I repeat here Mike Konczal's argument: see Mike Konczal, The hidden welfare state and private sector spending coalitions, *Rortybomb,* June 30, 2011, https://rortybomb.wordpress.com/2011/06/30/the-hidden-welfare-state-and-private-sector-spending-coalitions.

71. Butler, *The privatization option.*

72. Esping-Andersen, *The three worlds.*

7. REENGINEERING LESS ELIGIBILITY

1. Shlay & Rossi, Social science research, 130; Rossi, *Down and out in America;* Baxter & Hopper, The new mendicancy; Mitchell, The annihilation of space; Ellickson, The homelessness muddle, 56.

2. Culhane, Metraux, & Wachter, Homelessness and public shelter provision.

3. Culhane, Metraux, & Hadley, Public service reductions.

4. Tsemberis & Eisenberg, Pathways to housing.

5. Culhane & Metraux, Rearranging the deck chairs.

6. Victims have the option to go to a specific shelter with specialized social workers. These shelters' locations are secret to prevent abusers from finding the women. (Recent separation is a known predictor of further violence.) Stays at domestic violence shelters have a time limit of 180 days. See New York City Independent Budget Office, *The rising number,* 10.

7. Durham & Johnson, *Homelessness prevention.*

8. New York City Department of Investigation, *Probe of Department.*

9. New York City Independent Budget Office, *The rising number,* 7–9.

10. Grunberg & Eagle, Shelterization, 522.

11. Julie Bosman, City seeks new powers in its stalled fight against homelessness, *New York Times,* June 23, 2009, www.nytimes.com/2009/06/24/nyregion/24homeless.html.

12. Samuel H. Williamson, Seven ways to compute the relative value of a U.S. dollar amount, 1774 to present, *MeasuringWorth,* 2019, www.measuringworth.com/uscompare.

13. Bosman, City seeks new powers; Cara Buckley, City drops plan to charge rent to shelter residents, *New York Times,* June 4, 2010, www.nytimes.com/2010/06/05/nyregion/05homeless.html; see also New York City Department of Investigation, *Probe of Department,* 26.

14. Hansmann, The role of nonprofit enterprise.

15. Cindy Rodriguez, To create housing for homeless, landlords evict paying tenants, *WNYC News,* August 12, 2013, www.wnyc.org/story/311609-homeless-more-lucrative-landlords-their-own-paying-tenants.

16. Clarkson FlatBed, The scandal down the block, *The Q at Parkside,* July 5, 2012, http://theqatparkside.blogspot.nl/2012/07/scandal-down-block.html.

17. Nathan Tempey, Residents fight for right to remain in notorious Brooklyn homeless shelter, *Gothamist,* July 16, 2015, http://gothamist.com/2015/07/16/60_clarkson_homeless_brooklyn.php.

18. Lamotte, Du non-profit au for profit.

19. Bosman, City seeks new powers.

20. Nathan Tempey, Nearly 9 out of 10 family homeless shelters in NYC have an "immediately hazardous" problem, *Gothamist,* Jan. 6, 2016, http://gothamist.com/2016/01/06/homeless_shelters_still_decrepit.php.

21. Winnie Hu, Review of New York shelter system finds hundreds of violations, *New York Times,* March 12, 2015, www.nytimes.com/2015/03/13/nyregion/new-york-homeless-shelter-system-violations-report.html.

22. New York City Department of Investigation, *Probe of Department,* 5.

23. Thery, *Larry's clique.*

24. Hu, Review of New York shelter system.

25. New York City Department of Investigation, *Probe of Department,* 5–6.

26. J. David Goodman, Tensions over New York's homeless shelters explode after disputed rape accusation, *New York Times,* Feb. 22, 2016, www.nytimes.com/2016/02/23/nyregion/tensions-over-new-yorks-homeless-shelters-explode-after-disputed-rape-accusation.html.

27. Carl Campanile & Jamie Schram, Cuomo demands probe into alleged "gang rape" at Bellevue Men's Shelter, *New York Post,* Feb. 20, 2016, http://nypost.com/2016/02/20/cuomo-demands-probe-into-alleged-gang-rape-at-bellevue-mens-shelter.

28. FlatBed, The scandal down the block.

29. These tactics are described in Thery, *Larry's clique;* and Greenberg, Tenants under siege.

30. See Marwell, Privatizing the welfare state; Marwell, *Bargaining for Brooklyn;* and Marwell & Gullickson, Inequality in the spatial allocation.

31. Tom Robbins,He was the hope of East New York, *New York Daily News,* Feb. 8, 1998, www.nydailynews.com/archives/news/hope-east-new-york-ran-political-boss-played-brutal-game-hardball-brooklyn-article-1.801620.

32. Abdulai Bah, New York City's homeless find little comfort in shelter system, *Al Jazeera America,* March 30, 2015, http://america.aljazeera.com/watch/shows/fault-lines/articles/2015/3/30/new-york-citys-homeless-find-more-discomfort-in-shelter-system.html.

33. New York City Independent Budget Office, *The rising number.*

34. Tana Ganeva, Conditions were "bluntly Dickensian": The disgrace of New York's homeless shelters, *Salon,* July 10, 2015, www.salon.com/2015/07/09/homeless_in_nyc_partner.

35. New York City Independent Budget Office, *The rising number,* 3.

36. FlatBed, The scandal down the block.

37. Ian Frazier, Hidden city, *New Yorker,* Oct. 28, 2013, www.newyorker.com/magazine/2013/10/28/hidden-city

38. New York City Independent Budget Office, *The rising number,* 5.

39. New York City Independent Budget Office, 2.

40. Patrick Markee, Municipal shelter system in New York City fails to meet the needs of homeless individuals, *New York Daily News,* Feb. 17, 2015, www.nydailynews.com/new-york/municipal-shelter-system-nyc-fails-homeless-individuals-article-1.2117926.

41. See Markee.

42. Chauncey Alcorn, Molly Crane-Newman, Erin Durkin, & Jennifer Fermino, Horror stories show why NYC's homeless resist shelters despite frigid temperatures. *New York Daily News,* Jan. 4, 2016, www.nydailynews.com/new-york/horror-stories-show-homeless-avoid-nyc-shelters-article-1.2485417.

43. Baxter & Hopper, The new mendicancy.

44. Tempey, Residents fight.

45. FlatBed, The scandal down the block.

46. Thery, *Larry's clique.*

47. Bah, New York City's homeless.

48. Bosman, City seeks new powers.

49. Julie Bosman, A shelter for families in need of a push, *New York Times,* March 21, 2010, www.nytimes.com/2010/03/22/nyregion/22homeless.html?_r = 0.

50. Christopher Haire, Next step shelter program uses punitive measures, Brooklyn Ink, Dec. 17, 2011, http://brooklynink.org/2011/12/17/39204-next-step-shelter-program-uses-punitive-measures

51. Sarah Murphy, The "Next Step" punishment, *Safety Net* (Coalition for the Homeless newsletter), Autumn 2011, www.coalitionforthehomeless.org/the-next-step-punishment.

52. Frazier, Hidden city.

53. John Del Signore, Bloomberg: Problem with homeless shelters is they're too "pleasurable," *Gothamist,* August 24, 2012, http://gothamist.com/2012/08/24/bloomberg_problem_with_homeless_she.php.

54. Frazier, Hidden city.

55. McAllister & Berlin, Policymaking and caseload dynamics.

56. Main, Hard lessons on homelessness.

57. Culhane, Metraux, & Wachter, Homelessness and public shelter provision.

58. New York City Independent Budget Office, *The rising number.*

59. Cragg & O'Flaherty, Measuring the incentive.

60. Ellickson, The homelessness muddle.

61. Sam Roberts, What led to crackdown on homeless, *New York Times,* Oct. 28, 1991, www.nytimes.com/1991/10/28/nyregion/what-led-to-crackdown-on-homeless.html?pagewanted = all.

62. Mitchell, The annihilation of space; Beckett & Herbert, Dealing with disorder.

63. Benjaminsen & Dyb, The effectiveness of homeless policies; Hermans, The Dutch strategy; Benjaminsen, Homelessness.

64. Lindblom, Toward a comprehensive homeless-prevention strategy; Culhane, Metraux, & Byrne, A prevention-centered approach.

65. I draw this analogy and argument from Mike Konczal's commentary on Matt Desmond's *Evicted* (2016); see Konczal, The violence of eviction.

66. Diane Cardwell, City to clear homeless encampments, *New York Times,* July 18, 2006, www.nytimes.com/2006/07/18/nyregion/18homeless.html.

67. Metraux & Culhane, Recent incarceration history.

68. Metraux & Culhane, Homeless shelter use; Greenberg & Rosenheck, Jail incarceration.

69. Metraux & Culhane, Recent incarceration history; on the "institutional circuit" see Hopper et al., Homelessness.

70. Kohler-Hausmann, Guns and butter, 91, analyzes the movement of deinstitutionalization as the shift from a social to a penal treatment of mental illness.

CONCLUSION

1. Huntington, *Political order in changing societies.*

2. Hirschman, *The passions and the interests;* Hirschman, Rival interpretations of market society.

3. Adam Smith is not usually considered a hero of social democracy. But, at a time when Townsend and Malthus wrote horrible things about the poor, Smith wrote in the *Wealth of Nations:* "Where wages are high, accordingly, we shall always find the workmen more active, diligent, and expeditious, than where they are low" (cited in Ravallion, The idea of antipoverty policy, 15n22); and "Wherever there is great property, there is great inequality. . . . Civil government, so far as it is instituted for the security of property, is in reality instituted for the defence of the rich against the poor, or of those who have some property against those who have none at all" (book V, chapter I, part II).

4. For an argument that affirmative action should serve to break the association between minority status and lower-class status, see Sabbagh, *Equality and transparency.*

5. Autor et al., When work disappears.

6. Wilkinson & Pickett, *The spirit level*; Therborn, *The killing fields of inequality*; Atkinson, *Inequality.*

7. Lindert, *Growing public*; Ravallion, *The idea of antipoverty policy;* Atkinson, *Inequality;* Bourguignon, Revisiting the debate.

8. On the sufficiency view see Frankfurt, Equality as a moral ideal; on the Rawlsian position see Rawls, *A theory of justice.*

9. Brady & Bostic, Paradoxes of social policy.

10. Piketty, *Le capital au 21e siècle.*

11. Atkinson, *Inequality.*

12. Piketty, *Le capital au 21e siècle;* Milanovic, *Global inequality;* Scheidel, *The great leveler.*

13. Alesina & Glaeser, *Fighting poverty;* Finseraas, Immigration and preferences for redistribution; Gilens, *Why Americans hate welfare;* Eger, Even in Sweden.

ACKNOWLEDGMENTS

First, thank you to my father, Marc Bonnet, and my former student Quentin Batréau. They kept pressing for me to send them early drafts, and they provided encouragements and crucial feedback at the earliest stages of this project. They have read all the chapters in atrocious versions and deserve so much credit.

Thank you to Daniel Sabbagh, who read the full manuscript and brought his unusual sharpness to save me many an embarrassment. Patrick Le Galès also read the entire thing, 17 years after he had massacred drafts of my undergraduate thesis. I have never properly thanked Patrick, who taught me so much, for how much I owe him; let this be the occasion.

Marco Di Nunzio, Claire Dupuy, Catherine Höffler, Raul Magni-Berton, Sidonie Naulin, Julie Pollard, Patrick Präg, Francesco Ragazzi, and Pascale Trompette read chapters and gave great feedback. Thank you! Special thanks to Nicolas Martin-Breteau for accepting a last-minute reading mission and for giving great feedback.

Maura Roessner, my editor at the University of California Press, has been very helpful all along and found superb anonymous reviewers, to whom I am also thankful.

Thank you to my colleagues at Pacte, the research center at CNRS, Gilles Bastin, Céline Belot, Thierry Delpeuch, Alain Faure, Simon Godard, Isabelle Guinaudeau, Pierre Martin, Sebastian Roché, Guillaume Roux, and Pascale Trompette—and in particular to Claire Dupuy (who saw the good in my half-baked arguments), Raul Magni-Berton (pushed me to become truer to my scholarly self), and Sidonie Naulin (never too shy to attack my complacency). Claire and Sidonie have been incredibly supportive in these past four years. Thank you!

Over the years I have benefited from advice and support from Barbara Da Roit (taught me lifelong wisdom about organizations), Erhard Friedberg (taught me about human nature), Eloi Laurent (made me think about my responsibilities as a scholar), Raphaël Madinier (taught me how to write), Naïma Makri (provided me with reality checks), Nicole Marwell (transformed my understanding of social policy), Vincent Pasquini (provided me with reliable life wisdom), Mary Pattillo (taught me about race), Francesco Ragazzi (acted as my academic superego), Eva Rosen (explained to me countless American mysteries), Jessica Serraris (saw potential when it wasn't obvious), Clément Théry (taught me sociology), Sudhir Venkatesh (encouraged me to do fieldwork and to press on), Romain Vian (helped me to shake off some of my teenage cluelessness), and Mathieu Zagrodzki (made me rethink assumptions). Clément and Vincent have been enormously helpful in making it possible for me to do research in New York. Thank you.

Mistakes and sloppiness are, of course, my responsibility only.

I received funding and support from the Department of Sociology at Columbia University and from the Center for Urban and Policy Research, also at Columbia University (thank you, Sudhir Venkatesh); from CIRHUS, the CNRS research center at New York University (thank you, Nicolas Guilhot); from the Fondation pour les sciences sociales (thank you, François Héran); from Agence nationale de la recherche (thank you, Dominique Duprez); and from my research center, Pacte (thank you, Nicolas Buclet and Anne-Laure Amilhat-Szary). I am grateful to the colleagues who accepted roles as members of the jury for the "habilitation" dissertation: Daniel Cefaï, Fabien Jobard, Jacques de Maillard, Hélène Périvier, and Maud Simonet. Thank you also to Fatima Raja and Joe Abbott for excellent copyediting.

I have written this book at the public library of Leiden (Netherlands), near the tower. The heating is good, internet and restrooms free. The library is full of books that people actually read, self-help, cooking recipes, *Buying a House for Dummies.* The place reflects the unpretentiousness of the provincial middle class from a rich, social democratic, Western European country. It is open to the homeless and the mentally ill, functional and dignified, low and high culture side by side. It informs this book through and through.

Thanks to my little boy, Adri, and my wife, Migena, writing this book has been an incredibly happy and fulfilling journey, and this book is lovingly dedicated to them.

REFERENCES

Abramowitz, A., & Teixeira, R. (2009). The decline of the white working class and the rise of a mass upper-middle class. *Political Science Quarterly, 124*(3), 391–422.

Aebi, M. F., & Linde, A. (2010). Is there a crime drop in Western Europe? *European Journal on Criminal Policy and Research, 16*(4), 251–77.

Alesina, A., & Glaeser, E. L. (2004). *Fighting poverty in the U.S. and in Europe: A world of difference.* New York: Oxford University Press.

Alexander, M. (2010). *The new Jim Crow: Mass incarceration in the age of colorblindness.* New York: New Press.

Allard, Scott W. (2009). *Out of reach: Place, poverty, and the new American welfare state.* New Haven, CT: Yale University Press.

Allegretto, S. A., Doussard, M., Graham-Squire, D., Jacobs, K., Thompson, D., & Thompson, J. (2013). *Fast food, poverty wages: The public cost of low-wage jobs in the fast-food industry.* Berkeley, CA: UC Berkeley Center for Labor Research and Education.

Anderson, E. (1999). *Code of the street.* New York: Norton.

Atkinson, A. B. 2015). *Inequality.* Cambridge, MA: Harvard University Press.

Austin, M. J. (2003). The changing relationship between nonprofit organizations and public social service agencies in the era of welfare reform. *Nonprofit and Voluntary Sector Quarterly, 32*(1), 97–114.

Autor, D. H., Dorn, D., & Hanson, G. (2017). When work disappears: Manufacturing decline and the falling marriage-market value of men. *NBER Working Paper, 23173.*

Autor, D. H., Katz, L. F., & Kearney, M. S. (2006). The polarization of the US labor market. *American Economic Review, 96*(2), 189-94.

Autor, D. H., Katz, L. F., & Kearney, M. S. (2008). Trends in US wage inequality: Revising the revisionists. *Review of Economics and Statistics, 90*(2), 300–323.

Autor, D. H., Manning, A., & Smith, C. L. (2016). The contribution of the minimum wage to US wage inequality over three decades: A reassessment. *American Economic Journal: Applied Economics, 8*(1), 58–99.

Baldwin, J. (1960). Fifth Avenue, Uptown. *Esquire*, July. www.esquire.com/news-politics/a3638/fifth-avenue-uptown.

Balko, R. (2013). *Rise of the warrior cop: The militarization of America's police forces.* New York: PublicAffairs.

Barker, V. (2013). Nordic exceptionalism revisited: Explaining the paradox of a Janus-faced penal regime. *Theoretical Criminology, 17*(1), 5–25.

Baumer, E. P., & Wolff, K. T. (2014). Evaluating contemporary crime drop(s) in America, New York City, and many other places. *Justice Quarterly, 31*(1), 5–38.

Baxter, E., & Hopper, K. (1982). The new mendicancy: Homeless in New York City. *American Journal of Orthopsychiatry, 52*(3), 393–408.

Beaumont, Gustave de, & Tocqueville, Alexis de. (1833). *On the penitentiary system in the United States and its application in France.* Philadelphia, PA: Carey, Lea, and Blanchard.

Becker, G. S. (1968). Crime and punishment: An economic approach. *Journal of Political Economy, 76*(2), 169–217.

Beckett, K. (1999). *Making crime pay: Law and order in contemporary American politics.* New York: Oxford University Press.

Beckett, K., & Herbert, S. (2008). Dealing with disorder: Social control in the post-industrial city. *Theoretical Criminology, 12*(1), 5–30.

Beckett, K., & Western, B. (2001). Governing social marginality welfare, incarceration, and the transformation of state policy. *Punishment & Society, 3*(1), 43–59.

Been, V., Ellen, I., & Madar, J. (2009). The high cost of segregation: Exploring racial disparities in high-cost lending. *Fordham Urban Law Journal, 36*, 361–93.

Benjaminsen, L. (2016). Homelessness in a Scandinavian welfare state: The risk of shelter use in the Danish adult population. *Urban Studies, 53*(10), 2041–63.

Benjaminsen, L., & Dyb, E. (2008). The effectiveness of homeless policies—Variations among the Scandinavian countries. *European Journal of Homelessness, 2*, 45–67.

Besley, T., & Coate, S. (1992). Workfare versus welfare: Incentive arguments for work requirements in poverty-alleviation programs. *American Economic Review, 82*(1), 249–61.

Blaug, M. (1963). The myth of the old poor law and the making of the new. *Journal of Economic History, 23*(2), 151–84.

Block, F., & Somers, M. (2003). In the shadow of Speenhamland: Social policy and the old poor law. *Politics & Society, 31*(2), 283–323.

Bloom, N. D. (2012). Learning from New York: America's alternative high-rise public housing model. *Journal of the American Planning Association, 78*(4), 418–31.

Blumstein, A. (2006). The crime drop in America: An exploration of some recent crime trends. *Journal of Scandinavian Studies in Criminology and Crime Prevention, 7*(S1), 17–35.

Blumstein, A., & Rosenfeld, R. (1998). Explaining recent trends in US homicide rates. *Journal of Criminal Law & Criminology, 88*(2), 1175–1216.

Bosworth, B., Burtless, G., & Zhang, K. (2016). Later retirement, inequality in old age, and the growing gap in longevity between rich and poor. *Economic Studies at Brookings.* www.brookings.edu/wp-content/uploads/2016/02/BosworthBurtlessZhang_retirementinequalitylongevity_012815.pdf.

Bourguignon, F. (2015). Revisiting the debate on inequality and economic development. *Revue d'économie politique, 125*(5), 633–63.

Bowser, A. R. (2003). One strike and you're out—or are you? Rucker's influence on future eviction proceedings for Section 8 and public housing. *Penn State Law Review, 108,* 611.

Boyer, G. R. (1990). *An economic history of the English poor law, 1750–1850.* Cambridge: Cambridge University Press.

Brady, D. (2009). *Rich democracies, poor people: How politics explain poverty.* New York: Oxford University Press.

Brady, D., & Bostic, A. (2015). Paradoxes of social policy welfare transfers, relative poverty, and redistribution preferences. *American Sociological Review, 80*(2), 268–98.

Brady, D., Blome, A., & Kleider, H. (2016). How politics and institutions shape poverty and inequality. *The Oxford Handbook of the Social Science of Poverty,* ed. D. Brady and L. M. Burton, 117–40. Oxford : Oxford University Press.

Brady, D., Finnigan, R. M., & Hübgen, S. (2017). Rethinking the risks of poverty: A framework for analyzing prevalences and penalties. *American Journal of Sociology, 123*(3), 740–86.

Bratton, W. J., & Malinowski, S. W. (2008). Police performance management in practice: Taking COMPSTAT to the next level. *Policing, 2*(3), 259–65.

Brodkin, E. Z. (2007). Bureaucracy redux: Management reformism and the welfare state. *Journal of Public Administration Research and Theory, 17*(1), 1–17.

Brodkin, E. Z. (2011). Policy work: Street-level organizations under new managerialism. *Journal of Public Administration Research and Theory, 21*(suppl. 2), i253–77.

Bucklen, K. B., & Zajac, G. (2009). But some of them don't come back (to prison!): Resource deprivation and thinking errors as determinants of parole success and failure. *Prison Journal, 89*(3), 239–64.

Butler, S. M. (Ed.). (1985). *The privatization option: A strategy to shrink the size of government.* Washington, DC: Heritage Foundation.

Calabrese, T. D. (2012). The accumulation of nonprofit profits: A dynamic analysis. *Nonprofit and Voluntary Sector Quarterly, 41*(2), 300–324.

Campbell, M. C., & Schoenfeld, H. (2013). The transformation of America's penal order: A historicized political sociology of punishment. *American Journal of Sociology, 118*(5), 1375–1423.

Canela-Cacho, J. A., Blumstein, A., & Cohen, J. (1997). Relationship between the offending frequency (λ) of imprisoned and free offenders. *Criminology, 35*(1), 133–76.

Cantillon, B. (2011). The paradox of the social investment state: Growth, employment and poverty in the Lisbon era. *Journal of European Social Policy, 21*(5), 432–49.

Carré, J. (2016). *La prison des pauvres: L'expérience des workhouses en Angleterre.* Paris: Vendémiaire.

Case, A., & Deaton, A. (2015). Rising morbidity and mortality in midlife among white non-Hispanic Americans in the 21st century. *Proceedings of the National Academy of Sciences, 112*(49), 15078–83.

Case, A., & Deaton, A. (2017). Mortality and morbidity in the 21st century. *Brookings Papers on Economic Activity,* Spring 2017, 397–476.

Castel, Robert. (1995). *Les métamorphoses de la question sociale: Une chronique du salariat.* Paris: Fayard.

Cavadino, M., & Dignan, J. (2006). Penal policy and political economy. *Criminology and Criminal Justice, 6*(4), 435–56.

Center for NYC Neighborhoods. (2016). *The impact of property flipping on homeowners and renters in small buildings.* Center for NYC Neighborhoods. https://cnycn.org/wp-content/uploads/2016/04/CNYCN-NYC-Flipping-Analysis.pdf.

Charette, A., Herbert, C., Jakabovics, A., Marya, E. T., & McCue, D. T. (2015). *Projecting trends in severely cost-burdened renters: 2015–2025.* Cambridge, MA: Harvard University Joint Center for Housing Studies.

Child, C. (2010). Whither the turn? The ambiguous nature of nonprofits' commercial revenue. *Social Forces, 89*(1), 145–61.

Chioda, L., De Mello, J. M., & Soares, R. R. (2016). Spillovers from conditional cash transfer programs: Bolsa Família and crime in urban Brazil. *Economics of Education Review, 54,* 306–20.

Chiricos, T. G. (1987). Rates of crime and unemployment: An analysis of aggregate research evidence. *Social Problems, 34*(2), 187–12.

Clark, G. (2005). The condition of the working class in England, 1209–2004. *Journal of Political Economy, 113*(6), 1307–40.

Clark, G., & Page, M. E. (2018). Welfare reform, 1834: Did the New Poor Law in England produce significant economic gains? *Cliometrica,* doi:10.1007/s11698-018-0174-4.

Clarno, A. (2014). Beyond the state: Policing precariousness in South Africa and Palestine/Israel. *Ethnic and Racial Studies, 37*(10), 1725–31.

Cohen, S. (1985). *Visions of social control: Crime, punishment and classification.* Cambridge: Polity.

Cooper, D., & Kroeger, T. (2017). Employers steal billions from workers' paychecks each year. Washington, DC: Economic Policy Institute, www.epi.org/files/pdf/125116.pdf.

Crafts, N. F. R. (1985). English workers' living standards during the Industrial Revolution: Some remaining problems. *Journal of Economic History 45*(1), 139–44.

Cragg, M., & O'Flaherty, B. (1994). Measuring the incentive to be homeless. Columbia University Department of Economics Discussion Paper #714. www.columbia.edu/cu/libraries/inside/working/Econ/ldpd_econ_9495_714.pdf.

Culhane, D. P., & Metraux, S. (2008). Rearranging the deck chairs or reallocating the lifeboats? Homeless assistance and its alternatives. *Journal of the American Planning Association, 74,* 111–21.

Culhane, D. P., Metraux, S., & Byrne, T. (2011). A prevention-centered approach to homelessness assistance: A paradigm shift? *Housing Policy Debate, 21*(2), 295–315.

Culhane, D. P., Metraux, S., & Hadley, T. (2002). Public service reductions associated with placement of homeless persons with severe mental illness in supportive housing. *Housing Policy Debate, 13*(1), 107–63.

Culhane, D. P., Metraux, S., Park, J. M., Schretzman, M., & Valente, J. (2007). Testing a typology of family homelessness based on patterns of public shelter utilization in four US jurisdictions: Implications for policy and program planning. *Housing Policy Debate, 18*(1), 1–28.

Culhane, D. P., Metraux, S., & Wachter, S. M. (1999). Homelessness and public shelter provision in New York City. In M. H. Schill (Ed.), *Housing and Community Development in New York City: Facing the Future*, 203–32. Albany: State University of New York Press.

Currie, J. (2006). The take-up of social benefits. In A. Auerbach, D. Card, & J. Quigley (Eds.), *Poverty, the distribution of income, and public policy*, 80–148. New York: Sage.

Danziger, S. K. (2010). The decline of cash welfare and implications for social policy and poverty. *Annual Review of Sociology, 36*, 523–45.

Danziger, S., Haveman, R., & Plotnick, R. (1981). How income transfer programs affect work, savings, and the income distribution: A critical review. *Journal of Economic Literature, 19*(3), 975–1028.

Davis, G. F. (2013). After the corporation. *Politics & Society, 41*(2), 283–308.

Dawson, M. C. (2014). The hollow shell: Loïc Wacquant's vision of state, race and economics. *Ethnic and Racial Studies, 37*(10), 1767–75.

De Giorgi, A. (2006). *Re-thinking the political economy of punishment: Perspectives on post-Fordism and penal politics*. Aldershot: Ashgate.

De Giorgi, A. (2007). Toward a political economy of post-Fordist punishment. *Critical Criminology, 15*(3), 243–65.

De Giorgi, A. (2010). Immigration control, post-Fordism, and less eligibility. A materialist critique of the criminalization of immigration across Europe. *Punishment & Society, 12*(2), 147–67.

De Giorgi, A. (2012). Punishment and political economy. In J. Simon & R. Sparks (Eds.), *The Sage handbook of punishment and society*, 40–59. New York: Sage.

Deiana, C. (2016). *The bitter side of trade shocks: Local labour market conditions and crime in the US*. Working paper, Associazione Italiana Economisti del Lavoro.

Desmond, M. (2016). *Evicted: Poverty and profit in the American city*. New York: Crown.

De Swaan, A. (1988). *In care of the state: Health care, education, and welfare in Europe and the USA in the modern era*. Oxford: Oxford University Press.

Donzelot, J. (1977). *La police des familles*. Paris: Minuit.

Downes, B. T. (1968). Social and political characteristics of riot cities: A comparative study. *Social Science Quarterly, 49*(3), 504–20.

Downes, D., & Hansen, K. (2006). Welfare and punishment in comparative perspective. In S. Armstrong & L. McAra (Eds.), *Perspective on punishment: The contours of control*, 133–54. Oxford: Oxford University Press.

Draca, M., & Machin, S. (2015). Crime and economic incentives. *Annual Review of Economics, 7*(1), 389–408.

Duffield, M. R. (2001). *Global governance and the new wars: The merging of development and security*. London: Zed.

Duncan, G. J., Hill, M. S., & Hoffman, S. D. (1988). Welfare dependence within and across generations. *Science, 239*(4839), 467–71.

Durham, C., & Johnson, M. (2014). *Homelessness prevention, intake, and shelter for single adults and families*. Washington, DC: Urban Institute.

Duvoux, N. (2015). *Les oubliés du rêve américain: Philanthropie, État et pauvreté urbaine aux États-Unis*. Paris: PUF.

Dwyer, R. E. (2013). The care economy? Gender, economic restructuring, and job polarization in the US labor market. *American Sociological Review, 78*(3), 390–416.

Eberstadt, N. (2016). *Men without work: America's invisible crisis.* West Conshohocken, PA: Templeton Foundation Press.

Edin, K., & Kefalas, M. (2005). *Promises I can keep. Why poor women put motherhood before marriage.* Berkeley: University of California Press.

Edin, K., & Lein, L. (1997). *Making ends meet: How single mothers survive welfare and low-wage work.* New York: Sage.

Edin, K. J., & Shaefer, H. L. (2015). *$2.00 a day: Living on almost nothing in America.* New York: Houghton Mifflin Harcourt.

Edsall, T. B., & Edsall, M. D. (1992). *Chain reaction: The impact of race, rights, and taxes on American politics.* New York: Norton.

Edwards, F., Esposito, M. H., & Lee, H. (2018). Risk of police-involved death by race/ethnicity and place: United States, 2012–2018. *American Journal of Public Health, 108*(9), 1241–48.

Eger, M. A. (2010). Even in Sweden: The effect of immigration on support for welfare state spending. *European Sociological Review, 26*(2), 203–17.

Ehrlich, I. (1996). Crime, punishment and the market for offenses. *Journal of Economic Perpectives, 10*(1), 43–67.

Ekunwe, I. O., & Jones, R. S. (2012). Finnish criminal policy: From hard time to gentle justice. *Journal of Prisoners on Prisons, 21*(1/2), 173–89.

Ellen, I. G., Horn, K. M., & Reed, D. (2016). Has falling crime invited gentrification? *NYU Furman Center working paper,* Oct. 18.

Ellen, I. G., Lacoe, J., & Sharygin, C. A. (2013). Do foreclosures cause crime? *Journal of Urban Economics, 74,* 59–70.

Ellickson, R. C. (1990). The homelessness muddle. *Public Interest, 99,* 45–60.

Entorf, H., & Spengler H. (2000). Socio-economic and demographic factors of crime in Germany: Evidence from panel data of the German states. *International Review of Law and Economics, 20,* 75–106.

Esping-Andersen, G. (1990). *The three worlds of welfare capitalism.* Princeton, NJ: Princeton University Press.

Esping-Andersen, G., & Myles, J. (2009). Economic inequality and the welfare state. In W. Salverda, B. Nolan, & T. M. Smeeding (Eds.), *The Oxford handbook of economic inequality,* 639–64. Oxford: Oxford University Press.

Eterno, J. A., & Silverman, E. B. (2012). *The crime numbers game: Management by manipulation.* Boca Raton, FL: CRC Press.

Farrell, G., Tilley, N., & Tseloni, A. (2014). Why the crime drop? *Crime and Justice, 43*(1), 421–90.

Faucher-King, F., & Le Galès, P. (2010). *The New Labour experiment: Change and reform under Blair and Brown.* Palo Alto, CA: Stanford University Press.

Feinstein, C. H. (1998). Pessimism perpetuated: Real wages and the standard of living in Britain during and after the Industrial Revolution. *Journal of Economic History, 58*(3), 625–58.

Feler, L., & Senses, M. Z. (2016). Trade shocks and the provision of local public goods. IZA Discussion Papers, No. 10231.

Ferguson, J. (1990). *The anti-politics machine: "Development," depoliticization and bureaucratic power in Lesotho.* Cambridge: Cambridge University Press.

Finseraas, H. (2008). Immigration and preferences for redistribution: An empirical analysis of European survey data. *Comparative European Politics, 6*(4), 407–31.

Fisher, W. F. (1997). Doing good? The politics and antipolitics of NGO practices. *Annual Review of Anthropology, 26,* 439–64.

Flamm, M. W. (2005). *Law and order: Street crime, civil unrest, and the crisis of liberalism in the 1960s.* New York: Columbia University Press.

Floud, R., Wachter, K., & Gregory, A. *Height, health and history: Nutritional status in the United Kingdom, 1750–1980.* Cambridge: Cambridge University Press, 1990.

Foster, H., & Hagan, J. (2009). The mass incarceration of parents in America: Issues of race/ethnicity, collateral damage to children, and prisoner reentry. *The ANNALS of the American Academy of Political and Social Science, 623*(1), 179–94.

Fougère, D., Kramarz, F., & Pouget, J. (2009). Youth unemployment and crime in France. *Journal of the European Economic Association, 7*(5), 909–38.

Fox, J. A., & Zawitz, M. W. (2007). *Homicide trends in the US.* Washington, DC: Bureau of Justice Statistics.

Frankfurt, H. (1987). Equality as a moral ideal. *Ethics, 98*(1), 21–43.

Freeman, R. B. (1999). The economics of crime. In O. Ashenfelter & D. Card (Eds.), *Handbook of labor economics,* Vol 3C, 3529–71. North Holland: Elsevier.

Gainsborough, J. F. (2003). To devolve or not to devolve? Welfare reform in the states. *Policy studies journal, 31*(4), 603–23.

Gans, H. J. (1968). The ghetto rebellions and urban class conflict. *Proceedings of the Academy of Political Science, 29*(1), 42–51.

Garland, D. (1985). *Punishment and welfare: A history of penal strategies.* Aldershot: Gower.

Garland, D. (1990). *Punishment and modern society: A study in social theory.* Chicago: University of Chicago Press.

Garland, D. (2001). *The culture of control: Crime and social order in contemporary society.* Oxford: Oxford University Press.

Garland, D. (2013). Penality and the penal state. *Criminology, 51*(3), 475–517.

Garland, D. (2014). The welfare state: A fundamental dimension of modern government. *European Journal of Sociology, 55*(3), 327–64.

Garrow, E. E. (2010). Receipt of government revenue among nonprofit human service organizations. *Journal of Public Administration Research and Theory, 21*(3), 445–71.

Garrow, E. E. (2015). Racial and ethnic composition of the neighborhood and the disbanding of nonprofit human service organizations. *Du Bois Review: Social Science Research on Race, 12*(1), 161–85.

Geller, A., & Curtis, M. A. (2011). A sort of homecoming: Incarceration and the housing security of urban men. *Social Science Research, 40*(4), 1196–1213.

Gerardi, K., Shapiro, A. H., & Willen, P. (2007). Subprime outcomes: Risky mortgages, homeownership experiences, and foreclosures. *Federal Reserve of Boston Working Paper* No. 07-15.

Geremek, B. (1978). *Litość i szubienica.* French translation: *La potence ou la pitié: l'Europe et les pauvres du moyen âge à nos jours.* Paris: Gallimard, 1987; English translation: *Poverty: A History.* London: Blackwell, 1994.

Gilens, M. (2009). *Why Americans hate welfare: Race, media, and the politics of antipoverty policy.* Chicago: University of Chicago Press.

Girth, A. M., Hefetz, A., Johnston, J. M., & Warner, M. E. (2012). Outsourcing public service delivery: Management responses in noncompetitive markets. *Public Administration Review, 72*(6), 887–900.

Goffman, A. (2009). On the run: Wanted men in a Philadelphia ghetto. *American Sociological Review, 74*(3), 339–57.

Goffman, A. (2014). *On the run: Fugitive life in an American city.* Chicago: University of Chicago Press.

Goffman, A. (2015). When the police knock your door in. In J. Auyero, P. Bourgois, & N. Scheper-Hughes (Eds.), *Violence at the urban margins,* 212–47. New York: Oxford University Press.

Goldstein, H. (1979). Improving policing: A problem-oriented approach. *Crime and Delinquency, 25*(2): 236–58.

Gottschalk, M. (2006). *The prison and the gallows: The politics of mass incarceration in America.* Cambridge: Cambridge University Press.

Gottschalk, M. (2015). *Caught: The prison state and the lockdown of American politics.* Princeton, NJ: Princeton University Press.

Gottschalk, P., & Moffitt, R. (2009). The rising instability of US earnings. *Journal of Economic Perspectives, 23*(4), 3–24.

Gould, E. D., Weinberg, B. A., & Mustard, D. B. (2002). Crime rates and local labor market opportunities in the United States: 1979–1997. *Review of Economics and Statistics, 84*(1), 45–61.

Greenberg, G. A., & Rosenheck, R. A. (2008). Jail incarceration, homelessness, and mental health: A national study. *Psychiatric Services, 59*(2): 170–77.

Greenberg, M. (2012). New York: The police and the protesters. *New York Review of Books, 11,* 58–61.

Greenberg, M. (2017). Tenants under siege: Inside New York City's housing crisis. *New York Review of Books,* August 17. www.nybooks.com/articles/2017/08/17/tenants-under-siege-inside-new-york-city-housing-crisis.

Greenstein, Robert. (1985). Losing faith in "Losing Ground." *New Republic,* March 25, 12–17.

Gregory, J. N. (2006). *The southern diaspora: How the great migrations of black and white southerners transformed America.* Chapel Hill: University of North Carolina Press.

Grinstead, O., Faigeles, B., Bancroft, C., & Zack, B. (2001). The financial cost of maintaining relationships with incarcerated African American men: A survey of women prison visitors. *Journal of African American Men, 6*(1), 59–70.

Grogger, J. (1998). Market wages and youth crime. *Journal of Labor Economics, 16*(4), 756–91.

Grönqvist, H. (2013). Youth unemployment and crime: Lessons from longitudinal population records. Unpublished manuscript, Swedish Institute for Social Research, Stockholm.

Grossman, J. R. (1991). *Land of hope: Chicago, black southerners, and the Great Migration.* Chicago: University of Chicago Press.

Groves, L. H. (2016). Welfare reform and labor force exit by young, low-skilled single males. *Demography, 53*(2), 393–418.

Grunberg, J., & Eagle, P. F. (1990). Shelterization: How the homeless adapt to shelter living. *Psychiatric Services, 41*(5), 521–25.

Guo, B. (2006). Charity for profit? Exploring factors associated with the commercialization of human service nonprofits. *Nonprofit and Voluntary Sector Quarterly, 35*(1), 123–38.

Gustafson, K. (2009). The criminalization of poverty. *Journal of Criminal Law and Criminology, 99*(3), 643–716.

Hacker, J. S. (2004). Privatizing risk without privatizing the welfare state: The hidden politics of social policy retrenchment in the United States. *American Political Science Review, 98*(2), 243–60.

Halpern-Meekin, S., Edin, K., Tach, L., & Sykes, J. (2015). *It's not like I'm poor: How working families make ends meet in a post-welfare world.* Berkeley: University of California Press.

Hannon, L., & DeFronzo, J. (1998). The truly disadvantaged, public assistance, and crime. *Social Problems, 45*(3), 383–92.

Hansmann, H. B. (1980). The role of nonprofit enterprise. *Yale Law Journal, 89*(5), 835–901.

Harding, D. J. (2009). Collateral consequences of violence in disadvantaged neighborhoods. *Social Forces, 88*(2), 757–84.

Harding, D. J. (2010). *Living the drama: Community, conflict, and culture among inner-city boys.* Chicago: University of Chicago Press.

Harris, A. (2016). *A pound of flesh: Monetary sanctions as punishment for the poor.* New York: Sage.

Hasenfeld, Y. (2015). What exactly is human services management? *Human Service Organizations: Management, Leadership & Governance, 39*(1), 1–5.

Hasenfeld, Y., & Garrow, E. E. (2012). Nonprofit human-service organizations, social rights, and advocacy in a neoliberal welfare state. *Social Service Review, 86*(2), 295–322.

Hasenfeld, Y., Ghose, T., & Larson, K. (2004). The logic of sanctioning welfare recipients: An empirical assessment. *Social Service Review, 78*(2), 304–19.

Healy, K. (2017). Fuck nuance. *Sociological Theory, 35*(2), 118–27.

Heathcote, J., Perri, F., & Violante, G. L. (2010). Unequal we stand: An empirical analysis of economic inequality in the United States, 1967–2006. *Review of Economic dynamics, 13*(1), 15–51.

Hebert, T. (2005). *The invisible tenant: Living in federally assisted housing after prison.* New York: Family Justice.

Heclo, H. (1974). *Modern social politics in Britain and Sweden.* New Haven, CT: Yale University Press.

Helland, E., & Tabarrok, A. (2007). Does three strikes deter? A nonparametric estimation. *Journal of Human Resources, 42*(2), 309–30.

Hellegers, A. P. (1999). Reforming HUD's "one-strike" public housing evictions through tenant participation. *Journal of Criminal Law and Criminology, 90*(7), 323–62.

Herbert, S. (2009). *Citizens, cops, and power: Recognizing the limits of community.* Chicago: University of Chicago Press.

Hermans, K. (2012). The Dutch strategy to combat homelessness: From ambition to window dressing? *European Journal of Homelessness, 6*(2), 101-18.

Hinton, E. (2016). *From the War on Poverty to the war on crime: The making of mass incarceration in America.* Cambridge, MA: Harvard University Press.

Hipp, J. R. (2010). A dynamic view of neighborhoods: The reciprocal relationship between crime and neighborhood structural characteristics. *Social Problems, 57*(2), 205–30.

Hirsch, A. R. (1983). *Making the second ghetto: Race and housing in Chicago, 1940–1960.* Cambridge: Cambridge University Press.

Hirsch, F. (1977). *Social limits to growth.* London: Routledge & Kegan Paul.

Hirschman, A. O. (1977). *The passions and the interests.* Princeton, NJ: Princeton University Press.

Hirschman, A. O. (1982). Rival interpretations of market society: Civilizing, destructive, or feeble? *Journal of economic literature, 20*(4), 1463–84.

Hobsbawm, E. J. (1957). The British standard of living, 1790–1850. *Economic History Review, 10*(1), 46–68.

Hochschild, A. (2016). Our awful prisons: How they can be changed. *New York Review of Books,* May 26, www.nybooks.com/articles/2016/05/26/our-awful-prisons-how-they-can-be-changed.

Hollister, M. (2011). Employment stability in the US labor market: Rhetoric versus reality. *Annual Review of Sociology, 37,* 305–24.

Hood, C. (1991). A public management for all seasons? *Public administration, 69*(1), 3–19.

Hopper, K., Jost, J., Hay, T., Welber, S., and Haugland, G. 1997. Homelessness, severe mental illness, and the institutional circuit. *Psychiatric Services, 48*(5), 659–64.

Howard, C. (1997). *The hidden welfare state: Tax expenditures and social policy in the United States.* Princeton, NJ: Princeton University Press.

Hoynes, H. W., & Schanzenbach, D. W. (2012). Work incentives and the food stamp program. *Journal of Public Economics, 96*(1–2), 151–62.

Huck, P. (1995). Infant mortality and living standards of English workers during the Industrial Revolution. *Journal of Economic History, 55*(3), 528–50.

Human Rights Watch. (2004). *No second chance: People with criminal records denied access to public housing.* New York: Human Rights Watch.

Human Rights Watch. (2009). *Lethal force: Police violence and public security in Rio de Janeiro and São Paulo.* New York: Human Rights Watch. www.hrw.org/report/2009/12/08/lethal-force/police-violence-and-public-security-rio-de-janeiro-and-sao-paulo.

Human Services Council Commission. (2016). *New York nonprofits in the aftermath of FEGS: A call to action.* www.nysba.org/LessonsFromtheFEGSCollapse.

Huntington, S. P. (1968). *Political order in changing societies.* New Haven, CT: Yale University Press, 2006.

Hyra, D. S. (2006). Racial uplift? Intra-racial class conflict and the economic revitalization of Harlem and Bronzeville. *City & Community,* 5(1), 71–92.

Immergluck, D. (2013). Too little, too late, and too timid: The federal response to the foreclosure crisis at the five-year mark. *Housing Policy Debate, 23*(1), 199–232.

Jacobs, B. A., & Wright, R. (2006). *Street justice: Retaliation in the criminal underworld.* New York: Cambridge University Press.

Jacobs, D., & Jackson, A. L. (2010). On the politics of imprisonments: A review of systematic findings. *Annual Review of Law and Social Science, 6,* 129–49.

Jessop, B. (1993). Towards a Schumpeterian workfare state? Preliminary remarks on post-Fordist political economy. *Studies in Political Economy, 40*(1), 7–39.

Jobard, F. (2012). Proposition on the theory of policing, *Champ pénal/Penal field, 9,* http://journals.openedition.org/champpenal/8286.

Jones, J., & Schmitt, J. (2014). Update on low-wage workers. CEPR Blog, Center for Economic Policy and Research. http://cepr.net/blogs/cepr-blog/update-low-wage-worker–1979–2013.

Kaeble, D., Maruschak, L. M., Bonczar, T. P. (2015). *Probation and parole in the United States,* 2014. Washington, DC: Bureau of Justice Statistics (BJS), US Dept of Justice, & Office of Justice Programs.

Kalleberg, A. L. (2011). *Good jobs, bad jobs. The rise of polarized employment systems in the United States.* New York: Basic Books.

Kalleberg, A. L., Reskin, B. F., & Hudson, K. (2000). Bad jobs in America: Standard and nonstandard employment relations and job quality in the United States. *American Sociological Review,* 65(2), 256–78.

Kasy, M. (2017). Who wins, who loses? Identification of the welfare impact of changing wages. Unpublished manuscript, Harvard University.

Katz, L. F., & Krueger, A. B. (2016). The rise and nature of alternative work arrangements in the United States, 1995–2015. NBER Working Paper, No. w22667.

Katznelson, I. (2005). *When affirmative action was white: An untold history of racial inequality in twentieth-century America.* New York: Norton.

Kelley, R. D. (1990). *Hammer and hoe: Alabama communists during the Great Depression.* Chapel Hill: University of North Carolina Press.

Kelling, G. L., & Bratton, W. J. (1998). Declining crime rates: Insiders' views of the New York City story. *Journal of Criminal Law and Criminology (1973), 88*(4), 1217–32.

Kenworthy, L. (1999). Do social-welfare policies reduce poverty? A cross-national assessment. *Social Forces, 77*(3), 1119–39.

Kenworthy, L. (2011). *Progress for the poor.* New York: Oxford University Press.

Kenworthy, L., & Marx, I. (2017). *In-work poverty in the United States.* IZA Institute of Labor Economics Discussion Papers, No. 10638. ftp.iza.org/dp10638.pdf.

Kleiman, M. (2009). *When brute force fails: How to have less crime and less punishment.* Princeton, NJ: Princeton University Press.

Kohler-Hausmann, J. (2015). Guns and butter: The welfare state, the carceral state, and the politics of exclusion in the postwar United States. *Journal of American History, 102*(1), 87–99.

Kohler-Hausmann, J. (2017). *Getting tough: Welfare and imprisonment in 1970s America.* Princeton, NJ: Princeton University Press.

Konczal, M. (2011). The hidden welfare state and private sector spending coalitions. *Rortybomb,* June 30, https://rortybomb.wordpress.com/2011/06/30/the-hidden-welfare-state-and-private-sector-spending-coalitions.

Konczal, M. (2016). The violence of eviction. *Dissent,* Summer. www.dissentmagazine.org/article/the-violence-of-eviction-housing-market-foreclosure-gentrification-finance-capital.

Korpi, W. (1983). *The democratic class struggle.* London: Routledge.

Korpi, W., & Palme, J. (1998). The paradox of redistribution and strategies of equality: Welfare state institutions, inequality, and poverty in the Western countries. *American Sociological Review, 63*(5), 661–87.

Kraska, P. B., & Kappeler, V. E. (1997). Militarizing American police: The rise and normalization of paramilitary units. *Social Problems, 44*(1), 1–18.

Krause, M. (2014). *The good project: Humanitarian relief NGOs and the fragmentation of reason.* Chicago: University of Chicago Press.

Lacey, N. (2008). *The prisoners' dilemma: Political economy and punishment in contemporary democracies.* Cambridge: Cambridge University Press.

Lacey, N. (2012). Punishment, (neo)liberalism and social democracy. European University Institute: Max Weber Lecture Series, 2012/02. http://cadmus.eui.eu/bitstream/handle/1814/21134/MWP_LS_Lacey_2012_02.pdf?sequence = 1&isAllowed = y.

Lacey, N., & Soskice, D. (2013). Why are the truly disadvantaged American, when the UK is bad enough? A political economy analysis of local autonomy in criminal justice, education, residential zoning (May 14, 2013). London School of Economics Legal Studies Working Paper No. 11/2013.

Lacey, N., Soskice, D., & Hope, D. (2018). Understanding the determinants of penal policy: Crime, culture, and comparative political economy. *Annual Review of Criminology, 1,* 195–217.

LaFree, G. (1999). Declining violent crime rates in the 1990s: Predicting crime booms and busts. *Annual Review of Sociology, 25,* 145–68.

Lamotte, M. (2016). Du non-profit au for profit: Vers un "floutage" de la notion de public. *Lien Social et Politiques, 76,* 253–71.

Lappi-Seppälä, T. (2008). Trust, welfare, and political culture: Explaining differences in national penal policies. *Crime and Justice, 37*(1), 313–87.

Lappi-Seppälä, T. (2011). Explaining imprisonment in Europe. *European Journal of Criminology, 8*(4), 303–28.

Lappi-Seppälä, T., & Tonry, M. (2011). Crime, criminal justice, and criminology in the Nordic countries. *Crime and Justice, 40*(1), 1–32.

Lauritsen, J. L., Rezey, M. L., & Heimer, K. (2016). When choice of data matters: Analyses of US crime trends, 1973–2012. *Journal of Quantitative Criminology, 32*(3), 335–55.

Lee, B. A., Tyler, K. A., & Wright, J. D. (2010). The new homelessness revisited. *Annual Review of Sociology, 36*, 501.

Lee, C. S., & Koo, I. H. (2016). The welfare states and poverty. In D. Brady & L. M. Burton (Eds.), *The Oxford handbook of the social science of poverty*, 709–32. Oxford: Oxford University Press.

Lein, L., Danziger, S. K., Shaefer, H. L., & Tillotson, A. (2016). Social policy, transfers, programs, and assistance. In D. Brady & L. M. Burton (Eds.), *The Oxford handbook of the social science of poverty*, 733–50. Oxford: Oxford University Press.

Lerman, A. E., & Weaver, V. (2014). Staying out of sight? Concentrated policing and local political action. *The ANNALS of the American Academy of Political and Social Science, 651*(1), 202–19.

Levi-Strauss, C. (1963). The structural study of myth. In *Structural anthropology*, 206–31. New York: Basic Books.

Levy, S. D. (2008). Collateral consequences of seeking order through disorder: New York's narcotics eviction program. *Harvard Civil Rights-Civil Liberties Law Review, 43*, 539–80.

Lieberman, R. C. (1998). *Shifting the color line: Race and the American welfare state*. Cambridge, MA: Harvard University Press.

Liedka, R. V., Piehl, A. M., & Useem, B. (2006). The crime-control effect of incarceration: Does scale matter? *Criminology & Public Policy, 5*(2), 245–76.

Lindblom, E. N. (1991). Toward a comprehensive homeless-prevention strategy. *Housing Policy Debate, 2*(3), 957-1025.

Lindert, P. H. (2004). *Growing public: Social spending and economic growth since the eighteenth century*. Volume 1, *The Story*. Cambridge: Cambridge University Press.

Lindert, P. H., & Williamson, J. G. (1983). English workers' living standards during the Industrial Revolution: A new look. *Economic History Review, 36*(1), 1–25.

Lipsky, M., & Smith, S. R. (1993). *Nonprofits for hire: The welfare state in the age of contracting*. Cambridge, MA: Harvard University Press.

Liska, A. E., & Bellair, P. E. (1995). Violent-crime rates and racial composition: Convergence over time. *American Journal of Sociology, 101*(3), 578–610.

Lu, J. (2015). Which nonprofit gets more government funding? *Nonprofit Management and Leadership, 25*(3), 297–312.

Lubet, S. (2017). *Interrogating ethnography: Why evidence matters*. New York: Oxford University Press.

Luksetich, W. (2008). Government funding and nonprofit organizations. *Nonprofit and Voluntary Sector Quarterly, 37*(3), 434–42.

Machin, S., & Meghir, C. (2004). Crime and economic incentives. *Journal of Human Resources, 39*(4), 958–79.

Mahler, J. (2006). *Ladies and gentlemen, the Bronx is burning: 1977, baseball, politics, and the battle for the soul of a city*. New York: Macmillan.

Main, T. (1993). Hard lessons on homelessness. The education of David Dinkins. *City Journal*, Summer. www.city-journal.org/html/hard-lessons-homelessness–12629.html.

Mallik-Kane, K., & Visher, C. A. (2008). *Health and prisoner reentry: How physical, mental, and substance abuse conditions shape the process of reintegration.* Washington, DC: Urban Institute Justice Policy Center.

Mannheim, H. (1939). *The dilemma of penal reform.* London: George Allen and Unwin.

Manning, P. K. (1988). Community policing as a drama of control. In J. R, Greene & S. D. Mastrofski (Eds.), *Community policing: Rhetoric or reality,* 27–45. New York: Praeger.

Manning, P. K. (2001). Theorizing policing: The drama and myth of crime control in the NYPD. *Theoretical Criminology,* 5(3), 315–44.

Marical, F., d'Ercole, M. M., Vaalavuo, M., & Verbist, G. (2006). Publicly-provided services and the distribution of resources [Report]. *OECD Social, Employment and Migration Working Papers,* no. 45. Retrieved from www.oecd.org/els.

Marta, N., Perry, D., & Charlotte, A. (1999). The first month out: Post-incarceration experiences in New York City. New York: Vera Institute of Justice. Retrieved from www.vera.org/publications/the-first-month-out-post-incarceration-experiences-in-new-york-city.

Marwell, N. P. (2004). Privatizing the welfare state: Nonprofit community based organizations as political actors. *American Sociological Review,* 69, 265–91.

Marwell, N. P. (2007). *Bargaining for Brooklyn: Community organizations in the entrepreneurial city.* Chicago: University of Chicago Press.

Marwell, N. P., & Gullickson, A. (2013). Inequality in the spatial allocation of social services: Government contracts to nonprofit organizations in New York City. *Social Service Review,* 87(2), 319–53.

Marwell, N. P., & McInerney, P. B. (2005). The nonprofit/for-profit continuum: Theorizing the dynamics of mixed-form markets. *Nonprofit and Voluntary Sector Quarterly,* 34(1), 7–28.

Marx, I., Marchal, S., & Nolan, B. (2012). Mind the gap: Net incomes of minimum wage workers in the EU and the US. *Minimum income protection in the Flux.* Discussion Paper series, Forschungsinstitut zur Zukunft der Arbeit, No. 6510.

Marx, I., Salanauskaite, L., & Verbist, G. (2016). For the poor, but not only the poor: On optimal pro-poorness in redistributive policies. *Social Forces,* 95(1), 1–24.

Marx, K. (1867). *Capital.* Volume 1. London: Penguin Classics, 2004.

Mastrofski, S. D. (2006). Community policing: A skeptical view. In A. Braga & D. Weisburd (Eds.), *Police innovation: Contrasting perspectives,* 44–75. Cambridge University Press.

McAllister, W., & Berlin, G. (2004). Policymaking and caseload dynamics: Homeless shelters. ISERP Working Paper 04-04. http://academiccommons.columbia.edu/doi/10.7916/D8C53SQ7.

McDowall, D., & Loftin, C. (2005). Are US crime rate trends historically contingent? *Journal of Research in Crime and Delinquency,* 42(4), 359–83.

McDowall, D., & Loftin, C. (2009). Do US city crime rates follow a national trend? The influence of nationwide conditions on local crime patterns. *Journal of Quantitative Criminology,* 25(3), 307–24.

Melossi, D. (2012). Punishment and migration between Europe and the USA: A transnational "less eligibility"? In J. Simon & R. Sparks (Eds.), *The Sage handbook of punishment and society,* 416–33. Los Angeles: Sage.

Meltzer, A. H., & Richard, S. F. (1981). A rational theory of the size of government. *Journal of Political Economy, 89*(5), 914–27.

Meltzer, D. O., & Chen, Z. (2011). The impact of minimum wage rates on body weight in the United States. In M. Grossman & N. H. Mocan (Eds.), *Economic aspects of obesity,* 17–34. Chicago: University of Chicago Press.

Messner, S. F., & Baumer, E. P. (2014). Stop, question, and assess: Comments on Rosenfeld and Fornango. *Justice Quarterly, 31*(1), 123–28.

Messner, S. F., & Rosenfeld, R. (1997). Political restraint of the market and levels of criminal homicide: A cross-national application of institutional-anomie theory. *Social Forces, 75*(4), 1393–1416.

Metraux, S., & Culhane, D. P. (2004). Homeless shelter use and reincarceration following prison release. *Criminology & Public Policy, 3*(2), 139–60.

Metraux, S., & Culhane, D. P. (2006). Recent incarceration history among a sheltered homeless population. *Crime & Delinquency, 52*(3), 504–17.

Mettler, S. (2011). *The submerged state: How invisible government policies undermine American democracy.* Chicago: University of Chicago Press.

Milanovic, B. (2016). *Global inequality.* Cambridge, MA: Harvard University Press.

Milkman, R., González, A. L., & Ikeler, P. (2012). Wage and hour violations in urban labour markets: A comparison of Los Angeles, New York and Chicago. *Industrial Relations Journal, 43*(5), 378–98.

Miller, R. J. (2014). Devolving the carceral state: Race, prisoner reentry, and the micro-politics of urban poverty management. *Punishment & Society, 16*(3), 305–35.

Mishel, L., Bivens, J., Gould, E., & Shierholz, H. (2012). *The state of working America.* Ithaca, NY: Cornell University Press.

Mitchell, D. (1997). The annihilation of space by law: The roots and implications of anti-homeless laws in the United States. *Antipode, 29*(3), 303–35.

Mock, N. H. (1997). Punishing the innocent: No-fault eviction of public housing tenants for the actions of third parties. *Texas Law Review, 76,* 1495–1531.

Moffitt, R. A., & Pauley, G. (2018). Trends in the distribution of social safety net support after the Great Recession. Stanford Center on Poverty and Inequality, Stanford University. www.econ2.jhu.edu/people/Moffitt/safety_net_distribution_trends.pdf.

Moffitt, R. (1992). Incentive effects of the US welfare system: A review. *Journal of Economic Literature, 30*(1), 1–61.

Morsy, L., & Rothstein, R. (2016). *Mass incarceration and children's outcomes.* Washington, DC: Economic Policy Institute. www.epi.org/files/pdf/118615.pdf.

Moskos, P. (2008). *Cop in the hood: My year policing Baltimore's eastern district.* Princeton, NJ: Princeton University Press.

Mosley, J. E. (2012). Keeping the lights on: How government funding concerns drive the advocacy agendas of nonprofit homeless service providers. *Journal of Public Administration Research and Theory, 22*(4), 841–66.

Moynihan, D. P. (1973). *The politics of a guaranteed income: The Nixon administration and the family assistance plan.* New York: Vintage.

Murakawa, N. (2014). *The first civil right: How liberals built prison America.* New York: Oxford University Press.

Murray, C. (1984). *Losing ground: American social policy, 1950–1980*. New York: Basic Books.

Nagin, D. S. (2013). Deterrence: A review of the evidence by a criminologist for economists. *Annual Review of Economics, 5*(1), 83–105.

National Research Council. (2002). *The dynamics of disability: Measuring and monitoring disability for social security programs*. Washington, DC: National Academies Press.

Nelken, D. (2010). Denouncing the penal state. *Criminology and Criminal Justice, 10*(4), 331–40.

NELP. (2014). The low-wage recovery: Industry employment and wages four years into the recovery. National Employment Law Project data brief, April. www.nelp.org/content/uploads/2015/03/Low-Wage-Recovery-Industry-Employment-Wages–2014-Report.pdf.

New York City Department of Investigation. (2015). *Probe of Department of Homeless Services' shelters for families with children finds serious deficiencies*. www1.nyc.gov/assets/doi/reports/pdf/2015/2015-03-12-Pro8dhs.pdf.

New York City Independent Budget Office. (2014). The rising number of homeless families in NYC, 2002–2012: A look at why families were granted shelter, the housing they had lived in & where they came from. https://ibo.nyc.ny.us/iboreports/2014dhs.pdf.

Nicholas, S., & Steckel, R. H. (1991). Heights and living standards of English workers during the early years of industrializations, 1770–1815. *Journal of Economic History, 51*(4), 937–57.

NYCLU [New York Civil Liberties Union]. (2014). *Stop-and-frisk during the Bloomberg administration (2002–2013)*. August. www.nyclu.org/sites/default/files/publications/stopandfrisk_briefer_2002-2013_final.pdf.

Oberschall, A. (1968). The Los Angeles riot of August 1965. *Social Problems, 15*(3), 322–41.

O'Connor, J. (1973). *The fiscal crisis of the state*. New York: St. Martin's.

Offe, C. (1984). *Contradictions of the welfare state*. London: Hutchinson.

O'Flaherty, B., & Sethi, R. (2010). Homicide in black and white. *Journal of Urban Economics, 68*(3), 215–30.

Oliver, P. (2017a). White rural imprisonment rates. Race, Politics, Justice (Blog). July 7. www.ssc.wisc.edu/soc/racepoliticsjustice/2017/07/07/white-rural-imprisonment-rates/.

Oliver, P. (2017b). Education, poverty, and rural vs. urban incarceration rates. Race, Politics, Justice (Blog). July 14. www.ssc.wisc.edu/soc/racepoliticsjustice/2017/07/14/education-poverty-and-rural-vs-urban-incarceration-rates.

Ousey, G. C., & Kubrin, C. E. (2018). Immigration and crime: Assessing a contentious issue. *Annual Review of Criminology, 1*, 63–84.

Pager, D. (2003). The mark of a criminal record. *American Journal of Sociology, 108*(5), 937–75.

Pager, D., Western, B., & Sugie, N. (2009). Sequencing disadvantage: Barriers to employment facing young black and white men with criminal records. *ANNALS of the American Academy of Political and Social Science, 623*(1), 195–213.

Parker, M. (2002). *Against management: Organization in the age of managerialism.* Cambridge: Polity.

Pattillo, M. (2003). Negotiating blackness, for richer or for poorer. *Ethnography, 4*(1), 61–93.

Pattillo-McCoy, M. (1998). Church culture as a strategy of action in the black community. *American Sociological Review, 63*(6), 767–84.

Perrow, C. (1991). A society of organizations. *Theory and Society, 20*(6): 725–62.

Pfaff, J. (2017). *Locked in: The true causes of mass incarceration—and how to achieve real reform.* New York: Basic Books.

Phelps, M. S. (2011). Rehabilitation in the punitive era: The gap between rhetoric and reality in US prison programs. *Law & Society Review, 45*(1), 33–68.

Phillips-Fein, K. (2017). *Fear City: New York's fiscal crisis and the rise of austerity politics.* New York: Metropolitan.

Pierce, J. R., & Schott, P. K. (2016a). The surprisingly swift decline of US manufacturing employment. *American Economic Review, 106*(7), 1632–62.

Pierce, J. R., & Schott, P. K. (2016b). Trade liberalization and mortality: Evidence from US counties. NBER Working Paper, No. w22849.

Piketty, T. (2013). *Le capital au 21e siècle.* Paris: Seuil.

Piketty, T., Saez, E., & Zucman, G. (2017). Distributional national accounts: Methods and estimates for the United States. *Quarterly Journal of Economics, 133*(2), 553–609.

Pinard, M. (2010). Collateral consequences of criminal convictions: Confronting issues of race and dignity. *New York University Law Review, 85*, 457–534.

Piven, F. F., & Cloward, R. (1993). *Regulating the poor: The functions of public welfare.* New York: Vintage. [First edition 1971.]

Piven, F. F. (2010). A response to Wacquant. *Theoretical Criminology, 14*(1), 111–16.

Polanyi, K. (1944). *The great transformation.* New York: Beacon, 2001.

Pope, D. G., & Pope, J. C. (2012). Crime and property values: Evidence from the 1990s crime drop. *Regional Science and Urban Economics, 42*(1), 177–88.

Posner, R. A. (1985). An economic theory of the criminal law. *Columbia Law Review, 85*(6), 1193–1231.

Prasad, M. (2012). *The land of too much: American abundance and the paradox of poverty.* Cambridge, MA: Harvard University Press.

Pratt, J. (2008). Scandinavian exceptionalism in an era of penal excess, part 1: The nature and roots of Scandinavian exceptionalism. *British Journal of Criminology, 48*(2), 119–37.

Pratt, J., & Eriksson, A. (2013). *Contrasts in punishment: An explanation of Anglophone excess and Nordic exceptionalism.* London: Routledge.

Pritchett, W. E. (2002). *Brownsville, Brooklyn: Blacks, Jews, and the changing face of the ghetto.* Chicago: University of Chicago Press.

Procacci, G. (1993). *Gouverner la misère: La question sociale en France (1789–1848).* Paris: Seuil.

Quadagno, J. S. (1984). Welfare capitalism and the Social Security Act of 1935. *American Sociological Review, 49*(5), 632–47.

Ravallion, M. (2013). *The idea of antipoverty policy* (No. w19210). Cambridge, MA: National Bureau of Economic Research.

Rawls, J. (1971). *A theory of justice.* Cambridge, MA: Harvard University Press. [Revised, 1975.]

Reich, C. A. (1963). Midnight welfare searches and the Social Security Act. *Yale Law Journal, 72*(7), 1347–60.

Reich, C. A. (1964). The new property. *Yale Law Journal, 73*(5), 733–87.

Renzetti, C. M. (2001). "One strike and you're out!" Implications of a federal crime control policy for battered women. *Violence Against Women, 7*(6), 685–98.

Rieder, J. (1985). *Canarsie: The Jews and Italians of Brooklyn against liberalism.* Cambridge, MA: Harvard University Press.

Rios, V. M. (2011). *Punished: Policing the lives of black and Latino boys.* New York: New York University Press.

Roberts, D. (1963). How cruel was the Victorian Poor Law? *Historical Journal, 6*(1), 97–107.

Rodney, R. S. (2003). "Am I my mother's keeper?" The case against the use of juvenile arrest records in One-Strike public housing evictions. *Northwestern University Law Review, 98*(2), 739–72.

Roeder, O., Eisen, L. B., & Bowling, J. (2015). *What caused the crime decline?* New York: Brennan Center for Justice.

Römer, F. (2017). Generous to all or "insiders only"? The relationship between welfare state generosity and immigrant welfare rights. *Journal of European Social Policy, 27*(2), 173–96.

Rosenfeld, R., & Fornango, R. (2014). The impact of police stops on precinct robbery and burglary rates in New York City, 2003–2010. *Justice Quarterly, 31*(1), 96–122.

Rossi, P. H. (1991). *Down and out in America: The origins of homelessness.* Chicago: University of Chicago Press.

Rothstein, J. (2010). Is the EITC as good as an NIT? Conditional cash transfers and tax incidence. *American Economic Journal: Economic Policy,* 2, 177–208.

Rugh, J. S., & Massey, D. S. (2010). Racial segregation and the American foreclosure crisis. *American Sociological Review, 75*(5), 629–51.

Rusche, G. (1930/1980). Prison revolts or social policy lessons from America. *Crime and Social Justice,* (13), 41–44.

Rusche, G. (1933/1978). Labor market and penal sanction: Thoughts on the sociology of criminal justice. *Crime and Social Justice,* (10), 2–8.

Rusche, G., & Kirchheimer, O. (1939). *Punishment and social structure.* New York: Columbia University Press.

Sabbagh, D. (2007). *Equality and transparency: A strategic perspective on affirmative action in American Law.* Basingtoke: Palgrave.

Salamon, L. M. (1987). Of market failure, voluntary failure, and third-party government: Toward a theory of government-nonprofit relations in the modern welfare state. *Nonprofit and Voluntary Sector Quarterly, 16*(1–2), 29–49.

Sampson, R. J. (2012). *Great American city: Chicago and the enduring neighborhood effect.* Chicago: University of Chicago Press.

Sampson, R. J., Raudenbush, S. W., & Earls, F. (1997). Neighborhoods and violent crime: A multilevel study of collective efficacy. *Science, 277*(5328), 918–24.

Sanders, E. (1999). *Roots of reform: Farmers, workers, and the American state, 1877–1917.* Chicago: University of Chicago Press.

Sandoval, D. A., Rank, M. R., & Hirschl, T. A. (2009). The increasing risk of poverty across the American life course. *Demography, 46*(4), 717–37.

Savage, J., Bennett, R. R., & Danner, M. (2008). Economic assistance and crime: A cross-national investigation. *European Journal of Criminology, 5*(2), 217–38.

Savas, E. S. (2002). Competition and choice in New York City's social services. *Public Administration Review, 62*(1), 82–91.

Savelsberg, J. J. (1994). Knowledge, domination, and criminal punishment. *American Journal of Sociology, 99*(4), 911–43.

Scheidel, W. (2017). *The great leveler: Violence and the history of inequality from the stone age to the twenty-first century.* Princeton, NJ: Princeton University Press.

Scheper-Hughes, N. (1992). *Death without weeping. The violence of everyday life in Brazil.* Berkeley: University of California Press.

Schlager, M. D., & Robbins, K. (2008). Does Parole work?—Revisited: Reframing the discussion of the impact of postprison supervision on offender outcome. *Prison Journal, 88*(2), 234–51.

Schmid, H. (2004). The role of nonprofit human service organizations in providing social services: A prefatory essay. *Administration in Social Work, 28*(3–4), 1–21.

Schmitt, J., Warner, K., & Gupta, S. (2010). The high budgetary cost of incarceration. Washington, DC: Center for Economic and Policy Research. www.cepr.net/documents/publications/incarceration-2010-06.pdf.

Schnapper, E. (1985). Affirmative action and the legislative history of the Fourteenth Amendment. *Virginia Law Review, 71*(5), 753–98.

Schuetz, J., Been, V., & Ellen, I. G. (2008). Neighborhood effects of concentrated mortgage foreclosures. *Journal of Housing Economics, 17*(4), 306–19.

Schwartz, A. E., Susin, S., & Voicu, I. (2003). Has falling crime driven New York City's real estate boom? *Journal of Housing Research, 14*(1), 101-35.

Sen, A. (1983). Poor, relatively speaking. *Oxford Economic Papers, 35*(2), 153–69.

Shapiro, C., & Schwartz, M. (2001). Coming home: Building on family connections. *Corrections Management Quarterly, 5*(3), 52–61.

Sharkey, P. (2018). *Uneasy peace: The great crime decline, the renewal of city life, and the next war on violence.* New York: Norton.

Sharkey, P., & Torrats-Espinosa, G. (2017). The effect of violent crime on economic mobility. *Journal of Urban Economics, 102,* 22–33.

Sharkey, P., Torrats-Espinosa, G., & Takyar, D. (2017). Community and the crime decline: The causal effect of local nonprofits on violent crime. *American Sociological Review, 82*(6), 1214–40.

Shlay, A. B., & Rossi, P. H. (1992). Social science research and contemporary studies of homelessness. *Annual Review of Sociology, 18,* 129–60.

Shoesmith, G. L. (2017). Crime, teenage abortion, and unwantedness. *Crime & Delinquency, 63*(11), 1458–90.

Sieh, E. W. (1989). Less eligibility: The upper limits of penal policy. *Criminal Justice Policy Review, 3*(2), 159–83.

Simon, J. (1993). *Poor discipline: Parole and the social control of the underclass, 1890–1990.* Chicago: University of Chicago Press.

Skocpol, T. (1995). *Protecting soldiers and mothers.* Cambridge, MA: Harvard University Press.

Small, M. L. (2015). De-exoticizing ghetto poverty: On the ethics of representation in urban ethnography. *City & Community, 14*(4), 352–58.

Smith, A. (1776). *An inquiry into the nature and causes of the wealth of nations.* Adam Smith Reference Archive. www.marxists.org/reference/archive/smith-adam/works/wealth-of-nations/book05/ch01b.htm.

Smith, P. S. (2011). A critical look at Scandinavian exceptionalism: Welfare state theories, penal populism and prison conditions in Denmark and Scandinavia. In T. Ugelvik & J. Dullum (Eds.), *Penal exceptionalism? Nordic prison policy and practice*, 38–57. London: Routledge.

Solar, P. M. (1995). Poor relief and English economic development before the Industrial Revolution. *Economic History Review, 48*(1), 1–22.

Somers, M. R., & Block, F. (2005). From poverty to perversity: Ideas, markets, and institutions over 200 years of welfare debate. *American Sociological Review, 70*(2), 260–87.

Soss, J., Fording, R. C., & Schram, S. (2011). *Disciplining the poor: Neoliberal paternalism and the persistent power of race.* Chicago: University of Chicago Press.

Soss, J., & Weaver, V. (2016). Learning from Ferguson: Welfare, criminal justice, and the political science of race and class. In J. Hooker & A. B. Tillery Jr. (Eds.), *The double bind: The politics of racial and class inequalities in the Americas: A report of the Task Force on Racial and Social Class*, 1–28. ashington, DC: American Political Science Association.

Stanziani, A. (2008). Serfs, slaves, or wage earners? The legal status of labour in Russia from a comparative perspective, from the sixteenth to the nineteenth century. *Journal of Global History, 3*(2), 183–202.

Stanziani, A. (2009). The traveling panopticon: Labor institutions and labor practices in Russia and Britain in the eighteenth and nineteenth centuries. *Comparative Studies in Society and History, 51*(4), 715–41.

Stuart, F. (2016). Becoming "copwise": Policing, culture, and the collateral consequences of street-level criminalization. *Law & Society Review, 50*(2), 279–313.

Sugrue, T. J. (1996). *The origins of the urban crisis: Race and inequality in postwar Detroit.* Princeton, NJ: Princeton University Press.

Sullivan, E., Mino, M., Nelson, K., & Pope, J. (2002). *Families as a resource in recovery from drug abuse: An evaluation of La Bodega de la Familia.* New York: Vera Institute of Justice.

Surowiecki, J. (2013). The pay is too damn low. *New Yorker,* August 12–19. www.newyorker.com/magazine/2013/08/12/the-pay-is-too-damn-low.

Sykes, B. L., & Geller, A. (2016). Mass incarceration and the underground economy in America. Unpublished manuscript, Department of Criminology, Law and Society, University of California, Irvine.

Sykes, J., Križ, K., Edin, K., & Halpern-Meekin, S. (2015). Dignity and dreams: What the Earned Income Tax Credit (EITC) means to low-income families. *American Sociological Review, 80*(2), 243–67.

Tach, L., & Edin, K. (2017). The social safety net after welfare reform: Recent developments and consequences for household dynamics. *Annual Review of Sociology, 43*, 541–61.

tenBroek, J. (1964). California's dual system of family law: Its origin, development, and present status. *Stanford Law Review, 16*(2), 257–317.

Thabit, W. (2003). *How East New York became a ghetto.* New York: New York University Press.

Thacher, D. (2008). The rise of criminal background screening in rental housing. *Law & Social Inquiry, 33*(1), 5–30.

Therborn, G. (2014). *The killing fields of inequality.* New York: John Wiley & Sons.

Thery, C. (2014). *Larry's clique: The informal side of the housing market in low-income minority neighborhoods.* PhD diss., Columbia University.

Thompson, H. A. (2010). Why mass incarceration matters: Rethinking crisis, decline, and transformation in postwar American history. *Journal of American History, 97*(3), 703–34.

Titmuss, R. M. (1950). *Problems of social policy.* London: Kraus (Reprint, 1976).

Tonry, M. (2009). Explanations of American punishment policies: A national history. *Punishment & Society, 11*(3), 377–94.

Tonry, M. (2014). Why crime rates are falling throughout the Western world. *Crime and Justice, 43*(1), 1–63.

Tonry, M. (2016). *Sentencing fragments: Penal reform in America, 1975–2025.* New York: Oxford University Press.

Travis, J., & Lawrence, S. (2002). *Beyond the prison gates: The state of parole in America.* Urban Institute. Retrieved from http://webarchive.urban.org/UploadedPDF/310583_Beyond_prison_gates.pdf.

Trojanowicz, R. (1982). *An evaluation of the Neighborhood Foot Patrol program in Flint, Michigan.* East Lansing: National Neighborhood Foot Patrol Center, Michigan State University.

Tyler, T. R. (2005). Policing in black and white: Ethnic group differences in trust and confidence in the police. *Police Quarterly, 8*(3), 322–42.

Ugelvik, T., & Dullum, J. (Eds.). (2011). *Penal exceptionalism? Nordic prison policy and practice.* London: Routledge.

Uggen, C., & Manza, J. (2002). Democratic contraction? Political consequences of felon disenfranchisement in the United States. *American Sociological Review, 67*(6), 777–803.

Unnever, J. D., & Gabbidon, S. L. (2011). *A theory of African American offending: Race, racism, and crime.* London: Routledge.

U.S. Bureau of Labor Statistics. (2016). National compensation survey: Employee benefits in the United States, March 2016. Bulletin 2785. www.bls.gov/ncs/ebs/benefits/2016/ebbl0059.pdf.

Van Leeuwen, M. H. (1994). Logic of charity: Poor relief in preindustrial Europe. *Journal of Interdisciplinary History, 24*(4), 589–613.

Van Oorschot, W. (1991). Non-take-up of social security benefits in Europe. *Journal of European Social Policy, 1*(1), 15–30.

Van Parijs, P., & Vanderborght, Y. (2017). *Basic income: A radical proposal for a free society and a sane economy.* Cambridge, MA: Harvard University Press.

Vélez, M. B., & Richardson, K. (2012). The political economy of neighbourhood homicide in Chicago: The role of bank investment. *British Journal of Criminology, 52*(3), 490–513.

Venkatesh, S. A. (2000). *American project: The rise and fall of a modern ghetto.* Cambridge, MA: Harvard University Press.

Venkatesh, S. A. (2006). *Off the books.* Cambridge, MA: Harvard University Press.

Villarreal, A. (2015). Fear and spectacular drug violence in Monterrey. In J. Auyero, P. Bourgois, & N. Scheper-Hughes (Eds.), *Violence at the urban margins,* 135–61. New York: Oxford University Press.

Visher, C. A., & Travis, J. (2003). Transitions from prison to community: Understanding individual pathways. *Annual Review of Sociology, 29,* 89–113.

Von Hoffman, A. (2004). *House by house, block by block: The rebirth of America's urban neighborhoods.* New York: Oxford University Press.

Wacquant, L. (1997). Three pernicious premises in the study of the American ghetto. *International Journal of Urban and Regional Research, 21*(2), 341–53.

Wacquant, L. (1999). *Les prisons de la misère.* Paris: Liber.

Wacquant, L. (2001). Deadly symbiosis: When ghetto and prison meet and mesh. *Punishment & Society, 3*(1), 95–133.

Wacquant, L. (2001). The penalisation of poverty and the rise of neo-liberalism. *European Journal on Criminal Policy and Research, 9*(4), 401–12.

Wacquant, L. (2009). *Punishing the poor: The neoliberal government of social insecurity.* Durham, NC: Duke University Press.

Wacquant, L. (2010). Prisoner reentry as myth and ceremony. *Dialectical Anthropology, 34*(4), 605–20.

Waldinger, R. D. (1996). *Still the promised city? African-Americans and new immigrants in postindustrial New York.* Cambridge, MA: Harvard University Press.

Waldinger, R., & Lichter, M. I. (2003). *How the other half works: Immigration and the social organization of labor.* Berkeley: University of California Press.

Waldron, J. (1991). Homelessness and the issue of freedom. *UCLA Law Review, 39,* 295–324.

Ward, D. A. (1972). Inmate rights and prison reform in Sweden and Denmark. *Journal of Criminal Law, Criminology, and Police Science, 63*(2), 240–55.

Warin P. (2011). Le non-recours au RSA: Des éléments de comparaison. *Odenore,* Working paper no. 13. http://odenore.msh-alpes.fr/documents/odenorewp13.pdf.

Watkins, S. C., Swidler, A., & Hannan, T. (2012). Outsourcing social transformation: Development NGOs as organizations. *Annual Review of Sociology, 38,* 285–315.

Weaver, V. M. (2007). Frontlash: Race and the development of punitive crime policy. *Studies in American Political Development, 21*(2), 230–65.

Wehner, P., & Levin, Y. (2007). Crime, drugs, welfare, and other good news. *Commentary, 124*(5), 19–24.

Weisbrod, B. A. (Ed.). (1977). *The voluntary nonprofit sector: An economic analysis.* New York: Lexington Books.

Weisbrod, B. A. (1988). *The nonprofit economy.* Cambridge, MA: Harvard University Press.

Weisburd, D., Telep, C. W., & Lawton, B. A. (2014). Could innovations in policing have contributed to the New York City crime drop even in a period of declining police strength? The case of stop, question and frisk as a hot spots policing strategy. *Justice Quarterly, 31*(1), 129–53.

Weisburd, D., Wooditch, A., Weisburd, S., & Yang, S. M. (2016). Do stop, question, and frisk practices deter crime? *Criminology & Public Policy, 15*(1), 31–56.

Wen, H., Hockenberry, J. M., & Cummings, J. R. (2017). The effect of Medicaid expansion on crime reduction: Evidence from HIFA-waiver expansions. *Journal of Public Economics, 154*, 67–94.

Western, B. (2002). The impact of incarceration on wage mobility and inequality. *American Sociological Review, 67*(4), 526–46.

Western, B., & Beckett, K. (1999). How unregulated is the US labor market? The penal system as a labor market institution. *American Journal of Sociology, 104*(4), 1030–60.

Western, B., Bloome, D., Sosnaud, B., & Tach, L. (2012). Economic insecurity and social stratification. *Annual Review of Sociology, 38*, 341–59.

Western, B., & Rosenfeld, J. (2011). Unions, norms, and the rise in US wage inequality. *American Sociological Review, 76*(4), 513–37.

White, A. (2013). Creating collective capacity: New York City's social infrastructure and neighborhood-centered services. In J. H. Mollenkopf (Ed.), *Toward a 21st Century City for All: Progressive Policies for New York City in 2013 and Beyond* chap. 7. New York: Graduate Center, City University of New York.

White, M. D. (2014). The New York City Police Department, its crime control strategies and organizational changes, 1970–2009. *Justice Quarterly, 31*(1), 74–95.

Whitman, J. Q. (2003). *Harsh justice: Criminal punishment and the widening divide between America and Europe.* New York: Oxford University Press.

Wildeman, C. (2009). Parental imprisonment, the prison boom, and the concentration of childhood disadvantage. *Demography, 46*(2), 265–80.

Wilkinson, R. G., & Pickett, K. (2009). *The spirit level: Why more equal societies almost always do better.* London: Allen Lane.

Williams, M. R., Holcomb, J. E., Kovandzic, T. V., & Bullock, S. (2010). *Policing for profit: The abuse of civil asset forfeiture.* Arlington, VA: Institute for Justice.

Willis, J. J., Mastrofski, S. D., & Weisburd, D. (2007). Making sense of COMPSTAT: A theory-based analysis of organizational change in three police departments, *Law and Society Review, 41*(1), 147–88.

Wilson, J. Q. (1975). *Thinking about crime.* New York: Vintage. [Rev. ed., 1985].

Wilson, J. Q., & Kelling, G. (1982). Broken windows: The police and neighborhood safety. *Atlantic Monthly, 249*(3), 29–38.

Wilson, W. J. (1987). *The truly disadvantaged: The inner city, the underclass, and social policy.* Chicago: University of Chicago Press.

Wilson, W. J., & Aponte, R. (1985). Urban poverty. *Annual Review of Sociology, 11*, 231–58.

Wong, Y. L. I., Culhane, D. P., & Kuhn, R. (1997). Predictors of exit and reentry among family shelter users in New York City. *Social Service Review, 71*(3), 441–62.

Wyly, E., Newman, K., Schafran, A., & Lee, E. (2010). Displacing New York. *Environment and Planning A, 42*(11), 2602–23.

Zimring, F. E. (2011). *The city that became safe: New York's lessons for urban crime and its control.* New York: Oxford University Press.

Zmora, M. (2009). Between Rucker and a hard place: The due process void for Section 8 voucher holders in no-fault evictions. *Northwestern University Law Review, 103*(4), 1961–91.

INDEX